Hold-Outs

CONTEMPORARY NORTH AMERICAN POETRY SERIES

Series Editors Alan Golding, Lynn Keller, and Adalaide Morris

Preface and Acknowledgments

In 1968 I moved from Imperial Beach, California, to Los Angeles and ended up working as an editor and publisher for about a decade and a half while making my living as a blueprint machine operator and typesetter. If I had attempted this alone, I doubt my projects would have lasted longer than a year, but I had supportive comrades and allies: Jim Krusoe, Paul Vangelisti, Dennis Cooper, Leland Hickman, George Drury Smith, Aleida Rodríguez, Jack Grapes, Doren Robbins, Manazar Gamboa, Jack Skelley, Joan Jobe Smith, Victor Valle, Peter Schneidre, and Michael C. Ford. The magazines that each of these poets worked on, as well as institutional productions such as Clayton Eshleman's *Sulfur,* made Los Angeles for many years a place that an aspiring poet could enjoy living and writing. Rents were still relatively cheap. Poets from elsewhere started showing up in the late 1970s and early 1980s and were surprised to find that there were many good bookstores in Los Angeles, and several of them had poetry reading series. Even more surprising to new arrivals was the fact that numerous poets in Los Angeles not only read work quite unlike their own writing, but actually enjoyed and admired it.

Whether longtime residents or recent arrivals, few poets in Los Angeles by the late 1970s, though, seemed able to explain how the variety of poetry emanating from this region fit into any larger story or pattern of American literature. One major obstacle in acquiring this knowledge was that much of the work from earlier decades was not easily available. We knew Thomas McGrath's poems because they were in print, but in the early 1970s Don Gordon lived in Los Angeles almost *incognito*. In 1972 Stuart Perkoff had not had a book of poems out for over fifteen years. By that point none of the founding editors of Los Angeles poetry magazines in the 1950s were still active in this city, and almost all of them were either dead or had moved elsewhere. Alexandra Garrett, who had worked on *Coastlines* magazine in its final years, would occasionally mention the old days, but we did not take the hint enough to dig through back issues. While Perkoff, Gordon, and Bert Meyers are now in print, the writing of their comrades is still almost inaccessible. This project is an attempt to intermingle the remembered with the forgotten. At the same time, I have also tried to balance what I have learned with the suspicion that for every community of poets in Los Angeles examined in this study, how many dozen clusters on the West Coast remain yet to be accounted for?

The West Coast stretches from Seattle to San Diego, in terms of the mainland of the United States, and should also include Baja California; one should not conflate the California Canon and the West Coast Poetry Renaissance into an assumption that one need only magnify my argument to encompass the whole. Very likely one would end up replicating the same kinds of errors that critics committed in the past in making San Francisco and the West Coast synonymous. What is actually needed is a comprehensive history of the actual West Coast, which at the very least, in terms of a literary continuum, stretches from Tijuana to Vancouver, British Columbia. Barbara Wilson's Seal Press, for instance, has never received any significant acknowledgment for its contributions to the kind of analysis suggested by the context of this book's project. Wilson was born in Long Beach in 1950 and established Seal Press in Seattle in 1976. In turn, any account that includes Seal Press's presence on the West Coast would need to juxtapose her labor and accomplishments with that of artists all the way down Mexico through Central America and along the West Coast of South America. Cesar Vallejo and Pablo Neruda have had more influence on many West Coast poets than T. S. Eliot and Wallace Stevens.

My project is meant merely to prepare potential resources for the critic with designs on a micro-encyclopedia, for only a series of volumes will be capable of encompassing the accomplishments of poets such as Robert Duncan, Michael McClure, Bob Kaufman, Joanne Kyger, Gary Snyder, Philip Whalen, Jack Spicer, Madeline Gleason, and Lew Welch, all of whose work filters in direct and indirect ways through the labors of many poets cited in this book, who also deserve their roles acknowledged, no matter how peripheral they may have seemed to East Coast critics in the past. That future project will require, in addition to poets and especially the poet-editors frequently cited later on in this book, an attuned vision capable of accounting for Fred Voss, Ray Zepeda, Gene Fowler, Gloria Enedina Alvárez, Robert Mezey, Brooks Roddan, Marine Robert Warden, Laurel Ann Bogen, Nichola Manning, Anthony Seidman, Doren Robbins, Peter J. Harris, Timothy Steele, Leslie Monsour, Sarah Maclay, Harryette Mullen, Killarney Clary, Rick Smith, David James, Ed Smith, Dave

Alvin, Max Benavidez, Aya Tarlow, Philomene Long, Daniel Moore, Steve Richmond, A. P. Russo, Michael Dahlberg, Eileen Ireland, Uri Hertz, Ralph Angel, Sharon Doubiago, Harold Norse, Philip Lamantia, Stan Persky, Jerome Rothenberg, Alvaro Cardona-Hine, Gene Frumkin, Leslie Scalapino, Gary Young, Brenda Hillman, Guillermo Gomez-Peña, Jerry Ratch, Alta, George Hitchcock, Amy Uyematsu, Sesshu Foster, Christopher Buckley, Judy Grahn, Diane Di Prima, Robert Hass, Jim Gustafson, Kirby Doyle, Luis Campos, Jed Rasula, Morton Marcus, Raymond Carver, Richard Garcia, Nanos Valaoritis, Jim Grabill, Kathleen Fraser, Barbara Maloutas, Aram Saroyan, Julia Stein, Deena Metzger, Austin Straus, Landis Everson, Luis Omar Salinas, Juan Felipe Herrera, David Bromige, Jack Hirschman, Cecilia Woloch, Therese Bachand, Gary Soto, Robert Gluck, Ishmael Reed, Carol Lem, Bill Berkson, Steve Abbott, Bruce Boone, Ellen Bass, Nate Mackey, Duncan McNaughton, Greg Hall, Robin Blaser, William Witherup, Marilyn Chin, Clemens Starck, Will Alexander, Jack Marshall, Joe Safdie, David Meltzer, Jim Cushing, Doug Blazek, Steve Carey, Russell Leong, A. D. Winans, S. A. Griffin, Glover Davis, Scott Wannberg, Paul Mariah, Steve Richmond, Lynn Bronstein, Julie Vinograd, Al Young, Michael Hannon, Bill Vartnaw, Richard Silberg, Gerda Penfold, Linda King, Tom Clark, George Evans, Keith Abbott, Bruce Williams, Curtis Faville, Dinah Berland, Karen Holden, Jay Jenkins, Quincy Troupe, Hunce Voelcker, and Beverly Dahlen, as well as the prolific and substantial contingent of Language poets, within this larger context of artistic experimentation and resistance. In theory, it is an impossible undertaking within a single short volume, but for anyone who might be tempted, here's a pencil-sketch clue: begin with the poem that Witherup dedicated to Dahlen as a first tendril in this vast rhizomatic legacy, and then read Lawson Fusao Inada's *Legends from the Camp* and Mitsuye Yamada's *Desert Run* (which was published by Alta's Shameless Hussy Press), after which you begin to consider how Carolyn Kizer and Adrienne Rich swoop through these perimeters of possibility accompanied by Susan King's exquisite productions from her Paradise Press. At the very least, I hope I have begun to establish the literate pertinacity to enculturation of the task that awaits you (second person *plural*).

Between 1980 and 1995 I frequently made my living as a typesetter for weekly newspapers in Los Angeles such as the *Argonaut* and *Radio & Records*. My primary tool was a Compugraphic 7500, an unusually responsive workhorse of a print culture machine. By the mid-1990s, however, the computer industry had eviscerated typesetting as a career option, and heading into the Memorial Day weekend of 1995, I found myself without work. At the urging of my dear friend, Kathryn McMahon, I decided to go to graduate school. Without her indefatigable encouragement, I would never have pursued this project, which began as a research topic for a seminar about Los Angeles, sponsored by Getty Research Institute, in which I participated for two months in 1996 as a visiting scholar, along with David James, Tom Dumm, Brenda Bright, Phil Ethington, Alan Sekula, Robert Flick, Becky M. Nicolaides, Ramon Garcia, Susan Phillips, and Roger Friedlander. I had met David James when we gave a poetry reading together at Beyond Baroque in February 1974, and his unstinting support has been essential to the completion of this task. In particular, a small grant he secured from James Irvine Foundation allowed me to devote a month of research to a short version of the Beyond Baroque chapter which appeared in his book, *The Sons and Daughters of Los: Culture and Community in L.A.* Special thanks are also due to Paul Vangelisti, who has published my poetry and prose for thirty-five years in a wide variety of magazines. A version of the opening portion of *Hold-Outs* appeared in *New Review of Literature* in the fall of 2004. I also owe a substantial debt to Michael Davidson and Donald Wesling, who read early drafts of several chapters with vivid exactitude between 2001 and 2004. Kevin McNamara, Steve Axelrod, Stephen Motika, and the late Eric Schocket were enthusiastic allies in the final stages of this project. As I did research and presented papers at conferences, Brooks and Lea Ann Roddan, Bob and Judy Chinello, Laurel Ann Bogen, and Lenny Durso provided shelter, meals, and best of all, warm friendship. Charlotte Wright and Joe Parsons provided constant counsel to me with unflinching forbearance and made certain I had the assistance of a superb copyeditor, Alicia Chrest.

Hold-Outs makes use of archival material that was made available through the enthusiastic graciousness of many people, including Lynda Claassen, Brad Westbrook, and Steve Coy, all of whom also helped keep my spirits up when I worked at the Special Collections Department of Geisel Library at UCSD when I was a graduate student. Special thanks are due to Stuart Perkoff, Boris Pillin, Tina Gainsboro, and Cliff Hickman. Vicki Steele and Simon Elliott at UCLA's Special Collections Library, Claude Zachery at USC Special Collections, Susan Perry at CSU Fullerton's Special Collections Library, Ann Butler at New York University, and Jacque Sundstrom at the University of Nevada, Las Vegas were also of significant assistance. The Huntington Library and the Andrew W. Mellon Foundation also provided small but important grants that enabled me to engage in additional research. Both Cathy Jurca and Cindy Weinstain at California Institute of Technology helped immensely in organizing an inspiring seminar in the summer of 2000 at the Huntington Library. California State University, Long Beach provided me with some release time from my teaching duties as well as a summer stipend that provided me with crucial time to revise portions of this manuscript; both the release time and the stipends partially counterposed the imposition of what can only be characterized as an astonishing amount of committee work. Finally, I want to extend my fervent gratitude to Edward Brunner and Jed Rasula for reading early drafts of what I regarded as a complete manuscript. Whatever degree of conciseness and organizational felicity this study might possess is owed in large part to the acumen of their suggestions, which helped me rectify aspects neglected in my earlier drafts.

This book is dedicated to my parents and my brother, Jim, as well as to my beloved friend and wife, Linda, whose extended family has provided me with sustaining companionship throughout this undertaking.

Introduction

Marginal Communities and the Outlaws of the Revisionist Canon

The preeminent power of the United States at the end of the cold war obscured how recently this nation had firmed up its formal geographical boundaries. *Which states were united?* In the immediate aftermath of the Korean War and the McCarthy investigations, ninety-six senators, all white, voted on whether to approve assistance to France as its effort to recolonize Vietnam teetered on disaster. Less than a decade later, responding to South Vietnam's unwillingness to abide by the anticipated results of mandated free elections, four additional senators from Hawaii and Alaska were eligible to vote on military appropriations to reinforce the postcolonial government established in Saigon. In between these ratifications of neoimperialism, John F. Kennedy became the first president whose election was confirmed by an electoral college representing fifty states. In other words, although the flag of the United States seemed to verge on centennial ripeness as solemn firemen hoisted it on the rubble of the World Trade Center's girders in September 2001, that version of the stars and stripes had manifested its amplitude, at that point, for less than a half century. The United States remains the only charter member of the United Nations to have significantly expanded and retained, after World War II, the quantity and scope of the lands constituting the full-fledged membership of its central or federal government.

On one hand, I appear to be arguing that the cold war is only a few strides away from a period that still seems almost *contemporary*, and as such not yet ready for anything more than judicious opinion. On the other hand, we should remember that people living in the United States a century ago, who might have been debating the specious justifications of our prolonged invasion of the Philippines, were exactly as far away from the U.S.-Mexican

War as we are from the beginning of the cold war. The trick is somehow to imagine that we can see the fluctuations of the more recent period as clearly as we claim to be able to distinguish and analyze the social prosody of the former span of cultural change.

Even as the official political boundaries of the United States temporarily stabilized at the fantasized limits of manifest destiny, the canon of American literature became unable to continue its rejection of marginalized voices. Feminists, gay, ethnic, and working-class writers ensnared and rearticulated the memory of how the United States had reached its status as the most deadly protagonist of the cold war. Is it merely a coincidence that as the nation formally expanded its unity, the canon of literature became a more divisive issue? In delineating a period of artistic production of which a significant portion is often described as postmodern, the communities of poets on the West Coast, particularly those in the Bay Area and Los Angeles, need to be considered as coeval factors in a distinct artistic challenge to the military-industrial-entertainment complex. Although these communities are often perceived as being engaged in fierce sibling rivalry, their strategies and material circumstances are intermingled and yet discrete. The political economy of each region placed unique stresses on poets who lived, and moved between, each city during the cold war.

The resurgence of poetry during the cold war was in large part due to its perdurability as an instrument of protest from the medieval to modernist periods. Drawing on the tradition of ballads and folk songs as well as Dadaist-inflected satire, the multitudinous communities of poets that emerged and dissolved in both Los Angeles and San Francisco during the cold war constituted an intermingled narrative of cultural upheaval that challenged the death wish of the Enlightenment project. "Go fuck yourself with your atom bomb," Allen Ginsberg plaintively cursed in the fourth line of "America," a poem in which his humorous despair alleviates the vatic angst (Ginsberg 146). "I'm putting my queer shoulder to the wheel," he sighs at the poem's conclusion, yet in making his resistance complicit with hegemonic discourse, he also realigns the centrality of his skewed poetics (148). Ginsberg and his friends, however, were only a small portion of the dispersed underground that was assaulting the zero-sum endgame of modern science's alliance with militaristic agendas. In presenting the West Coast Poetry Renaissance as a distinct area of imaginative exile, I propose to examine a wide range of poet-editors, including many World War II veterans, such as Thomas McGrath, James Boyer May, Leslie Woolf Hedley, and Alan Swallow, who defined themselves as an alternative to both the Beats and academic poets. In studying how this variegated insurgency affected the development of contemporary American poetry, I will argue that the relationship of artistic community formation to institutional power is an enduring problem of social value, especially since the outlaw status of some of these poets is not a literary construction but an actual interdiction of their lives and work.

Poetry is a relatively cheap form of art to produce, and it became a major artistic vehicle for protest against America's war in Vietnam. If the audience for poetry has subsided again, the critical interest in its social role has become more intense. The appointment of Dana Gioia as director of the Literature Program of the National Endowment for the Arts during George Bush's regime brought a new round of attention to his book, *Can Poetry Matter?*, in which Gioia argued that poetry has become a subculture that "has lost the confidence that it speaks to and for the general culture" (6). In positioning poetry as a marginal art form, however, Gioia neglects to consider whether any art form speaks to and for the general culture, and whether any such creature as the general culture actually exists. Poetry, along with other art forms such as theater, painting, dance, and video, has been important in the second half of the twentieth century precisely because it interrogated the notion that addressing an homogenous entity such as the general culture should be the primary goal of an artist. If poetry operates in a marginal manner, it also blends with these other arts by consciously destabilizing itself in an ongoing struggle between social institutions and individuals to define each other's contracted relationships in an historically contingent ecology.

Gioia's assessment of contemporary poetry as a subculture involves several errors, not the least of which is his misunderstanding of how subcultures operate. "Subcultures usually require institutions" (12), he claims in *Can Poetry Matter?* and yet what marks the vitality of most subcultures is their formation and growth as geodes of resistance that are outside of significant institutional support and regulation. Many poets, especially on the West Coast after World War II, emerged and matured as writers who either had few, if any, formal sources of support or lost or endangered those affiliations due to their acerbic social critique. These poets are often regarded as marginal, but marginality, whether cast in gender, race, or class terms and context, has unfortunately developed into a category invoked without any awareness of its historical contingency. The paradoxical strength of a marginal position has become willy-nilly an ideological assumption of modern literary criticism. As Michael Bérubé points out *Marginal Forces/Cultural Centers*: "It is by now axiomatic to post-Romantic thought that the rhetoric of marginality can be a powerful enabling device, even though marginality itself is synonymous with disempowerment: to claim to speak from the margin is paradoxically to claim to speak from a position of authority, and to describe a margin is to describe an authoritative challenge to hegemony"

(16–17). Bérubé employs this notion of marginality as he examines the work of African American poet Melvin Tolson, who sees "the goal of the margin" as achieving "access to the center in the hope of reconstructing the center" (143). Marginality, however, in being "post-Romantic," is as much a social construction as any other rubric. A perusal of the 1755 edition of Samuel Johnson's *Dictionary*, in fact, shows that the word, if it were in use, had not yet been recorded. While margin is by then embedded in English vocabulary, with one of its meanings being "a surgeon's wound," the emergence of *marginality* as a social category appears to be an understanding of relative social position congruent with other social formations such as "class" generated by the welter of the Industrial Revolution.

If the marginality of a poet is often configured as an indication of her or his capacity to critique the society that has pushed her or him to its fringes, it is also a position of flexibility and mobility.[1] Maria Damon's study of vanguard poetry after World War II, *The Dark End of the Street*, points out that marginality is inherently fluid: "no one can be in the perpetual and unqualified 'outside,' not only because it is difficult enough to strain ordinary human resources beyond their limits but because such a 'place' does not even exist.'" Damon further asserts that "the margin is not a habitat but an event, a state of becoming and devolving in constant flux. . . . The dark end of the street is not a geopolitical locale but a condition of subversive passion" (2). Damon's division of poetry into the "dark side," seething with "counterhegemonic elements" (10), and an implicit bright side, undefined but most probably a gentrified zone of accommodating quietude, replicates the mid-century binary of "cooked" versus "raw," or "Beat" versus "academic." These contrasts provide efficient ways to understand upheavals in recent and contemporary poetry, but the reductive impulse inherent in such binaries can easily erase what Damon admits is a "key issue" in analyzing marginality: the "utter physicality of place and placelessness . . . in each poet's oeuvre, though the *way* in which this is so is exquisitely peculiar and unique for each poet" (16). The singularity of each poet's blend of contingency and choice is the factor that causes Damon to admit that marginality as a synchronic device lacks sufficient clarity: the kinds of writers who are frequently perceived as marginal manage to chalk up more than a single instance of displacement (11). Class? Race? Gender?—The question of which aspect of marginality is highlighted directly affects the selection of work for a canon of literature.

Literary Access and Diversity

A canon is in part a distillation of the process by which some people have more initiating access to the fundamental tools of literacy and literary knowledge than others, and to pretend otherwise is to lend support to those who benefit from the suppression of the mechanics of the process. That amnesia is a significant tool within the discourse should not come as a surprise: cultural knowledge and artistic accomplishment are part of the prodigious symbolic and cultural capital produced daily in the United States, and the desire to separate the source of that symbolic capital from the quotidian requirements for its production is proportionately intense. Cultural capital portends not just economic resources, however, but also the means by which those who possess those resources separate the labor required to produce culture from the product itself, and then deny that labor deserves to be a factor in the evaluation of that culture. Edward Said's admonishment remains more pertinent than ever: "As it is practiced in the American academy today, literary theory has for the most part isolated textuality from the circumstances, the world, the physical means that make it possible, and render it intelligible as the result of human work" (4). Said's diagnosis revivifies Marx's classic aphorism, "No one can tell from the taste of the oats the conditions under which it was grown." Marx may still be read in the academy, but apparently his most genuine insights are not relevant to the production of contemporary poetry. A history, therefore, which does not take into serious account the material basis and practice of the art being examined perpetuates the "hidden injuries of class" interwoven within the very production of symbolic capital. In assessing the evolution of the West Coast Poetry Renaissance, not only will the keyboards of typesetting equipment at the West Coast Print Center in Oakland and NewComp Graphics Center at Beyond Baroque be part of the historical account, but specific fingertips at work on those keyboards will be called upon to contribute their testimony. The brusque subtleties of "the form and pressure of the age," as Hamlet formulated, are to be found at that passionate conjuncture of technology and human commitment.

John Guillory's *Cultural Capital* configures literary production as a field defined by institutions of learning, but I would point to an earlier stage of that process, long before the critique of textual production begins its counterpoint, in fact, and instantiate the actual experience of producing texts for cultural circulation as deserving at least equal prominence. I agree with Guillory that "the fact of class determines whether and how individuals gain access to the means of literary production," which includes the social magnifications by which one gains the self-confidence to become an agent of imaginative literacy (ix). The access to literary production, however, is not merely a matter of putting one's hands on the physical means of production, but of solidifying the possibility of action into a coherent, efficacious belief system. Class seems like a minor obstacle to everyone except those who are wiggling within its nets. Unfettered access to the subjunctive is, unfortunately, not part of every person's alleged endowment of natural rights. The potential legitimation of any literary effort is fundamentally based on one's relationship to cultural capital, which is not to say that people with relatively little reserves are doomed to be subservient to the hegemonic order. As Richard Brodhead has pointed out, human beings are extremely resourceful in finding ways to generate various kinds of narrative, but the "how" of the circulation of these texts is the crucial matter.[2] If I have chosen a group of writers whose intertwining is almost unknown to those who confer major literary awards, grants, and institutional validation in the United States, I do so in part because the need to investigate the issue of literary access promises to expand the dialogue between those who have access and those with much more limited access. African American poet Wanda Coleman, who has described the city of her birth and life-long residence as "the baddest piece of ass on the west coast," has managed to elude those restrictions enough to gain a measure of respect and significant awards, but becoming indisputably canonical is a much more challenging trek (22).

The struggle of poets in Los Angeles to define the value of their work has occurred within a larger debate in literature during the past half century. Disagreements have reached metaphorical boiling points in which critics claim that basic terms have been badly defined. "American critical theory," says Barbara Herrnstein Smith, "has been unable to acknowledge the most fundamental character of literary value, which is its mutability and diversity" (von Hallberg 14). By claiming that diversity is the essence of literary worth instead of merely an acknowledgment of one's generous eclecticism, she shifts the entire gravitational field of imaginative evaluation. Instead of strict aesthetic procedures favored by institutions, Herrnstein Smith levels the playing field so that the "circumstantial constraints" of individuals in "specific local conditions" have to be regarded as fundamentally divaricating forces shaping the canon and literary history. Personal struggle is no longer a matter of the colorful anecdote, of use primarily as the basis for entertaining banter or dinner party gossip.

One consequence of testing value by an emphasis on diversity is the necessity of reexamining the actual process by which literature is generated and circulated. The means by which literary writing has recombinant places made for it within print culture are not simply book reviews in newspapers or Weblogs, but the more quotidian, practical, and even tedious moments of the physical production of print culture: typesetting, glue-sticks, lightboards, proofreading. Diversity can only be said to be palpably represented when the time and labor required to convert authorial intent into social dialogue is included in the trajectory of canon formation.

Revisionist Canon, Revisionist Creativity

Updating and transplanting Emerson's call for an American literature in *American Scholar*, poet and publisher William Everson claimed that, while the East peruses and ponders the canon of judgment, the West exudes canonical creativity (118).[3] I do not believe that Everson intends this dichotomy to be absolute or to justify any implied dismissal of the Midwest or the South from the balancing act. Rather, I would suggest that his regional characterization alludes to a profoundly felt antinomian tendency on the West Coast as regarding its inherent right to determine the self-worth and legitimacy of its literary communities. The West Coast, Everson implies, needs to form its own canon separate from the hierarchical tradition that has developed on the East Coast, though an intense conversation between the two regions should continue to strengthen each other's adaptability to intermingled change.

Regardless of which side one might take in regard to Everson's distinction between the imaginative powers of the East Coast and West Coast, the term "canon" remains the pivot point of the debate. In *From Outlaw to Classic: Canons in American Poetry* Alan Golding argues that anthologies are the central agents in shifting weight between creativity and judgement. In particular, Golding proposes the "revisionist anthology" (30) as the crucial intervention in bringing readers to reconsider the magnitude of any given poem and its contemporary audience within the spectrum that Alastair Fowler categorizes as the potential, accessible, and useful canons (3). Revisionist anthologies, at their best, are deliberate affronts to the audiences for the most valorized writing.

In *The American Poetry Wax Museum* Jed Rasula concurs with much of Golding's analysis and in examining the canonical impact of anthologies observes that marginality is "most worth talking about not when it is the calculation of qualifications and merits in the honor-roll of oppressions suffered, nor is it the disappointment of being left out or unrecognized; rather *marginality* most tellingly names the disadvantage of having to bear the brunt of material and ideological labor that replenishes the center" (471). This labor, most often performed at a pay scale below the legal minimum wage, should be configured as involving physical exertion and not allowed to evanesce into the realm of narcissistic intellectual effort. My accounts and analysis intend to include the specific kinds of labor required to make the practice of poetry visible. In the case of a poet such as Leland Hickman, who edited three magazines (*Bachy*, *Boxcar*, and *Temblor*) in Los Angeles between 1978 and 1989, the enormous labor that sustained these projects was precisely that kind of disproportion suggested in Rasula's framework of marginality.

In suggesting that some anthologies be categorized as revisionist, Golding infers that one could assemble these anthologies on one's bookshelf and begin the process of considering a revisionist canon. (In contrast to the anxiety of influence, I would suggest that many poets experience the pleasure of belonging, the reciprocity of affection between siblings and distant cousins.) Similar to the kinds of contestation involved in establishing a canon of a period's works, the revisionist canon could be said to have three parts, the potential, the accessible, and the selective. Vatic in its motivation, the revisionist canon tends to hover in a liminal position between the potential and the accessible. The people or communities who are most active within the potential archives of the revisionist canon are far more cognizant of its size that those who endlessly reiterate the selective canon as represented in anthologies such as Poulin and Water's *Contemporary American Poetry* and its variants of fervent quietude.

The revisionist canon as a flexible and very permeable entity also offers another way to understand Everson's suggestion of the two kinds of canon, in that the West Coast is not so much a haven of more imaginatively inspired artists, but is the site of *revisionist creativity*. Partly by choice as well as contingency, the poets on the West Coast of the United States continue to provoke reassessments of the academic canon in that the prolific diversity of poetry being published and read in this region over the past century exerts an almost tectonic pressure on the fault lines of the canon. However, I would sound an important cautionary note at this point. Writing that seems central to a revisionist canon may have more than one social target, and may retain interest in being central to concerns and projects other than the putative canon of "established" literature that it supposedly so yearns to belong to and influence. This is to say that the division between the aesthetic canon and the institutional canon, the former being writer-driven and the latter pedagogically oriented, cannot be construed as the only point of departure. As Golding points out, the drift toward the institutional canon has been occurring for some time, but its dominance within the textbook marketplace can easily obscure the variety of audiences whose pleasure in being part of revisionist creativity includes the didactic aftermath of their collaboration with poets as agents of alternative liaisons of identity.

In the first chapter, "The Cartography of Dissidence," I will examine the literary history of Los Angeles, and consider how Southern California in general and Los Angeles in particular are erased from or minimized in the literary history of the West Coast. The second chapter, "Thinking Alone in Company," will examine the impact of the cold war on the first wave of literary magazines based in Los Angeles, which published a wide variety of poems and styles, ranging from the rhymed couplets of Ann Stanford to the meditative free verse of Philip Whalen. The third chapter will examine a community of anarchist poets in Venice, California, who are usually associated with the Beat movement. The title of the third chapter, "I Cannot Even Begin to Imagine the Extent of Their Aloneness," comes from the concluding lines of a poem by Stuart Perkoff that juxtaposes the poetic career of Louis Zukofsky and the lives of Dynamo poets such as Sol Funerol ("Variation on a Letter to Jonathan Williams," *Voices of the Lady: Collected Poems* 323–325). Perkoff himself pushed his life and art to the limits of Rimbaud's *voyant*, and he did not live to see the community he hoped for in Venice fully renew itself in a variant form. Venice West was one of the most notorious Beat hangouts a half century ago; its renown also faded the most quickly from view during the 1970s and 1980s, in part due to the deliberately negligible, sporadic efforts made by its members to get their work into print. Whereas other Beat scenes were certainly sincere about their alienation from the success-driven ethos of American society, they were also equally sincere about their commitment to seeing their alienation in print, with as many copies as possible in circulation. Adamantly suspicious of celebrity, the poets of Venice West perhaps had more in common with the coterie of poets clustered around Jack Spicer than with any other group. In fact, a founding member of the Venice West poetry community, Bruce Boyd, was a member of both coteries. Their reluctance to seek out publication and demonstrably outlaw behavior has combined to forestall any genuine assessment of their accomplishment. The lack of published materials continues to haunt evaluations of Venice West. The publication of Perkoff's *Voices of the Lady*, for instance, was an important first step, but it contains major errors in the chronology of the poems.

The fourth chapter is an account of the founding and development of Beyond Baroque, a literary arts center in Venice. During the 1970s independent bookstores multiplied in Los Angeles as places of cultural activism. Almost every one of the bookstores has folded, but Beyond Baroque has managed to survive into the second decade of the twenty-first century. This chapter will focus on the first half of Beyond Baroque's history, although its recently departed artistic director, Fred Dewey, has probably done more than anyone since its founder, George Drury Smith, to make Beyond Baroque a place that enables many different communities to connect. Under Dewey, for example, Beyond Baroque staged a collaborative festival with The World Stage in Leimert Park, and published a substantial collection of poetry by an original member of the Watts Writers Workshop, the group of writers that emerged from the Watts Rebellion in 1965. This chapter includes my own recollections of editing and publishing poetry as well as a brief account of the impact of another important small press, Little Caesar, which flourished along with Beyond Baroque under the artistic direction of Dennis Cooper.

The final chapter will examine several magazines or presses that were published or edited in Los Angeles between 1968 and 1990, a period that established Los Angeles as perhaps one of the most active sites for literary magazine production in the entire United States. All of these magazines have ceased publication, but many of the poets most associated with these magazines have continued to produce significant bodies of work, and my conclusion will examine the contrast between their frequent appearance in local anthologies and their continued absence from collections that are recognized as being the primary shapers of a contemporary canon.

In attempting to classify the writing and publishing activities of these poets, editors, and publishers, the need to distinguish between subversive and dissident as formative impulses within overlapping communities will continually recur. In *Faultlines: Cultural Materialism and the Politics of Dissident Reading* Alan Sinfield argues that the limited scope of dissidence, which he defines as the "refusal of an aspect of the dominant, without prejudging an outcome" (49), has more potential as a means for a subculture to generate an enduring response from the "prevailing system." Subversion is configured as more ambitious by Sinfield, and also more likely to be contained, and perhaps even be put to use by the dominant order. In either case, even a failed effort can produce a delayed change.

> Because subcultures are made to constitute the other, even because they
> are stigmatized and policed, they gain subversive leverage. Precisely their
> outlaw status may exert a fascination for the dominant, focusing subversive
> fantasies of freedom, vitality, even squalor. So they form points from which
> repression may be become apparent, silences audible. In focusing our work
> there is a withdrawal to base, it is a base from which the prevailing system
> may yet be discomposed, unsettled, obliged to acknowledge a larger con-
> ception of humanity. (299)

I would suggest that Sinfield's "larger conception of humanity" has a real object that reflects the expansion or diminution of a "conception of humanity," and that object is the canon of literature, a thing which is always open to revision and realignment. The development of any given canon of literature, whether constructed by genre or period or categorical affiliations, constitutes a narrative that tends to get lost within the ideological camouflage provided by institutional rewards and privileges. In the past half century the institutional canon of American literature has undergone serious revision, but much of the labor performed by poet-editors that contributed to this revision, needs to be reinscribed in accounts of contemporary literature. "All stories comprise within themselves," says Sinfield, "the ghosts of the alternative stories they are trying to exclude" (47). Dissidence and subversion often make their first moves by coaxing the alternative stories into some measure of visibility, and I propose that there are more ghosts impatient for their story to be told in Los Angeles than in any other American city of the past century.[4]

ONE

The Cartography of Dissidence

Los Angeles and Literary History
on the West Coast

Minor Literature in a Major Light: Representational Space and the Chronotope in Los Angeles

An abundance of resonant, palpitating daylight appears to have been a determining factor in nurturing the development of the film industry in Southern California, but the uses to which other artists have put this light constitutes a sustained alternative narrative of culture in Los Angeles. Although the metaphorical cameras of poets often prefer skies the gray of crystal rather than a steady cascade of light, I suggested a quarter century ago in my introduction to an anthology of writers, musicians, actors, and performance artists that the variegated quality of light in L.A. has served to attract or retain poets in a city whose cultural economy regards poetry as irrelevant (*"Poetry Loves Poetry"*). Lawrence Weschler subsequently confirmed my hunch about the alluring power of the region's incandescence, and how its indigenous radiance, despite massive doses of industrial fumes, strikes many artisans in Los Angeles as being unique. "There's something about the environment here—the air, the atmosphere, the light—that makes *everything* shimmer. There's a kind of glowing thickness to the world—the diaphanous soup I was talking about, which, in turn, grounds a magic-meditative sense of presence," says architect Coy Howard in Weschler's article. Yet this light is not uniform, and *everything* does not shimmer to the same degree; the disparities in the reproduction of social life in Los Angeles affect the visibility of its citizens' lives, both to each other directly and in the shared representations of their daily lives.

If any group of residents in Los Angeles can be said to engage in a critique of the social layers and auras of their city, the poets would be among the most prominent sources of that urban self-examination. Paul Vangelisti, a poet-editor-publisher who has lived and worked in Los Angeles since 1968, argues that the light in Los Angeles "is perhaps the single most distinguishing characteristic" (8) for writers in Los Angeles. In a brief introduction to *L.A. Exile*, Vangelisti describes the appeal that living there can have for writers as "alluring . . . It is precisely the extreme presence and absence, the simultaneous up close and far away of things the light yields, drawing the writer to lose oneself inward in a most tangible way, not in the least nostalgic or metaphysical" (17). The simultaneous "up close and far away" of Vangelisti's description is also the bifurcation that occurs to poets practicing their craft: "In Los Angeles, we write as necessarily absent and present: present to the fundamental passion for the craft perhaps felt no more intimately and immediately than in such 'splendid isolation'; absent from the fake history, the boosterism, the ever-more insidious banality of what most familiarly, in this town, is called the Business" (16).

If Vangelisti assesses the literary writer's attitude toward the Business as indifference, Julian Murphet adds in *Literature and Race in Los Angeles* what he regards as the haughtiness of the East Coast literary establishment to the already substantial burden of poets and fiction writers in Los Angeles. Los Angeles may have great light, but you can't eat it. Revealing a hint of visceral sympathy for the plight of Los Angeles poets, Murphet says that the literary writer in L.A. is "predisposed to glaring back at the world of established Letters and visual entertainment with all the menace of an underclass on a hot day" (5). (On a cold, damp February night, too, I would add.) Murphet draws on Delueze and Guattari's notion of a minor literature to establish his first axiom: "Los Angeles is already there. It is the place where all literature is minor" (6). In configuring literature this way in a city in which representation is the most problematic social force, Murphet reminds us that "the concept of the 'minor' only makes sense in determinate relation to what excludes it: governmentality, wealth, power, hegemony, or whatever shorthand you use for the concentration of might under late capitalism" (2). Murphet's study largely concentrates "on those efforts of the last fifteen years or so which have made 'postmodern Los Angeles' the object of their chronotopic labours" (32). This timeline allows him to concentrate on poets whose work he identifies as representative of "the point of view of the ethnic, working-class oppressed," such as Wanda Coleman and Sesshu Foster. In examining these writers, he urges us to consider Los Angeles "not as a reified fetish, but *as a* product—the product of its forgotten working class." His reading of a major poet such as Wanda Coleman is a long overdue consideration of her work, but his choice of her work is explicitly made as an either-or selection between white, middle-class writers or the ethnic, working-class.[1] Coleman herself, however, in a self-portrait that Murphet quotes, shows that the wheel of postmodern identity has many spokes: "My poverty level steadily climbs. I pay blood for everything. Open my pages and read my bleed: the essence of racism is survival; the primary mechanism, economics. The power to have is the power to do. I, black worker 'womon' poet angelena, disadvantaged first by skin, second by class, third by sex, fourth by craft . . . , fifth by regionality" (*African Sleeping Sickness* 218). Race, class, sex, craft, region. Coleman enunciates each of these categories as a disadvantage, and while in her case they accumulate into an implied indictment of the odds she confronts, they also imbricate themselves as points of contact with a significant number of other poets in Los Angeles. Class, region, and craft (meant both as choice of genre and quality of execution) make for an invigorating overlap between Coleman and her "group affiliations."

> Up at Lee's new apartment on Griffith, back in the early 80s, we watch the first documentary video tape of our maturing literary scene—another failed attempt to get any documentation on the new Southern California bards on Public Broadcasting. Before leaving I tell Lee that one day those video tapes, and the poets on them, will be very important. That we're *the* generation. Like Hemingway and Gertrude, like Virginia Woolf and Bloomsbury, like Henry (Miller) and Anais (Nin), Kerouac and Ginsberg. We're a group a movement a happening. I'm not bragging, I'm describing what I believe, the place where I've invested my future. Lee buries his hands deep in his pockets and goes into thoughtful silence as he walks me to my car. The night is clear, the stars twinkle, I can see the observatory from where we stand.
> "I've never thought of us quite that way, Wanda."
> I'm surprised and not sure I believe him. I'd always assumed Lee had more ego. My laughter fills the street. "Thank about it Lee, we're literary L.A., baby." (*Native in a Strange Land* 114)

"Lee" refers to Leland Hickman, a gay poet and editor who probably published more of Coleman's work in the 1970s than any other magazine editor in the United States. The stature that Coleman attributes to the work being done in Los Angeles would probably strike most critics as being a considerable overestimate of the actual accomplishment. Even Murphet, the most enthusiastic apologist for contemporary writers in Los Angeles, admits that "there are no masterpieces here, no great artificers, just intensities of immanence and becoming-minor" (6–7).[2] Murphet, however, regards that standard as simply an impoverished excuse offered by those who are not willing to admit that "we are not at any rate in need of 'classics' or 'masters', only of sober enunciations of what goes unvoiced, the 'people's concerns' in this time of an ever more purified dominance." At this point, I must part company with Murphet. "What goes unvoiced" is a far more complicated story than can be reduced to "the people's concerns." Indeed, to consider the lives and work of Coleman and Hickman would serve as a basic illustration of how difficult it is to define what constitutes "the people's concerns." If artists in any way give voice to the intimate obsessions of bonded individuals, the voices we hear will reflect the diversity of their needs and abilities. There is no reason to expect that "the people" would be any less wanting or more unified than writers, whose "fractured community . . . is exemplary of the general experience of neglect, prejudice, lack of achieved solidarity and self-laceration experienced by almost all the minorities under an unremitting domination" (3).

Murphet alludes to "a few of the difficulties faced by the writers themselves, in achieving recognition locally and at large" (3). Both Hickman and Coleman participated in the Beyond Baroque Poetry Workshop, and both had mixed experiences with the organization, which is now well into its fifth decade as the oldest major alternative literary arts center in Southern California. Murphet makes one very brief passing reference to Beyond Baroque and does not mention the Woman's Building at all. In estimating the heft of cultural work, Raymond Williams urged us to continually remember "the immediate conditions of a practice—the signalled places, occasions and terms of specifically indicated types of cultural activity" (Thurston 28). In Los Angeles the many difficulties of serious, non-academic poets—whether it be any combination of class, race, and gender—in gaining attention for their work have more to do with the disparity between their reputations in Los Angeles and their anonymity elsewhere.

Los Angeles fiction writers, or those who use the city as their primary staging ground, on the other hand, seem to find that their native or adopted landscape replenishes their reputations. Indeed, in terms of fiction, Los Angeles has overcome its position of the younger literary sibling on the West Coast. Between the gold rush and the Wall Street crash in 1929, San Francisco flourished as an attractive site for writers ranging from Mark Twain to Frank Norris; since then, however, Los Angeles has increasingly served as a provocative and often cynical muse to a distinguished ensemble of fiction writers.[3] In part, this respect for its fiction writers derives from the city's splayed aura of depravity within the public sphere. However little else the communities of poets and writers in Los Angeles during the cold war had in common, they shared an awareness that their city was perceived elsewhere as a quintessential site of _noir_ narrative. In fact, perhaps no other city in the United States is so emphatically associated with protagonists whose prime task is to solve violent crimes. The association of Los Angeles and murder mysteries shows little evidence of declining. If Horace McCoy, James M. Cain, Dorothy B. Hughes, Raymond Chandler, and Chester Himes were among the earliest writers to deploy Los Angeles as the milieu for their stories of

surroundings

seething betrayal and ironic punishment, more recent writers, such as Ross Macdonald, Joseph Hansen, John Gregory Dunne, James Ellroy, Walter Mosley, T. Jefferson Parker, and Tyler Dilts, have continued to depict Los Angeles as a place in which prevarication and violence engage in a mutually hypnotic *pas de deux*. Richard Lehan has argued that "probably no city in the western world has a more negative image than Los Angeles, depicted as it is on nightly TV as one vast freeway system, enshrouded in smog, carrying thousands of dreamers to a kind of spiritual and physical dereliction. We often move in this world from a sense of promise to a sense of the grotesque, and hence to the violent and the apocalyptic" (quoted in Fine 1995). If by the final decade of the past century the Los Angeles novel had become stigmatized by its "phantasmagoric quality," according to the primary chronicler of California history, Kevin Starr, the poetry scenes in Los Angeles had contrastingly produced a body of work that yielded "a most extraordinary connection between poetry and life, between poetry and the daily facts of Los Angeles" (480–481). Starr then optimistically conjectures that "someday, someone would figure out why the L.A. novel went one way while poetry took another path" (481). Starr's emphasis on the development of poetry as "popular vernacular art" in Southern California, especially in the anthology he cites, *Grand Passion: The Poets of Los Angeles and Beyond* (1995), is probably the reason why "path" is singular in his prediction. He seems unaware of the contributions of poets and editors such as Leland Hickman, Paul Vangelisti, and Douglas Messerli, all of whom were left out of *Grand Passion*, to the emergence of a maverick avant-garde in Los Angeles between 1970 and the end of the century, and so the paths which poets from San Francisco and Los Angeles share end up being left off the map.[4]

In terms of an accurate social critique, the distinction between writers in San Francisco and Los Angeles quickly dissolves into a superficial rivalry. Both cities simultaneously serve as sites to rebuke American exceptionalism in an alternating pincer attack; at any given moment, Los Angeles provides the main assault and San Francisco conducts extraordinarily effective guerilla insurgency, and six months later, the roles are reversed. The story of the emergence of poetic communities on the West Coast, therefore, is more complex than the prevalent version of poetic northern California and prosaic Southern California can accommodate.

The term "West Coast Poetry Renaissance" is my own description of the plenitude of poetic activity on the West Coast for close to a half century. I have appropriated the term "renaissance" from its usual postmodern partner, San Francisco, and applied it to a larger spatial increment of coastline, something akin to a fertile crescent's elongated delta, in order to provide a familiar

*being revived   *full of complaints*

crucial

rubric for a reviviscency, a term that lacks felicity, but at least partially evades the potentially querulous cultural overtones that accompany renaissance. Poetry did come to life again, especially on the West Coast, after World War II, and it did so at a particularly low point for the art form. "Although poets frequently find themselves at odds with mainstream culture," Hilene Flanzbaum has noted, "at no time in American literary history did they feel more embattled and more on the brink of extinction than in the years following World War II" (25). That apparent fate was avoided in large part because the eruption of poetic activity in both Los Angeles and San Francisco during the next several decades was more than the sum of individual careers, but proved to be a sustained inquiry into the relationship between community formation to institutional power during the cold war. The conjunction of rapidly proliferating small presses, independent bookstores, and alternative production spaces on the West Coast was, in particular, a renitent counterattack against the pedagogical uses of literature by the New Criticism. If, as Ross Chambers argues, "Literature is the discourse of power made readable" (18), the small press movement enabled poet-editor-publishers to question both the social form and content of that discourse's legibility.

Some contemporary poets might argue that the scenes that emerged during this decades following World War II are still flourishing, and that if such an entity as the West Coast Poetry Renaissance ever existed, it is still flourishing. Poetry certainly entered the twenty-first century in much better shape than it was at the midpoint of the previous one, and if anyone wishes to proclaim that the West Coast Poetry Renaissance is still in full steam, I will be happy to bask in their optimism, even though the small press movement that was a central element of that renaissance is now only a small fraction of its previous strength. In any reconnaissance of the production, distribution, and analysis of American poetry after World War II, however, one must be constantly alert to the metonymic tendency to equate northern California with the West Coast. This caution is rarely needed when one discusses poetic production on the East Coast; the poets in New York City are never conflated with all of New England, let alone the East Coast. In writing about poets on the West Coast, though, many critics unreflectively attribute the activity in the San Francisco Bay Area to the entire West Coast, constricting a narrative of literary legitimation about the region between Seattle and San Diego to an epicenter of San Francisco-Berkeley-Oakland. A typical example would be Lee Bartlett's lament: "While the work of postwar West Coast poets has a wide readership both in this country and abroad, the critical response has been generally disappointing" (xii). The representative figures he chooses to connote "three generations" of West Coast poetic experimentation are all white males associated with northern California: Rexroth, Everson, Duncan,

Patchen, Spicer, Jeffers, Snyder, McClure, Gunn, Tarn, Palmer, and Silliman. Linda Hamalian expands this list to include poets such as Bob Kaufman, Lenore Kandel, and Joanne Kyger in her article, "Regionalism Makes Good: The San Francisco Renaissance," but she equates that renaissance and the West Coast as exclusively identical signifiers.

> With the San Francisco Renaissance, the looming homogenization of the United States was suspended. With the emergence of the West Coast as a literary center, a kind of "multiregionalism" took over, which perhaps formed a prototype for the current multiculturalism (with the old boys network short-circuited). Certainly, the flowering of countless poetry journals and small quality private presses on the West Coast, and throughout the country for that matter, has offered evidence of that. (Kowalewski 228–229)

While I am not disputing the efficacy of the San Francisco Renaissance as a major point of cultural intervention, the "emergence of the West Coast" as a literary center during the cold war can hardly be surveyed, let alone investigated, by limiting the boundaries to less than four hundred square miles. Instead, the cartography of poetic dissidence in Los Angeles and San Francisco reveals overlapping contours of intense juridical and institutional hostility toward artists who identify themselves with informal communities. If "multiregionalism" took over, a proposition that requires substantial qualification, it did so because numerous communities of poets on the West Coast, including those in Los Angeles, were already engaged by the mid-1950s in defining their own specific opposition to the "looming homogenization" of the United States. The trial of Allen Ginsberg and Lawrence Ferlinghetti for *Howl and Other Poems* may have gotten the most publicity, but the blacklisting of poets such as Thomas McGrath and Don Gordon, and the trial and conviction of Wallace Berman in Los Angeles, constitute equally integral parts of the artistic struggle to establish the social legitimacy of art that protested political and sexual censorship.

The artists in Los Angeles, it could be argued, paid a higher price for their defiance than their counterparts in northern California. As Richard Cándida Smith recounts in *Utopia and Dissent: Art, Poetry, and Politics in California*, Los Angeles artist Connor Everts not only was put on trial for exhibiting obscene paintings, but lost teaching jobs. In a subsequent confrontation with undercover police officers, he was beaten so badly that nine out of twelve jurors voted to convict the police officers of violating Everts's civil rights. During the trial, his art studio was trashed, and a message was left that implied the police planned to deal more harshly with him in the future. In adding this instance of the penalties inflicted by the police and the justice system to better-known prosecutions in Los Angeles of writing, theater, and visual art such as Michael McClure's *The Beard* in 1968 and Wallace Berman's conviction, Cándida Smith expands the scope of artistic rebellion on the West Coast to include both northern and Southern California.

"Enabling fictions (of) inaugural moments," to use one of Michael Davidson's many felicitous phrases in *The San Francisco Renaissance*, are important for any movement or period. The reading at the Six Gallery in October 1955 by Allen Ginsberg, Philip Whalen, Michael McClure, Philip Lamantia, and Gary Snyder is often cited as a pivotal event. Thomas Parkinson in *Poets, Poems, Movements* reminds us, though, "when Lawrence Ferlinghetti came to San Francisco in 1953 and Allen Ginsberg in 1954, they were not entering a cultural void. . . . They found a sounding board . . . The audience and structure of public address were there, and the literary atmosphere was receptive" (176–177).[5] The affirmation was more than local, however: in 1955, for instance, the West Coast had only one well-established magazine willing to print members of the Beat generation such as Ginsberg, Kerouac, and Whalen; it was located in Los Angeles. Grover Jacoby, Jr., the editor of *Variegation* magazine, accepted the poems by Kerouac and Ginsberg before the Six Gallery reading took place, indicating that at least one editor in the nation was open to their work before any publicity about the Beat generation occurred. In approaching its sixtieth anniversary, Lawrence Ferlinghetti's City Lights Bookstore certainly deserves its international reputation, but it is not the poetic cynosure of the West Coast; rather, the contingent of poets, editors, and publishers in Long Beach, Santa Barbara, San Luis Obispo, and Santa Cruz, as well as San Francisco and Los Angeles, who contributed in a collective manner during the entire cold war to the development of the current diversity of American poetry, deserves that honor.

Clayton Eshleman has described the aftermath of this diaspora as:

> more complexly adversarial than in the past. . . . (The) positions that have divided poets against their peers (and against themselves) have scattered into a kind of archipelago of sites . . . that could also be described as a blizzard made up of academic poets, vagabond poets, student poets, Buddhist poets, eco-poets, surrealists, language poets, Neo-Formalists, haiku clubs, deaf signing poets, and poetry slams. In a fragmentary and confusing way, we are approaching what Robert Duncan called "a symposium of the whole." (263–265)

The metaphor of the "archipelago" seems more accurate to me, although if one preferred the notion of a blizzard, it is worth remembering that the wind that drives the storm is feminist poetry, absent from Eshleman's partial census. In contrast, feminist poetry is at the core of Maria Damon's suggestion that "island culture . . . is in fact a useful paradigm . . . Californian poetry can and has traveled and become cross-germinal for and with other movements and other locales. . . ." (258). Building on Mary Louise Pratt and Hakim Bey, Damon suggests that California poetry could be imagined as "a temporary autonomous contact zone," but other than mentioning tropes of constant movement and hybridity, Damon provides no more details of how a particular scene in northern California can elucidate all of California poetry. I wish to emphasize that I am not interested in setting up a contest that smacks of bragging rights. At any given moment, San Francisco or Los Angeles might have more poetry magazines or more reading series or more poets being published in magazines outside their so-called local efforts. (I would note that a magazine with a print run of five hundred copies in New York City would never regard itself as simply "local.") My point is that all of the poetic work done on the West Coast needs to be considered as contributing to a much more coherent and interwoven history than has previously been presented. In a sense, both San Francisco and Los Angeles cheat each other when the story of West Cost poetry is split up. The astonishing amount of work produced in both cities—and how much it had in common—should be the focus of critics who wish to come to terms with the most prolonged single renaissance in the literature of the United States. Until that happens, cognizant literary chorographers should feel abashed and ambivalent about any praise, no matter how effusive, extended to one terminus that implicitly relies on the exclusion of the other.

In contrast with the pattern of poetry critics allowing one local scene to subsume an entire coast, theater critics are much more specific about place and organizations in correlating a similar movement to disperse canonical power into a spectrum of communities. In American theater, beginning in the 1960s, regional stages began to challenge Broadway as being more than out-of-town tryout plays or outlets for summer revival festivals. Gordon Davidson, artistic director of the Mark Taper Forum for over thirty years, insists that the "decentralization of the American theater is the most challenging and enduring transformation of the last three decades" (Kolin/Kullman 162). If white male playwrights such as Eugene O'Neil, Tennessee Williams, Arthur Miller, and Edward Albee tended to dominate the playbills in previous decades, then the emergence of feminist, Chicano and African American playwrights after 1970 provides an invigorating parallel with transformation in authorial identity and region in poetry. In the case of theater's transformation, however, this decentralization was accompanied by widespread artistic experimentation. Unlike poetry, in which the avant-garde languished during the 1960s, theater provided the most memorable experimental interventions simultaneously with this decentralization. In noting that "the sixties literary avant-garde was strongest in the performing arts which united radical studies of the actor's physical and psychological capacities with the collective experience of political and aesthetic activism," Charles Russell names specific groups that served as avant-garde investigations: the Living Theater, the Performance Group, the Open Theater, the San Francisco Mime Troup, the Bodacious Buggerilla, *El Teatro* Campesino (245). The Company Theater in Los Angeles, as well as its offshoot, the Provisional Theater, could be added to Russell's list.[6] A survey of contemporary American playwrights which would regard itself as in any degree comprehensive would inevitably have to mention the Padua Hills Theater Festival in Los Angeles.

In examining poetry after the Second World War, therefore, I wish to follow the more generous model of acknowledgment and inclusion seen in assessments of the cultural work in theater. As is the case with poetry, theater is often perceived as a relatively marginal art; the entertainment industry of movies and popular music appears to make both superfluous, and both have almost simultaneously become areas of minor consideration within the field of literature. Nevertheless, by being a prime example of the decentralization of art during the past half century, theater is poised to remind us of the need to expand the context if we are to address the crucial question that concludes Cary Nelson's *Repression and Recovery: Modern American Poetry and the Politics of Cultural Memory 1910–1945* (246): what is "the social meaning of a life lived on poetry's behalf"? Accompanying this question about extrapolating a significant pattern from the struggles of an individual artist is Nelson's argument "that what is at stake in the varied poetic discourses of modern American poetry is not only the aesthetics of an individual cultural domain but also the network of relations that define the nature and boundaries of that domain, and grant it influence or irrelevance elsewhere in social life" (245). In acknowledging that "poetry is the literary genre that is most consistently, thoroughly, and unreflectively idealized" (245–246), Nelson is implicitly suggesting that the answer to his question involves some measure of heroism. With a bifurcating pun emanating from its pair of syllables, behalf's active and passive overtones subvert its own proposed idealism: lingering in the word's unctuous sincerity are both self-empowered agency and that which lacks the ability to participate resoundingly in public discourse. One part of Nelson's question involves determining what qualities comprise a representative poet, but he also knows that question cannot be separated from the potential or real audience whose work the poet addresses. Laboring on behalf of a small audience whose gratitude may be limited by their own economics to very limited purchases of books or audiotapes does require a certain amount of selflessness, and this would constitute a fairly common image of a poet's fate. A more difficult question is how does this fortitude affect the ability of a poet and her audience to intervene in the public sphere, or in a more likely scenario, poets and their audiences, many of which will be overlapping and even possibly in direct conflict.

The constant fluctuation of poet and audience is a significant factor in the instantiation of any "poetry scene," a term that Joseph Harrington puts in quotation marks to suggest a certain degree of indeterminacy. Building on criticism by Ernesto Leclau and Chantal Mouffe of Jürgen Habermas's notion of the public sphere, Harrington defines "poetry scene" in *Poetry and the Public* as "an empty space that is not defined in advance" (13). Harrington's description of a "poetry scene," however, does not include how one determines access to this space, or even what might be required for a space to empty out to a point where "fluid types of poetries and poetry communities could compete to determine the meaning of poetry (which they never do, once and for all)" (13). Harrington makes it sound as if anyone and everyone has equal access to this empty space, but one can be forgiven, I think, for suspecting that this empty space might prove as restricted as the "public sphere" of Habermas. If we choose to look at particular scene in answering these questions, the most useful part of his definition deserves to be kept foremost in any response: in a poetry scene, Harrington asserts, "any clear distinction between public and private has dissolved—except (and this is crucial) in the discourse employed by some of the contestants in the struggle" (13). For Harrington, therefore, the relationship between any given audience and a specific poet, whether a hermetic figure or a vatic provocateur, occurs in a space imbued with the romanticism of John Keats's "negative capability." Akin with marginality, the "empty space" that Harrington invokes ultimately harks back to the suspension of certainty that Keats believed to be the quickening factor of an imagination embedded in the subjunctive mode. In the final instance, I would argue that not only should the empty space not be defined in advance, but even in retrospect, it should be allowed to flow back into whatever provisional calculations emerge from dialogues about the events of any given scene.

Los Angeles and Literary History on the West Coast

The distinction between the public and the private as I examine various poetry scenes in Southern California as empty spaces has some immediate import. In consideration of full disclosure regarding partisanship, I need to state that I was a participant in some of these events. However, a very significant portion of this book addresses the lives and work of writers who were active in Los Angeles long before my own involvement began in the early 1970s. In attempting to be both partial participant and impartial critic, I am joining a growing movement among literary artists to reclaim their own domain, a critical insurgency that began with the Language writers in the mid-seventies. Bob Perelman's *The Marginalization of Poetry* is a prime example of a poet and academic critic addressing a period and literary movement in which he himself took part. While Perelman's book focuses on the period of the cold war that began with the protracted withdrawal of American troops from Vietnam, *Hold-Outs* will consider a much larger portion of the cold war period as the context for major transitions in American poetry.

In a section entitled "Overthrowing and Entering Literary History," Perelman notes that "literary history is normally a retrospective category of bureaucratic struggle and consensus, and not a site for active writing" (11). "Normally," however, is not always. As David Perkins points out in *Is Literary History Possible?* "one very important type of literary history is written for the purpose of distorting, attacking, or revising the past, or repressing a portion of it. Poets and novelists frequently generate such literary history in order to clear space for their own work" (21). I would argue that this kind of history is not so much a deliberate attempt to prevaricate, as when George W. Bush claimed that Iraq possessed weapons of mass destruction. Rather, portions of the past are deleted because, as Perkins notes elsewhere, analytical accounts of any given group of writers could be subject to a volatile, and almost infinite sequence of potential contexts for their work that could indefinitely forestall any conclusions. "For practical reasons," Perkins goes on to say, "each book or article describes only a small piece of the context. But then a convincing argument must be given for privileging the bit of context we choose" (128). The irony, of course, of *privilege* is that the word is all too often turned loose like a surly attack dog on those who have had the least privilege in the academy.

In studying this period, I propose to be as inclusive as possible, in so far as I am able to present distinctions between communities that avoid oversimplified or reductive binaries. Perelman's account, which approximately encompasses the years between 1972 and 1995, seems to hark back to stark divisions between groups of poets that characterized earlier critical assessments of American poetry (cooked vs. raw). In citing Robert von Hallberg's opinion that a "poetry of accommodation" (13) dominated the mainstream of American poetry after the United States was defeated in Vietnam, Perelman privileges Language writing as the primary center of opposition to mainstream poetics. Perelman is certainly spot on when he acknowledges the "unaccommodating poetics" of Language writing, which did serve to provoke fierce denunciations from poets associated with what Charles Bernstein has called "official verse culture" (Lazer 28). But is that the only contest going on within American poetry during that time?

Perelman's brief account of the literary history of Language writing concludes with remarks on the process of entering and overthrowing literary history; specifically, he notes the importance of "specific venues, magazines and publishing ventures . . . in forming the sense of a group project and making that project various." He summarizes this "initial phase of language writing" in his penultimate paragraph:

> The development of presses—Lyn Hejinian's Tuumba chapbook series, Geoff Young's press, The Figures; Barrett Watten's This Press; James Sherry's Roof Press—established something *of a complete literary environment* for language writing. This development can be interpreted variously. *The completeness of its self-management allowed for immediate access to publication* and review, which in turn encouraged large-scale projects and formal variety. Most importantly, this created a sense that writing was public, breaking open new territory and entering changing literary history seemed synonymous. (16–17, my italics)

Perelman's emphasis on the role of presses and publishing in the development of Language writing is an important part of the narrative, but he is leaving out the context in which these presses operated, and within which these gestures gained immediate legitimacy. If Language writers decided to start their own publications, they did so after hundreds of other poets, experimental writers, and social activists had already engaged in that strategy. The starting point of Young's The Figures was his magazine, *Stooge*, which was one of a couple hundred publishing efforts to take out a full-page ad in a catalog published by COSMEP (Committee of Small Magazine Editors and Publishers) in 1973. If the Berkeley Poetry Conference in 1965 is often considered the culmination of the crescendo of poets whose work appeared in Donald Allen's *The New American Poetry* anthology in 1960, the COSMEP conference in Berkeley in 1968 can be said to mark the formal beginning of a movement of small press editors and publishers that continued to accelerate for the next dozen years.

One of COSMEP's founders, Len Fulton, asserted in 1973 in the *Whole COSMEP Catalog* (*WCC*) that "the small press movement in its present form started during 1963–1964, between the cold stagnation of the Fifties and the heated Sixties" (Higgins 6).[7] Fulton, however, was referring to more than poetry magazines in assigning this date to the small press movement, which was a double-pronged attack on every major social institution in the United States on the part of both underground newspapers and small magazines. "We considered it a last desperate assertion of the individual against the giant machine—social, military, academic, cultural, spiritual. The word was do-it-yourself, and in publishing it took two main directions: towards poetry and art (in the small mags/presses), and towards journalism (in the underground newspapers)" (*WCC*, "Peopleship," lead editorial article in unpaginated catalog, page 6 from title page). The confluence of the underground newspapers and small press poetry magazines is the larger context in which eighty small press editors and publishers gathered in Berkeley between May 23–26, 1968.[8] The meeting was an especially contentious gathering, mainly because of antagonism between West Coast poets and the representative of the Coordinating Council of Literary Magazines (CCLM), Caroline Herron. CCLM was headquartered in New York City, and was perceived by many participants at the conference as primarily affiliated with university magazines. Alexandra Garrett, a representative of *Trace* magazine in Los Angeles, recalled the conference, until its final hours, was a prolonged stalemate:

> At the first meeting, and for two days thereafter, the Berkeley radical poets shouted down every attempt to hold a meeting; Carolyn [*sic*] Herron . . . was shouted into silence, but the people who had organized the conference waited for two days until the shouters went away, and then only on the last day was it possible to organize COSMEP. Among the principal organizers were Hugh Fox, Jerry Burns, Len Fulton, Richard Morris, Doug Blazek, and D. R. Wagner. (Peattie 146)

Garrett's account of the turbulence of the first two days is confirmed by John Oliver Simon, one of the editors of an anthology featuring poets who read during the course of the conference. In a brief introduction, Simon recalls the open structure of the readings, classifying two of them as "semi-scheduled" and another pair as open readings.

> Sometime history will say/ ah those were the days. Literary history which always takes then more seriously than now, will catch up to this point eventually also. I had a nice time at the conference. It also pulled my head way down. No blame, I guess, tho I screamed a couple times, once at caroline heron [*sic*] from the cclm/cia saying "That's the way it goes". . . . What cld you expect from dozens of random poets, editors, local & national paranoid madmen assembled in a very heavy locale. 5 weeks later the people were fighting the cops outside shakespeare's.
>
> it always takes so long to go out of egypt. (Krech and Simon, 1968, unpaginated)

The blending of East Coast institutional organizations (the National Endowment for the Arts dispersed its funds to little magazines through CCLM) with the Central Intelligence Agency may appear to be an extreme position to take, but Simon's association of institutional regimentation with bureaucratic centrality is expanded on by a manifesto-poem by Ron Silliman which appears in the anthology.

> The libraries are filled with the wrong books. . . . The college classes are even worse. . . . It is time to govern ourselves. Poetry is still the most advanced of the arts. 70,000 students on college campuses are taking courses in writing poetry. How many will be destroyed by their . . . profs? 69,995? Poets must rise above negation, it is the poets who will bring in the new world. Will you ever get to Grail Castle? Will I?
>
> You need not write about the war, only about the world! In a world of wars, of racists, of thieves leading nations, all poems relate directly. Be with yourself, you are what is needed, the word is you. (Krech and Simon, 1968, unpaginated)

Despite the youthful insouciance of his rhetoric, Silliman's assertion that "it is time to govern ourselves" is worth noting because it sums up the fundamental attitude of the poets and publishers at this conference. COSMEP expanded rapidly, going from 110 paid members in the fall of 1968 to 540 paid members five years later. In the ten years following its founding, annual conferences were held in almost every region across the country, with San Diego, Buffalo, Ann Arbor, Madison (Wisconsin), New York, Austin, and New Orleans hosting the gatherings. Headquartered in San Francisco, the development of COSMEP provides a chart of significant changes in the small press world of poets who also functioned as editors and publishers.[9]

In the ninth edition of *International Directory of Little Magazines & Small Presses*, its editor, Len Fulton, reports on a survey of 589 presses about circulation and printing. The number of issues that an average little magazine was putting into the hands of readers was still a tiny fraction of the general readership. The median circulation was 779 in 1973. A significant change had occurred, however, between the mid-sixties and the early seventies in regard to the printing process. "Presses using mimeo dropped almost in half between 1965 and 1973. (23% in 1965 to 12% in 1973). Furthermore, in the thirteen years between 1960 and 1973, small presses using letterpress dropped from 78% to 19%, whereas small presses using offset lithography to publish their authors increased from 17% to 69%" (158–159). This change in production reflects what should be addressed if one is to consider the notion that

Perelman suggests in a phrase such as "complete literary environment." I do not believe that one can describe a complete literary environment, any more than one can produce a complete literary history, but if the literary history of avant-garde poets at the end of the Vietnam War is to possess any degree of insightful perspective, the efforts of the poets and small press editors who founded and nurtured COSMEP needs to be an essential part of the story.

COSMEP grew out of Fulton's experiences as the editor of a little magazine, *Dust*, that he founded in 1963. His experience in producing the magazine led him to become: "self-consciously interested in the *production of literature*. . . . I found it terribly agreeable to be in touch with other small pressmen, to know what they were doing. Something in me dispermits my holding focus on just my own things. . . . The human drama of *how* literature gets produced is fascinating and vital as an art form laid over other art forms" (Peattie 37). Perhaps a variant definition of community can be extracted from the motivations of Fulton's impetuous curiosity: Community is self-conscious curiosity in which praxis never becomes subordinate to theory. The projects involved in any community formation will inherently be heterogeneous.

> I have been plotting this publishing process; and some of what gets done around here is the rudimentary form of it—like the *Directory of Little Magazines* which started in 1964–65. . . . Some of what I do on the other hand is more fully a part of the very process which it seems to plot—like the *Small Press Review*, which started in 1966. . . . The Committee of Small Magazine Editors and Publishers (COSMEP) is an outgrowth of this too—I'm not alone, you know, in these self-conscious interests. When Jerry Burns moved to Berkeley in mid-1967 the idea of a conference of editors was about the first thing that came up between us. (Peattie 37)

If we want to find a context for Bob Perelman's statement about the "development of presses," one of the best places is the *Whole COSMEP Catalog*, published in 1973. Consisting of one-page advertisements for small press operations and magazines, *WCC* marks the fifth anniversary of COSMEP as a pivotal point in small press culture. Numerous projects were merely at their nascent stage. At that point, *Stooge* magazine was a precursor for the greater project of The Figures press; John Crawford's *West End* is advertised only as a magazine in the catalog. Crawford juxtaposed the cover of volume 1, issue number 4, with a list of contributors accompanied by a poem by Denise Levertov, "Prayer for Revolutionary Love." There is no hint whatsoever that Crawford's *West End* is destined to become a major small press with an exceptionally distinguished back list of working-class poets and writers of color.

While little magazines had played a significant role in the emergence of many modernist writers, the women and men who produced these magazines did not necessarily see themselves as constituting a distinct challenge separate from the genre of work they were publishing. The small press movement after the Second World War, on the other hand, developed an understanding of itself as an alternative to the direction of American publishing capital. As outlandish as that claim may seem now, given the power of multinationals, the editors of many small magazines had the fantasy that they could present a model of empowerment to other people that would change the culture as a whole. "It is time to govern ourselves," was meant as more than a self-contained imperative by feminist journals and publishing outfits such as Violet Press, KNOW (Pittsburgh, Pennsylvania), Gay Sunshine, *Women: A Journal of Liberation, Matrix: She of the New Aeon*, and *Shameless Hussy*. Two of the publications dedicated their whole page to a demand for the impeachment of Richard Nixon, or for criminal charges to be filed against him for nuclear pollution. Other presses and magazines that contributed advertisements included Black Sparrow, *Wormwood Review, Greenfield Review, Vagabond, Sumac, Panjandrum, Bastard Angel, Invisible City, Wetlands, Blue Wind*, and *Nausea One*.

For a few years, this fantasy did have a minimal impact. Small presses were able to organize and acquire access to typesetting equipment that enabled them to increase the number of their publications. The West Coast Print Center, for instance, in Oakland, provided typesetting equipment on which issues of *This* magazine and *Hills* were typeset.[10] It was only the critical mass of a large number of small presses and little magazines on the West Coast that made the West Coast Print Center possible. If, as Perelman says, there was "immediate access to publication," this was in part because the small press movement of which the Language writers were a part provided actual material support for this production. The majority of people who made use of the West Coast Print Center may not have shared an equal interest in formal experimentation derived from an emphasis on theory, but the praxis of the avant-garde directly includes them as community and not merely as context. In a similar manner, independent bookstores that stocked the publications of Language writers had established themselves as outlets for the work of small presses and counterculture publications well before Language writing emerged. The valorization provided by little magazine publishing in the 1970s was due to the contumacious integrity shown by a huge number of writers and editors on the West Coast whose work contributed to "the role the twentieth-century avant-garde played in developing a politics of joy and resistance" (Kane xiii).

Expanding the context for the development of the avant-garde on the West Coast is a necessary intervention at this point, as is an understanding of the context itself as avant-garde. While David Perkins may very well be correct in arguing that "a true story cannot be told" in regards to literary history, I would like to suggest that inaugural fictions are central to the arguments in canon formation about the comparative significance of absolute and relative value. These fictions depend upon context, which is acknowledged by Alan Golding when he argues for the continued importance of terms such as "margin" and "center" in "mapping the poetic field. . . . Language writing, for instance, arose in the context of—though not necessarily *in reaction to*—a hegemonic poetic ideology of anti-theoretical lyric individualism" (Roberts and Allison 134). I agree with Golding, but at best it only tells half the story. The larger context was the small press movement.

The Counter-Attack

In academic accounts of this period, everything I have just mentioned is erased with thoroughness worthy of revisionist editorial work in an encyclopedia in USSR in 1938. The comparison will no doubt sting, and given the hideousness of Stalin's reign, I am no doubt overreaching in my criticism. Yet I need to make it clear that one cannot simply discard the heroic labor of hundreds of people, and then pretend that such cavalier privileging of the academy is not being done out of anything other than deliberate, egregious suppression of facts or flagrant incompetence. "During this period (1977–1983), the postwar movement of American poetry into the academy accelerated," writes Jahan Ramazani in *The Norton Anthology of Modern and Contemporary Poetry.*[11] On a literal level, the statement is not false: someone driving a car at twenty-five miles per hour slowly pushing down on the gas pedal to go thirty-five miles per hour could be said to be "accelerating;" in 1978 and 1979, the academic poetry acceleration rate was about three miles per hour per year. Meanwhile, the small press movement, especially on the West Coast, had reached its top speed, and by 1979 the academy was not even visible in its rearview mirror. The Association of Writers and Writing Programs (AWP) reports that there were only eighteen MFA programs in the United States in 1975. Ten years later there were thirty-one. Rivaling a handful of MFA programs in the late 1970s was a massive and unprecedented explosion in small press activity. I can assure you that the overwhelming majority of the poets who sustained this movement did not have MFAs, nor did the poets they published. The primary development of American poetry in the 1970s was the development of the small press movement.

One motive for writing this particular chapter is to remind people of a period before MFA workshops became the normative experience of young writers. In order to establish a ground-level sense of the literary terrain outside of Random House and FSG, we need to examine literary magazines of the period, and fortunately, they provide direct choreographic evidence. My primary hope is to call attention to writers who were working with very little institutional support or validation back in that period. Despite writing intriguing, challenging poetry that ranges from accessible to difficult, most of these poets have still not received any sustained attention in critical articles.

In considering the landscape of American poetry in the pivotal decade of the cold war, however, one should be cautious about citing the AWP's census of MFA programs. Willmore City, for instance, put out a double issue (number six and seven) in 1978, in which the first half featured the poetry of Southern California poets such as Holly Prado, Kate Braverman, Gerry Locklin, Joan Jobe Smith, Carol Lewis, and Steve Kowit, a variation on a lineup that appeared in numerous magazines; the concluding portion concentrated on the faculty and students at an MFA program in Massachusetts. The issue notes that a total of fifteen MFA programs were active in the United States at that time, and the back of the issue contains a directory of these programs. Whether there were eighteen or fifteen programs in 1978 is fundamentally irrelevant. In a country of over two hundred million people and at least five thousand people actively engaged in publishing their poetry, either number of MFA programs hardly constitutes a hegemonic position in a field churning with small press projects. This is not to say that MFA programs in 1975 did not exert any measurable influence on American poetry. Daniel Halpern's uneven anthology of younger American poets in 1975 was the forerunner of a slew of collections that modeled very narrow notions of what could constitute contemporary poetry.[12]

In this account of literary history, I will inevitably be accused of setting up a good guys/bad guys binary, but I see no other way to remind young poets in the twenty-first century that the success of the MFA programs by the end of the century was not a foregone conclusion in 1974 or 1978. Naïve as it might seem in retrospect, we truly hoped that people would read more and more creative work, and that this work would be published by small presses and sold in independently owned bookstores. We saw this as part of a change that included the women's movement and the emergence of the third world in confrontation with the neoimperialism of terrorist organizations such as the Central Intelligence Agency. That the American people turned their backs on the possibility of a literate, creative citizenship and opted to affirm state-sponsored terrorism, funded by illegal arms deals, profoundly dismayed us. I cannot speak for the votes that put the Reagan-Bush bureaucracy of the past quarter century into power. I can only vouch for how it felt in the mid-1970s to be part of the small press movement. The record at that time shows I was not alone:

I was struck by the seriousness of intent of most present; of the desire to get past polemics and keep our eye on the "small press commonweal." I think the whole conference had a new feeling about it; a new awareness of our role in our country and our culture's life; perhaps in world history. We are less and less underground; more and more concerned to get our ideas and our material across to the rest of the world. This new spirit, which was incipient in New Orleans last year, and was felt in the newsletter this past year, is definitely growing. One important cause is the number of women's presses joining. If we can now attract the third world, and can keep ourselves keeping it together, what will stop us from posing a serious threat to the Establishment of Publishing in this country, so that it, too, will have to reform or step down? At times, I just sat quietly and felt the stir of new breath, new blood about me. People might explode with wild-eyed opinions, but there was a basic determination both to accept such right to explode and to get on with the real work of pulling ourselves together and making our work, those we publish, felt in the world. Yours sincerely, Judy Hogan[13]

None of this happened without an extraordinary effort, and the process of learning how to do the work was in itself one of the major challenges everyone in the small press poetry movement confronted. Editing, design, production, distribution, publicity: the biggest challenge, then as now, in starting a poetry magazine or launching an independent literary press is acquiring all the simultaneous skills that one needs in order to make this kind of thing happen. (I was fortunate enough to be given the opportunity to learn what I needed in a sequence that permitted a generous margin of error at the start.)

The conjunction of small presses, independent bookstores, and production facilities for small presses was a unique period in American poetry. Certainly, this particular blend will never occur again. The typesetting equipment is obsolete, and unlike letterpress, is extremely unlikely to survive as a means of production for any future cottage industry. The determination of the people involved in these projects was fueled by their own mutual lack of accommodation to the ideological strategies of capitalism in the United States. If the Language writers echoed the phrase "The author is dead" as a battle cry, the small press editors and publishers at this time acted on a much more radical belief that "the publisher is dead."[14]

Donald Allen's anthology, *The New American Poetry*, is often considered the crucial turning point in presenting the first flowering of little magazines after World War II, and subsequently inspiring a new generation of writers.[15] Allen superbly assembled a considerable number of poets, but he falls considerably short of depicting the full extent of what he termed the "creative rebellion" of that era.

Poets in Donald Allen's 1960 *New American Poetry* Anthology

Adam, Helen	Jones, LeRoi (Amiri Baraka)
Antoninus, Brother (William Everson)	Kerouac, Jack
Ashbery, John	Koch, Kenneth
Blackburn, Paul	Lamantia, Philip
Blaser, Robin	Levertov, Denise
Borregaard, Ebbe	Loewinsohn, Ron
Boyd, Bruce	Marshall, Edward
Bremser, Ray	McClure, Michael
Broughton, James	Meltzer, David
Carroll, Paul	O'Hara, Frank
Corso, Gregory	Olson, Charles
Creeley, Robert	Oppenheimer, Joel
Dorn, Edward	Orlovsky, Peter
Doyle, Kirby	Perkoff, Stuart Z.
Duerden, Richard	Schuyler, James
Duncan, Robert	Snyder, Gary
Eigner, Larry	Sorrentino, Gilbert
Ferlinghetti, Lawrence	Spicer, Jack
Field, Edward	Welch, Lew
Ginsberg, Allen	Whalen, Philip
Gleason, Madeline	Wieners, John
Guest, Barbara	Williams, Jonathan

Of course, in all fairness to Allen, no subsequent anthology has managed to be even half as adept at representing the range of work produced by the mid-century's most vital poetic dissidents. It is worth considering that well over a half century after the Six Gallery poetry reading, no single anthology has yet to present anything close to an overview of the eruption that occurred in the two decades following the detonation of atomic weapons in Japan. Such a book would have to include poets almost every potential editor for this project would initially consider fundamentally incompatible. The task of assembling a volume of this magnitude is daunting, for where can an editor or editors be found capable of selecting the most representative pieces of Charles Bukowski as well as Jack Spicer, who can juxtapose Bob Kaufman and Robert Duncan with equal felicity? This deft anthology must include Stuart Perkoff as well as Kenneth Patchen, Philip Lamantia as well as John Thomas, Diane Di Prima alongside Jack Hirschman, and devise a strategy for segueing from the complete text of Langston Hughes's "Montage of a Dream Deferred" to the earliest *Tablets* by Armand Schwerner. Donald Allen faced an immense task in organizing the multiplicity of poetic scenes that existed in the mid to late 1950s, but even with cunning retrospection, how is it possible to present in a proportionate manner Diane Wakoski, Edward Field, Lawrence Ferlinghetti, Lenore Kandel, Robert Creeley, Kenneth Rexroth, George Hitchcock, Helen Adam, Amiri Baraka, Bruce Boyd, Gary Snyder, Leslie Woolf Hedley, Richard Brautigan, Ruth Weiss, Thomas McGrath, Naomi Replansky, Muriel Rukeyser, Don Gordon, A. B. Spellman, William Pillin, Clarence Major, Barbara Moraff, Jack Micheline, Sue Abbott Boyd, and Clayton Eshleman? Of course the reader familiar with this particular delineation of a poetic strain will note instantly that Ed Dorn and Frank O'Hara have not been mentioned yet, while those less familiar will need to be reminded that *Howl* was not the only book scrutinized by the prosecutor and judge during the most famous obscenity trial of the 1950s. Where, in fact, do Bill Margolis, the publisher and editor of the *Miscellaneous Man*, and Gil Orlovitz, the poet, whose work was also being subjected to interdiction, fit into this imaginary volume? Anyone tempted to take on this project should be forewarned that it will require a thorough review of magazines such as the *Outsider*, which was published in New Orleans and Tucson, as well as *Yugen* and the *Floating Bear*. This revisionist anthology is very much still in the potential canon.

Regardless of how familiar many of these names might be to critics, the most pertinent common attribution that one could assign to the overwhelming majority of the poets listed above is their identification, either by themselves or their readers, with the West Coast at significant points in their lives or careers. While the best-known names are associated with northern California, the lesser-known names are precisely the ones whose writing disturbs the most common binaries of the period, such as "Beat vs. Academic." In order to gain some perspective on the extent of the internecine disputes that eventually had a profound impact on the evolution of poetic communities on the West Coast, I have constructed a chart in which I have placed groups of poets whose work and lives intertwined with each other in ways that were visible to members of at least one other group, if not two or three. This chart is meant as a sketch, in the way that one might draw a series of mountain ranges traversed by a number of earthquake faults. These groups abut each other, and slippage and jostling occur rapidly.

The poets whose work was included in *The New American Poetry*, which Allen began editing in 1958, appear in bold; names of poets who were also editors and/or publishers appear in italics. If we consider the four columns as representing the full range of non-institutional poetic work being done on the West Coast, then one can begin to recover a sense of how much is

Poets of the West Coast Poetry Renaissance, 1946–1966

BEATS	SF RENAISSANCE	VENICE WEST	MAVERICKS
Lawrence Ferlinghetti	**Helen Adam**	**Bruce Boyd**	Josephine Ain
Allen Ginsberg	**Robin Blaser**	Eileen Ireland	John Beecher
Bob Kaufman	**Ebbe Borregaard**	Maurice Lacy	Richard Brautigan
Jack Kerouac	**James Broughton**	Lawrence Lipton	Charles Bukowski
Joanne Kyger	**Robert Duncan**	Charles Newman	Alvaro Cardona-Hine
Philip Lamantia	**William Everson/ Brother Antoninus**	**Stuart Z. Perkoff**	*Gene Frumkin*
Michael McClure	Stan Persky	Frankie Rios	Jack Gilbert
David Meltzer	*Jack Spicer*	Tony Scibella	Don Gordon
Gary Snyder		John Thomas	*Leslie Woolf Hedley*
William Wantling		Saul White	Jack Hirschman
Lew Welch			*George Hitchcock*
Philip Whalen			*Grover Jacoby, Jr.*
			Robinson Jeffers
			Hanson Kellogg
			Carl Larsen
			Bill Margolis
			James Boyer May
			Thomas McGrath
			Bert Meyers
			Josephine Miles
			Daniel Moore
			Kenneth Patchen
			William Pillin
			Kenneth Rexroth
			Edwin Rolfe
			Muriel Rukeyser
			James Scheville
			Ann Stanford
			Edmund Teske
			Mel Weisburd
			Peter Yates
			Curtis Zahn

left out of *The New American Poetry* in terms of the "creative rebellion" of the period. My choice of rubric for each column makes use of the familiar movements (Beat, San Francisco Renaissance, and Venice West) as well as the less familiar "mavericks"—poets not particularly identified by any of those movements but whose works were published in such San Francisco or Los Angeles literary magazines as *Inferno, Trace, California Quarterly,* and *Coastlines* between 1951 and 1964. My emphasis on poet-editors and poet-publishers in this chart is designed to reveal the role of editing as a central tenet of the entire renaissance. Indeed, the effusive interest by almost all of the poets who also worked as editors in the writing of individuals from the other categories is the congregating predicate in this renaissance. I have italicized the names of the poet-editors and poet-publishers. Many poets in each group had active, enduring relationships with the members in other groups. William Pillin, for instance, was associated with the "Inferno coterie," according to a letter from Stuart Perkoff to Donald Allen, but was also a primary contributor to *Coastlines* magazine.[16] Bruce Boyd knew Jack Spicer for many years and corresponded with Gary Snyder for several years; in addition to being published in Spicer's *J* magazine, his work also appeared in Margolis's *Mendicant.*[17] As might be expected, the individuals in the "mavericks" list provide some of the most unanticipated extensions in the rhizomes of minor scenes in a major shift. Grover Jacoby, Jr., primarily published poets such Ann Stanford and Josephine Miles and was a constant advocate of Lawrence Hart's Activist poets group, but he was also the first editor anywhere in the United States to accept poems by three poets in the Beat category. Richard Brautigan was first published by Leslie Woolf Hedley and had a follow-up collection receive its first major review in *Coastlines,* but he also dedicated one of his novels to Jack Spicer in appreciation for Spicer's editorial assistance.

In looking at this list, one is struck by how few of the poets were included in the book that supposedly defines the period, *The New American Poetry,* and yet the confluence, if not at least partial compatibility, can be seen in the issues of the *Outsider* magazine, edited by Jon and Louise ("Gypsy Lou") Webb.[18] In the following list of contributors to the *Outsider,* poets associated with the West Coast or who contributed significantly to it are listed in italics.

The *Outsider* included work by an equal number of poets who were in *The New American Poetry,* and lived and worked elsewhere in the country beside the West Coast. For Jon and Louise Webb to present poets from each of the above categories indicates that from at least one specific vantage point outside of the New York-San Francisco-Los Angeles triangle, all of these cities were contributing to the groundswell of subversive passion. "The

Contributors to *Outsider*

BEATS	MAVERICKS	BLACK MOUNTAIN POETS
Gregory Corso	*Charles Bukowski*	Cid Corman
Diane Di Prima	Larry Eigner	Robert Creeley
Lawrence Ferlinghetti	*Gene Frumkin*	Edward Dorn
Allen Ginsberg	*Leslie Woolf Hedley*	Charles Olson
Michael McClure	Langston Hughes	Joel Oppenheimer
Gary Snyder	*Philip Lamantia*	Jonathan Williams
	James Boyer May	
	Thomas McGrath	
	Harold Norse	
	Kenneth Patchen	
	Margaret Randall	
	Gilbert Sorrentino	
	Curtis Zahn	

Outsider" is a poet whose work resists the easy entrance into respectability; some element of scandal, negation, or vehement defiance is propped in plain view. In looking at the West Coast and the poets who wrote and published there between the end of World War II and the beginning of direct American involvement in Vietnam, we should prepare to defy our own expectations as much these poets challenged the social authority and order of their time.

TWO

Thinking Alone in Company

L.A. Literary Magazines during the Cold War

"The missing term in modernist thinking" observes Frank Lentricchia at the end of *Modernist Quartet*, "is community: something larger, something more valuable from isolate selfhood. But where in the secular and liberal West are models for this to be found?" (291) If World War I utterly transformed the modernist groundswell unleashed by Baudelaire and Whitman in the mid-nineteenth century, the cold war further eroded any Enlightenment pretense to an enduring social contract and accelerated the fragmentation of a poetics of identity as improvised autonomy. In the earliest years of the cold war, however, poets in at least one area of the United States felt a sense of communal recrudescence that was palpable enough to be visible even to Simone de Beauvoir, who recorded a visit to a bookstore in Berkeley, California in March 1947, a conversation with an unnamed young writer who edited an avant-garde literary magazine influenced by a combination of surrealism and Henry Miller (*L'Amérique au jour le jour* 199). Miller's books, as de Beauvoir notes, were banned in the United States, but that interdiction only served to reinforce what she called a "regional intellectualism."[1] De Beauvoir's assessment was that, compared to the coteries that exist in France, the writers in Berkeley were audacious. She did not mention by name Robert Duncan, whose *Earthly City, Heavenly City*, was published in 1947 by a former atomic bomb scientist, Bern Porter, nor did she appear to have met others who became known for their role in the Berkeley Renaissance, such as Jack Spicer (1925–1965). Their presence in their environs must have been evident enough to those she talked with, though, because according to her estimate the scene had gone beyond adumbration: "almost everybody agrees that there is a great poetic renewal at the moment" (200). As a stranger from another country, de

Beauvoir's glimpse of the Berkeley Renaissance is especially valuable because it objectively confirms what might possibly be regarded as the nostalgic exaggerations of the participants in that scene.

As unlikely as it might seem, however, the model for "something more valuable than isolate selfhood," was also to be found in Los Angeles. De Beauvoir had begun her cross-continental trip in New York City in late January, and before arriving in Berkeley, she had spent the last week of February in Los Angeles, staying with a screenwriter and his wife, a friend identified only by the initial, "N," with whom she visited Venice, which she describes as a "dreary amusement park by the beach" in which the "throughfares are glowing but deserted. The vendors look as though they were holding a vigil over a corpse" (166). De Beauvoir did not meet any poets while she was in Los Angeles, nor did she talk with anyone who suggested that a poetic renaissance had begun in Southern California. However, one literary magazine, *Variegation*, had been launched the year before she arrived. Its editor was a young poet named Grover Jacoby, Jr., who was born and raised in Los Angeles, and who published his first book of poetry, *The Human Patina*, in Los Angeles in 1939. Jacoby was a member of a poetry group, founded by Frona Lane, which gathered at the Los Angeles Public Library.[2] At a meeting in the fall of 1945, Jacoby blurted out that he was going to start publishing a magazine featuring only free verse. According to Kimmis Hendrick, a reporter for the *Christian Science Monitor*, Jacoby "hadn't planned to do anything of the kind. But having said so publicly, he had to carry through." Jacoby came from a family that had lived in Los Angeles for several generations, and he had the financial means to follow up on his apparently spontaneous announcement.[3]

Variegation began appearing on a quarterly basis in 1946, and Jacoby's own essay, "The Prosody of Free Verse," opened the first issue. One of the poets he mailed a copy to was William Carlos Williams, who in early February 1947, wrote back enthusiastically about the magazine and Jacoby's essay. Pointing to Jacoby's phrase, "the mysteries lying at the metrical core," Williams responded: "I can't tell you what a satisfaction it is to me to see a beginning being made here. . . . you have put out a magazine built explicitly upon the physical aspect of the poem as a field of study and invention: that is a tremendous advance on anything that anyone else is doing anywhere today, so far as I know." (Jacoby, Box 1) Williams concluded his letter by telling Jacoby, "All you need now is genius—and plenty of it." Jacoby's essay will never challenge Olson's "Projective Verse" essay as a primary document of alternative poetics in this period, but it does provide evidence that a formal consideration of technique was part of the earliest days of the West Coast Poetry Renaissance.

Jacoby did not publish any further essays on the mysteries at the metrical core. In fact, he partially succumbed to the predilection for formal poetry in the United States in the early 1950s by starting a second poetry magazine in 1950, *Recurrence*, which declared itself to be a "magazine of rhyme" in its subtitle, and ran concurrently with *Variegation* for a half-dozen years. Nevertheless, Jacoby's first magazine distinguishes itself in many ways, not the least of which is that his saddle-stitched magazine lasted more than a decade, and came out on its seasonal schedule on a remarkably reliable basis. His perseverance would have been largely self-motivated and required more than financial assiduity. His only publishing reinforcement in Southern California during the first five years of publication was *Line* magazine, which lasted three issues (April 1948–May 1949).[4] Secondly, it is important to emphasize it was not a local magazine, either in the selection of its authors or in its circulation. Even though only a few libraries subscribed to it, the magazine reached a wide audience through such outlets as the *New York Herald-Tribune*, which republished poems from literary journals every Sunday in its column, "Week in Poetry."[5]

Jacoby's editorial choices were also very unusual for the period in that a comparatively large percentage of the contributors were women, several of whom were published or praised by Alan Swallow, including poetry workshop leader Frona Lane. One could amplify the earlier charts I presented to gain some perspective on Jacoby's interest in women's poetry, though this expansion will also include a concurrent representative list of the poets published in America's best-known poetry magazine, *Poetry*.

One does not tend to think of Los Angeles at the midcentury as having a poetry magazine that would be publishing writers whose work was also appearing in *Poetry* magazine, but Jacoby published many of these women poets not once or twice, but several times.

Of the poets in his roster whom he shared with *Poetry* magazine, Josephine Miles is among the most underappreciated, but perhaps her work and influence as a teacher has led critics to overlook the deft brushwork of her social commentary. Jacoby published five of her poems in all, including this ecological satire:

These putrefactive chemicals muddle the gulls' feet.
The purple assuages, green corrodes.
Crystalline forms decline a kind of powder,
Spraying at the beak, clinging the nodes.

O deceit. It would be better, says my teacher,
If the gulls would get out of this factory yard.
The natural storms of ocean winter
Will teach them that life is hard.
("The Gulls," *Recurrence*, Spring 1953, 86)[6]

Midcentury Interplay between Three L.A. Literary Magazines and *Poetry* Magazine

POET	VARIEGATION/RECURRENCE	CALIFORNIA QUARTERLY	COASTLINES	POETRY
Josephine Ain	X		X	
Eric Barker	X			
John Berryman				X
Irene Bruce	X			
Jean Burden	X			X
Hayden Carruth				X
Gene Frumkin		X	X	
Allen Ginsberg	X		X	
Don Gordon		X	X	
Thom Gunn				X
Anthony Hecht				X
Leslie W. Hedley	X	X	X	
Josephine Jacobsen	X			X
Randall Jerrell				X
Weldon Kees				X
Hanson Kellogg	X			X
Jean-Louis Kerouac	X			
Frona Lane	X			
Joanne de Longchamps			X	X
Walter Lowenfels		X	X	
Marcia Masters	X			X
Thomas McGrath		X	X	
Eve Merriam	X		X	
W. S. Merwin				X
Josephine Miles	X			X
Rosalie Moore	X			X
Frank O'Hara				X
Naomi Replansky		X	X	
Theodore Roethke				X
James Schevill	X		X	X
Ruth Forbes Sherry	X			X
Muriel Spark	X			X
Lawrence Spingarn	X		X	X
Ann Stanford	X		X	X
Wallace Stevens				X
Melvin Tolson				X
Philip Whalen	X		X	
Harold V. Witt	X		X	X

While none of the magazines produced in Los Angeles during the decade and a half after World War II were founded by women, Jacoby not only published many women, but also selected work that addressed the political crisis of the McCarthy witch-hunts. Ann Stanford contributed a total of twenty poems to Jacoby's pair of magazines. In *Recurrence*'s summer issue of 1953, Stanford's "The Trolley" was the first of her three poems, and its shift in implied political critique from concise aphorism to stinging irony is reinforced when one notices Jacoby's editorial juxtaposition. At some other time in the history of the United States, the poem immediately preceding "The Trolley" might seem innocuously self-involved, but the final stanza of Hanson Kellogg's "Assembly Line" can hardly elude the political context of that year, though it makes no direct references to HUAC:[7]

> Guilt of reflection, guilt of offbeat drum,
> Face me clear with what I have become:
> Shadows for the stage set, black against gray stone;
> Shadows the jury, with movements of their own,
> Always the same gestures—and the smoke, the spiral hum.
> (*Recurrence*, Summer 1953, 5)

In establishing how technological control is imbricated with social corruption, lines five and six of "The Trolley" reiterate and amplify the tone that Kellogg has just established:

> By drugstore and café
> Warehouse and chimneystack
> Flanged to a rigid way
> I follow down the track.
>
> Though rot and favor gnaw
> Upon the civic heart,
> Obedient to law
> On schedule I depart.
> (*Recurrence*, Summer 1953, 6)

Stanford's disappearance from contemporary anthologies is especially puzzling and even ironic in that she was the first woman to edit a historical anthology of women poets. She was born in 1916 in La Habra, California, and graduated from Stanford University in 1938. While at Stanford University, she studied with Yvor Winters, a poet whom Swallow reminded her that "no one is rational about . . . one of his great feats has been to disturb people, to shake them so that they become angry" (Claire 23). The association with Winters haunted critical analysis of Stanford's poetry, provoking unwarranted negative reactions throughout her career to the point that when she worked on the dust jacket material for her fifth book, *The Descent*, she instructed her editor to leave out any mention of Winters.

> If you could leave off the Yvor Winters label somehow, it might be better. Last time some reviewer in the Carolinas saw the Winters thing and took off about my formalism, as a kind of conditioned reflex. My work, much of it in *The Weathercock*, and most of it in the new volume, goes back to a style I was developing just before I entered college and got into the Winters thing. Actually I've been working away from the Winters approach for the past twenty years. (Letter to Barbara Brag, Correspondence File of the Archive of Ann Stanford)

Revealing much more than metrical fluidity, Stanford's early poetry has exceptional resonance and depth. The influence of Winters in terms of organizing a metrical argument is undeniable, and yet there is an emotional poignancy in these poems that lets a hint of nihilism seep in.

> Red bluff, sheer blue are blent
> Despite the mind's intent,
> And I forget the green
> Enlivening the scene.
> Through shards of light and shade,
> The sharp impressions fade,
> While slanting hours erase
> My hand, your heart, your face.
> ("The Canyon," *The White Bird* 25)

Within a span of eight lines, Stanford completes a metrical circle; the first and last lines are almost rhythmically equivalent in their stresses, but a wedge of transformation divides their images' effects, with the first line suggesting unity and the final line dissolution. The reference in lines three and four to Andrew Marvell's most famous couplet is the kind of literary strategy that Stanford would begin to eliminate as she matured.

One might assume that a poet with these kinds of credentials, affiliations, and portfolio would feel safe in the 1950s, but on the contrary, Ann Stanford showed extraordinary courage in making the decisions about what poets to be associated with. In retrospect, it is easy to say that she was not in significant danger, but that assessment is almost pathetically naïve. She chose to give her work to a magazine, *Coastlines*, that had opened its first issue with a poem by Don Gordon, a blacklisted poet. Indeed, a copy of that issue was found in the FBI files of Alice Greenfield McGrath, the second wife of Tom McGrath. Walter Lowenfels, a poet who was convicted and sentenced to jail on charges of being an active Communist, and Naomi Replansky, whose passport was lifted in the early 1950s, were other contributors. The decision of whom to associate with was not a minor matter of putative allegiance or fealty. As Stanford noted in her diary in 1955:

> The "Epilogue" to my Magellan was read at the Unitarian Church Festival of Arts this evening. I had had some hesitation when they asked to contribute something because of the blacklisting of people who even associate with people who are suspected of leftist leanings these days, and Tom McGrath and his wife always participate so prominently in these affairs. In fact, Alice McGrath was in charge of this one. Such an association might impede Ron's clearance in case he had the chance to design any government buildings. (Novak 2)

Stanford's diary notation provides a means of gauging the accuracy of Warren French's assessment of *Coastlines* magazine in *The San Francisco Renaissance, 1955–1960*, in which he dismisses the magazine as provincial: "a number of literary journals were launched in the area (Los Angeles) during the period between 1955 and 1960. The most notable was the slick and eye-catching *Coastlines* . . . Los Angelenos could always come up with the money to package their inferior product more glossily than the usually out-of-pocket San Franciscans, but none of their efforts attracted much more than local interest" (88). On the contrary, Alan Swallow in Colorado was very interested in the work of the poets who were publishing not only in *Coastlines*, but in its direct predecessor, *California Quarterly*, as well as in other Los Angeles magazines that managed to attract more than local interest: to say that the FBI represents an instance of a nationally based readership hardly requires elaboration.

Jacoby was very partial to the Activist poets associated with Lawrence Hart, whom Jacoby regarded as the best teacher of creative writing on the West Coast. In the final years of *Variegation*'s publication, other poets in the San Francisco area began noticing the magazine as they started their literary careers. I have not been able to determine how Allen Ginsberg first happened to have heard of *Variegation*. Perhaps he noticed that the name of the magazine when the *New York Herald-Tribune* reprinted his father's poems from the magazine. However he encountered it, by the spring of 1955, he had begun submitting poems from a pre-"Howl" manuscript to Jacoby, who printed four of them by the winter of 1956. In the issues between Ginsberg's appearances, Jacoby selected a poem, "Everything is in the same moment," by a writer known only for a single novel at that point, *The Town and the City*, though Jack Kerouac chose to present himself as Jean-Louis Kerouac in *Variegation*. Kerouac's poem is part of a sequence, *Mexico Choruses*, published by Grove Press in 1959. Another participant in the Six Gallery reading who also published in *Variegation* was Philip Whalen, who had two poems in the summer 1956 issue. Whalen submitted these poems to Jacoby after he attended a reading that Whalen gave in San Francisco.

Jacoby edited *Variegation* for eleven years and *Recurrence* for seven, a remarkable amount of time for a practicing poet to devote to tasks focused on others' talents. When he began publishing a poetry magazine in Los Angeles, he was completely alone in Los Angeles in his willingness to speak up for poets. By the time that Jacoby was publishing Ginsberg, Whalen, and Kerouac, other editorial voices had firmly established themselves in Los Angeles, making this city one of the few places in America that offered non-academic writers a variety of possible outlets.

California Quarterly and Blacklisted Poets in Los Angeles

Of the major blacklisted poets of the early 1950s, Thomas McGrath remains the best known, in part due to his ambitious long poem, *Letter to an Imaginary Friend*. McGrath had grown up on a farm in North Dakota, during a time of intense of left-wing and progressive political activity in that state, as well as Minnesota and Wisconsin. He attended North Dakota State University and won a Rhodes Fellowship, but Hitler's invasion of France and bombing raids in England forced McGrath instead to matriculate to Louisiana State University, where he met his future publisher, Alan Swallow, with whom he shared a rural background. Swallow enjoyed McGrath's poetry and set the type for McGrath's first book himself. After the United States entered the war, McGrath was drafted and stationed at a remote outpost in Alaska for two years. McGrath eventually did go to England and studied there, but after a stay in France where he wrote a novel, he moved back to the United States and took a teaching job at Los Angeles State College. Swallow would go on to publish several of McGrath's collections of poetry, including the first part of *Letter to an Imaginary Friend*, as well as *To Walk a Crooked Mile* and *Figures of a Double World*.

In "Homage to Thomas McGrath," E. P. Thompson claims that "McGrath is a master-poet to his last fingernail. . . . (His) poetry will be remembered in one hundred years when many more fashionable voices have been forgotten" (104–105) but he makes this claim knowing that McGrath's work "is not, and never has been, ... in anyone's fashionable party. His trajectory has been that of a willful defiance of every fashion" (104). As Thompson points out, this includes "a good deal of what has been offered as counterculture also" (104). McGrath's intransigent alienation from the prevalent New Criticism of the midcentury was equaled by his refusal to accommodate his poetics to the ideological needs of the Communist Party, which he had joined in the 1930s, for which he was called to the stand in April 1953. Even after he lost his teaching job and found himself reduced to working for a pittance in a factory producing wooden animals, he continued editing *California Quarterly*. In a gesture of unrepentant defiance to HUAC, he gave the cover of an issue in the Fall of 1954 to Edwin Rolfe, a veteran of the Abraham Lincoln Brigade of the Spanish Civil War who had died earlier that year in May. From the summer of 1937 until the end of 1938, Rolfe had served in the field as well as worked as the editor and publisher of *Volunteer for Liberty*, the publication of the International Brigade. When Rolfe returned to the United States, he wrote a definitive account of his generation's response to fascism, *The Lincoln Battalion: The Story of the Americans who Fought in Spain*. Rolfe was drafted into the U.S. Army during World War II, but was discharged due to ill health. He moved to Los Angeles with his wife, in part because he hoped to get work in Hollywood. Rolfe had some success at first, including coauthoring a novel, *The Glass Room*, with Lester Fuller which Warner Brothers planned to turn into a film starring Humphrey Bogart and Lauren Bacall. The last half-dozen years of Rolfe's life involved illness and little work. Larry Edmunds Bookshop published his first collection of poetry in fifteen years, *First Love and other poems*, in an edition of 375 copies that contained some of the poems written while he was in Spain. McGrath published a posthumous collection of Rolfe's work, *Permit Me Refuge*, in 1955 in a volume that proved to be the final publication of *California Quarterly*.

Hollywood's attempt to purge Communists from the industry had resulted in prison sentences for the Hollywood Ten, including Edwin Rolfe's friend and fellow soldier in the Spanish Civil War, Albert Maltz, but soon after getting out of prison, several of the Hollywood Ten, including Herbert Bieberman, Paul Jarrico, and Adrian Scott, formed their own film company, the Independent Production Corporation. Their first production was a film script by Michael Wilson that recounted a prolonged, but successful, strike by Mexican American miners in Grant County, New Mexico. Despite intense efforts by the studio system to stop the shooting of *Salt of the Earth*, which used actual miners, their spouses, and children, as well as union organizers as actors, the film was finally completed, but distribution of the film was also met with serious impediments, and screenings were confined to a few theaters in Los Angeles and New York. The publication of the script in the summer

1953 issue of *California Quarterly* was more successful than expected. A subsequent issue claimed that ten thousand copies of the magazine had been sold. According to James J. Lorence's *The Suppression of "Salt of the Earth,"* 5 percent of these copies were purchased by the International Union of Mine, Mill and Smelter Workers (IUMMSW) in hopes of gaining union support for the public distribution of the film about their strike. As Lorence points out, the Federal Bureau of Investigation monitored this film through the process of its creation, including its publication, and the elimination of the film from the public sphere could be summed up in Pauline Kael's dismissal of *Salt* as "as clear a piece of Communist propaganda as we have had in many years" (195). Her categorization of the film suggests the degree to which the entrenched witch-hunt of the Left in post-WWII America ensnared critics as well as film processing laboratories.

McGrath was hardly the only World War II veteran on the West Coast who challenged the discourse surrounding Hollywood's collaboration with right-wing repression and containment culture. Challenging the well-intentioned fantasy of a film such as *The Best Years of Our Lives*, for instance, combat veteran Leslie Woolf Hedley's first book of poems after the war denied that *any* representation of war's dirty secrets is possible. About two-thirds of the way through *The Edge of Insanity*, Hedley presents us with a page dominated by a large, empty rectangle above a three line faux ekphrastic poem depicting the consequences of "people . . . killing each other" (19). The blank space in the book serves temporarily as the projective denial of the ability of language to represent the experience of a soldier. Hedley's demarcation line seems to indicate the boundary of a community in which those who have shared an experience cannot represent it, and those outside the community are regarded as inherently incapable of perceiving any representation whatsoever of that trauma. Hedley's book was published in Los Angeles; he moved to San Francisco shortly afterward, where he started a magazine, *Inferno*, the first issue of which was printed in his basement. Among the most forthright, blunt statements in any poetry magazine on the West Coast during the height of McCarthy investigations, Hedley's introductory editorial in an early issue diagnoses the crisis of American culture and political life at the start of the Korean War, during which the military draft that had been reinstituted in the late 1940s wasted little time in efficiently recalling to front-line duty in Korea a massive number of World War II veterans, some of whom were only just beginning to recover from post-traumatic stress syndrome, as well as mobilizing successive waves of younger males. "America, you know, pathologically hates poets. . . . We interfere with the business of sucking dry all the resources, the humanities the creative ability of the entire planet—and other planets as soon as they get to them. But if we don't let them frighten us, we're bound to be heard. . . . Unfortunately, we're all waiting for an explosion. If you find a tinge of that terror and death on these pages, it's a sign of these times" (*Inferno*, Winter 1952). The first poem in that issue, James Boyer May's "Lamia, 1950," explicitly names the kind of explosion that Hedley notes "we're all waiting for," but goes a step further in pointing to the accomplices of atomic warfare, "the ivy-hid prognosticators" who cite Spengler and Toynbee as they imply that the mass murder of civilians at Hiroshima generated no permanent ecological damage: "didn't all the green come back?"—to which May responds, "Yes, nitwits too."

Foaming the Length of This Seaboard: James Boyer May and *Trace* Magazine

The most astute readers of contemporary poetry in 1953 and 1954 would have sensed that a new convergence was thickening on the West Coast. No other region in America had four independent literary magazines of the feisty caliber of *California Quarterly*, *Variegation*, *Inferno*, and *Golden Goose*, with a fifth magazine, *Trace*, serving as a facilitator of commentary and change-of-address reference guide. These magazines and their editors' projects addressed through their own poems and the material they selected for the magazine everything from labor issues to the atomic bomb to apartheid in South Africa. As such, the various eruptions of Beat poets, whether in North Beach or Venice West, between late 1955 and 1960 were more like tossing dry wood on hot coals than an unpredictable and spontaneous combustion.

Unfortunately, within less than a decade, the critical reaction to Donald Allen's *The New American Poetry* appeared to confirm, if not solidify, an incredibly oversimplified claim of an irreconcilable division within American poetry; readers and critics were expected to choose between two configurations in a very uneven contest: one side seemed to possess immense institutional resources, while the challenger had an inventory that Allen Ginsberg half-seriously spoofed in his poem "America" as consisting of two joints. Over forty years later, this reductionist binary still forestalls consideration of the sizable number of poets, especially on the West Coast, who chose a third course of poetics. Indeed, the old schema still has most critics in its sway. In *Cold War Poetry*, for instance, Edward Brunner contrasts Robert Pack, Louis Simpson, and Donald Hall's *New Poets of England and America* (1957) and Donald Allen's "counteranthology" as if these two volumes were the only reading options whatsoever for everyone (185). While Brunner does acknowledge poets not recognized in either anthology, his retention of these two anthologies as a fundamental binary forestalls any discussion of the debate taking place among those who equally loathed academic formalism and Allen's roster, and in particular ignores the location of the voices that refused to offer their definitive allegiance to one side or the other.

Of the poet-editors producing a magazine during this period which ran for at least sixty issues, James Boyer May's *Trace* magazine perhaps best records the public disputes that mark the boundaries between these two groups. Beginning with "Towards Print," an editorial column of literary reflections and book reviews which first appeared in a mimeographed magazine called *Matrix* magazine in 1950, May's evaluation of the turbulence in American culture in general and West Coast poetry in particular over a twenty-year period points to the third path that many poets took. May (1904–1972) spent World War II as a military policeman in Louisiana. After the war, he moved to Los Angeles and went to work for the Department of Employment. Having graduated from Beloit College in 1926, May had little inclination to sit in a classroom again. After Alan Swallow published his collection of short stories, *For a New Age of Hate*, in 1947, he had hopes of getting a novel about his experiences at Camp Ponchantrain published, but when his career as a novelist faltered, he focused instead on nurturing connections between disparate clusters of poets. Although May regarded *Trace* primarily as an outgrowth of his bibliographical knowledge of little magazines, it was meant as more than a glorified address book. If poets felt isolated, the editors of small poetry magazines had even fewer places to congregate and exchange their thoughts on their projects and the state of culture. May decided very early on to make *Trace* a place for dialogue between editors.[8] By issue number 10 (February 1955), May included letters from ten editors, addressing a compulsion to share this knowledge and amplify a dialogue about topics such as a distinction between art and non-art, the disparity of quality in experimental writing, the value of Ezra Pound's work, and the length of time needed to consider and return submissions. One indication of both the circulation of *Trace* and May's willingness to give exposure to talented but unknown writers is the entry after the letters, a statement by Larry Eigner about his process of revision which is longer than any of the editor's statements. Housebound due to cerebral palsy, Eigner lived in Swampscott, Massachusetts. By late 1954, *Trace* had become the most visible and widely circulated magazine of its kind. It would eventually attract more than two thousand subscribers.

As writers and editors, both Hedley and May represent World War II veterans who challenged both the theory and the practice of the New Criticism, the pedagogical model that most veterans were being subjected to as they took advantage of the G.I. bill. Nor was May shy about expressing his opinion of mainstream magazines. Months before any police officer entered City Lights Bookstore in hopes of launching a prosecution against Ginsberg and Orlovitz, James Boyer May bluntly stated his contempt for the superficiality of cultural analysis launched by *Time* and *Life* magazines on June 11, 1956: "If the editor were to vomit, it would be naturally and from simple reaction to the day's glances at such 'educational' features" as a thing in *Time* titled "Parnassus, Coast to Coast" (*Trace*, August 1956, 10). May was equally caustic about *Life*'s article, "Advice to and From Writers," calling it "basically idiotic."[9]

One might reasonably expect that May would be a champion of the Beat writers, given this degree of outspoken contempt for conventional and standard publications, but instead he consistently emphasized that the most important poets on the West Coast were those outside of both Allen and Hall's anthologies: Robinson Jeffers, Kenneth Patchen, William Pillin, Leslie Woolf Hedley, William Margolis, Gil Orlovitz. Six months after charges against *The Statement of Erika Keith* had been dismissed and *Howl* had been acquitted by Judge Horn, May used his column to correct what he regarded as major misconceptions about West Coast poetry. On the first page of issue 26, May reflects that for several months he has been receiving letters which contain "extremely discoloured pictures of the Coast scene," and makes three basic points:

> First, there has been and IS no 'movement,' no 'underground,' no 'school,' however inchoate. There HAS been widening interest in experimental writing of many sorts not slanted for mass consumption. . . . Next the active writers exhibit intense individualities which have been confirmed by their failure to hold together any of the groups which have each disappeared almost before defined. . . . Thus, and third, there is no leader and no voice; and each poet has spoken mainly for his personal ideas. . . . One valid generalization, at least must be that a romantic chaos of creativities foams the length of this seaboard. (*Trace*, April 1958, 1)

May's rejection of an incipient master narrative of hipness is reinforced by his subsequent list of crucial "familiar figures," of which the poets listed above are praised for their roles in creating "an un-Pacific Coast," implying a disputed region. Jeffers and Patchen, in particular are acknowledged as the senior poets in the "recent furor," while Kenneth Rexroth is pointed to as "another who stands alone." May cites only two women in his list of those who are "ignored" in the "recent furor," Josephine Miles and Jean Garrigue. With the exception of Thomas McGrath, all dozen of the poets whom May regards as the core of this ferment were not included in either Hall or Allen's anthology.

May concedes that Jeffers has stayed "aloof during all the excitements," but the omission of Patchen from anthologies published in his lifetime that have received the most critical response has been replicated by the failure of critics in the twenty-first century to acknowledge him as a role model of the poetics of stoic protest for an entire generation of West Coast poets.[10] May asserts that Patchen is the one "who has influenced more (poets) than any," and in fact is "flagrantly imitated by many . . . He . . . has kept his own course; and this has held as well for his pioneering endeavors in combining the reading of poetry with jazz" (*Trace*, April 1958, 1). In the same issue, May reviews Patchen's *Selected Poems*, noting Patchen's "unique mastery of the American idiom—he has built, in the past two decades, a profound philosophical realisation of our time" (18). The Los Angeles police had less respect for Patchen, however, raiding a movie theater and seizing a print of *Plague Summer*, an antiwar film with a script based on Patchen's *Journal of Albion Moonlight*. Issue 26 of *Trace* concludes by reporting that on February 20th, 1958, the film was found "guilty" on obscenity charges, though the next issue reported that verdict had been overturned on a technicality (*Trace*, June 1958, 23).

Patchen's absence from Allen's anthology was perhaps due to his unwillingness to become part of a school or movement. Allen Ginsberg remembers encountering Patchen at City Lights Bookstore, and that he loaned Ginsberg his copy of Blaise Cendrar's *Voyage Transiberiene*, but their acquaintance turned into sour disdain when they met again in New York City in the lobby of the Living Theater, "Patchen disapproved Kerouac's poetics, and didn't seem to like—in fact actively disapproved—all the new work of composition that later entered Donald Allen's *New American Poetry 1945–1960*. It may be that he thought it too commercial. . . ." (*Outsider*, Winter 1968–1969, 99–100). Regardless of what caused Patchen to disassociate himself from the poets in Allen's anthology, the actual literary situation was far more complex than a confrontation in a theater lobby. For one thing, Patchen's *Selected Poems* was published by Ferlinghetti, and his work continued to appear in many magazines such as the *Outsider* and Clarence Major's the *Coercion Review*.[11] The reluctance, and in some cases caustic alienation, felt by many prominent poets on the West Coast as they interacted with a young generation should be taken as an indication of how accurate May's assessment of "no school" was. In the final issue of *Trace* magazine in 1972, May admitted that he had underestimated the capacity of the poets of the Beat generation to influence an even younger generation of artists and social rebels, but he also insisted that his original claim was still valid.

May regarded the publication of opinions that differed from his evaluations to be one of the most important aspects of his magazine, but since some poets receive good or bad reviews regardless of whether they are written by May or someone else, one can hardly but conclude that *Trace* favored an identifiably eclectic group of writers. If May loathed the mainstream, he was at best ambivalent about many of the poets whose work appeared in Allen's anthology, running negative reviews of Robert Duncan and Denise Levertov, but in doing so, he also praises poets, such as Mina Loy, whose work had been virtually forgotten by everyone except Jonathan Williams. In a similar manner, May dismissed most of the work that appeared in the early issues of *Evergreen Review*, which would include work of Charles Olson, but praised the experimental prose of Arlene Zekowski and Stanley Berne.[12]

The First "No School" Anthology of Los Angeles Poets

A year before Grover Jacoby's pair of magazines ceased publication, two young poets who had studied under Tom McGrath started their own magazine, *Coastlines*, a title intended to suggest its commitment to place and genre. The founding editors of *Coastlines*, Gene Frumkin and Mel Weisburd, were working as assistant editors on *California Quarterly* toward the end of its four-year run, and the overlap of their editorial projects extended to the roster of poets published in both magazines. In fact, as one can see from referring back to the chart on page 30, Frumkin and Weisburd also published a significant number of poets who had appeared in Jacoby's magazines. *Coastlines* lasted a total of twenty-two issues, with its final one appearing in 1964, which means that Los Angeles had at least two poetry magazines being regularly produced for almost a decade and a half. Perhaps most remarkable of all, none of these magazines had any institutional support whatsoever. Frumkin worked as a journalist and editor for a garment industry publication in downtown Los Angeles and Weisburd spent his time trying to monitor the deteriorating air quality in Los Angeles for the AQMD. In maturing from mimeographed beginnings to national recognition, the total number of issues produced by McGrath, Frumkin, and Weisburd far exceeds the lifespan of the average little magazine cited in Donald Allen's *The New American Poetry*.

Estelle Gershgoren Novak's *Poets of the Non-Existent City: Los Angeles in the McCarthy Era* (*PNEC*) borrows its title from the proclamation on the cover of double issue number 14-15 of *Coastlines* magazine in 1960. Playing off the familiar reputation of Los Angeles as a massive, constantly expanding collage, the editors of *Coastlines* decided to turn an urban conundrum into a context that suggested the virtuosity of survival, if not the virtue of their art. Novak's book is a conscientious anthology of poems and articles that appeared in either *California Quarterly* (1951–1956) or *Coastlines* (1955-1964) magazine.

Novak chose nineteen poets as the representative figures for a period ("the McCarthy Era") that is insufficiently defined in her long introductory essay. She points to the investigations of the House Un-American Activities Committee (HUAC) as an obvious starting point, but other than referring to the long-term effects of blacklisting and job losses, one has no sense of when the McCarthy era comes to an end, or when its stranglehold finally began to exhaust itself. A more important question than the chronological span, though, is the relationship between the poets and the city, "non-existent" or not. What is it that makes these poets identifiable with Los Angeles other than a mailing address? Are they *primarily* Los Angeles poets? Is the place where they write, or write about, so crucial that it overrides any other description of their work? Or is "Los Angeles" a code word for marginality, an ironic inflection of their relationship to the culture at large as well as to the layers of poets and artists elsewhere, both experimental and traditional? Above all, what advantage do we gain by categorizing them as Los Angeles poets?

The first difficulty is one that I have already noted: many of these poets had previously received significant attention outside of Southern California. The problem of the dichotomy of local versus national has its roots in a contradictory standard in which regional identity and literary significance are played off against each other in such a way that each category can be invoked to negate the other. If a poet produces a body of work aligned as a material or performative text with other poets living in her or his region, then the first question concerns whether this work is significant in any way outside of this group. If the value of the work to readers and writers outside of that region can be demonstrated in a variety of ways, then the challenge to dismiss the regional affiliation of the poet is raised, or at least the evidence supporting the poet's supposedly wider importance is then marshaled to dilute any primary emphasis on the poet's involvement with a local community. In other words, if a poet has a reputation outside of the local, she or he forfeits any significant role or participation in the social realignments that a locally based publication is endeavoring to develop or accentuate. One of the most praised poets in Novak's book, Don Gordon, is a good example of this problem: in considering authorial identity within a context of a renaissance of resistance and critique in Los Angeles, is he simply a poet protesting the compulsory directives of the police and military state, or he is primarily a poet of a community? If *Howl* could be said to have come out of North Beach and City Lights Bookstore, and Venice West gave Stuart Perkoff and his compatriots a community of common references, was there anything other than a literary magazine that bound the disaffiliates of *Coastlines* together? Beginning with the second issue, *Coastlines* moved its editorial office to a house owned by one of its contributors, a short story writer named Barding Dahl. The back pages of the third issue contained a formal announcement of Dahl's art organization, The Community Forum of Los Angeles (CFLA), and an open invitation to meetings on Thursday evenings that focused on scheduling events.[13]

The extent of the ruckus midway through a poetry reading at that house, during which Allen Ginsberg, challenged by a drunk, allegedly took off all his clothes, is still a matter of dispute. Neither Ginsberg nor Gregory Corso, the other poet who read, seemed to care whose version should be believed, but then again, they may have preferred or even enjoyed conflicting accounts since the longer people talked about it, the more volatile the incident became in memory. Lawrence Lipton turned Ginsberg's gesture of innocuous vulnerability into a crisis that supposedly gauged who in the audience was Beat or square. Lawrence Lipton's account of the evening would appear three years after it happened in *The Holy Barbarians*, permanently severing any artistic affiliation or sense of common cause that Venice West and the editors of *Coastlines* shared. The quarrel between Lipton and *Coastlines* had started as early as the sixth issue, when Lipton's article, "America's Literary Underground," nominated the writers who were "blowing the whistle on the Social Lie." Lipton's article, however, did make an important distinction about the underground as a modern artistic category. To be a member of the underground, according to Lipton, was more than a matter of being a young and hungry artist who was enduring poverty while establishing one's career:

> It (the underground) was not a matter of selling few books before you sell many, of being an unknown before you became a well-known. Most writers have to travel that road, some slowly, some swiftly. It was a matter of basic assumptions, basic attitudes. The underground writer, as distinguished from the merely unknown writer, rejected all "the well known facts" that the conformist writer accepted as part of the Social Contract, if not the natural Order. Implicit when it was not explicit in every word he wrote was the assumption that profit is immoral and exploitation of every kind cannibalistic, that the State is the punitive arm of whatever class happens to be in power, and war is compulsory mass murder. (*Coastlines*, Winter 1956–1957, 4)

Following this distinction, Lipton provides a paragraph-long list of the contemporary underground, consisting of twenty-three men. Only one of them, Chester Himes, is not white. Lipton's underground consists of two generations, both of which have confronted the most difficult trick of belonging to the underground: "to emerge from (it) without leaving the best of you behind in the process." Lipton notes that "a few died trying, Dylan Thomas, Weldon Kees. And a few are only now emerging—intact. Paul Goodman, Hugh MacDiarmid, Kenneth Patchen, Richard Eberhart, Kenneth Rexroth, Louis Zukofsky." Lipton's willingness to construct an enormous tent for poetry grew out of a conviction that these poets, along with more recently emerging ones he cites such as Duncan, Lamantia, Levertov, Creeley, Olson, Hedley,

May, Corso, Ginsberg, Ferlinghetti, Perkoff, and Jonathan Williams, "do not in any sense constitute a 'school.' Some of them are not even on family fighting terms with one another. But they are all conscious of belonging to a literary underground" (*Coastlines*, Winter 1956–1957, 5).

In the same issue of *Coastlines*, as well the next one, Mel Weisburd challenged Lipton's nominations by claiming his version of an "underground" could be said to constitute a school: the Sensible School of Poetry, a name that was too disingenuous to be effective, but which scooped up an equally disparate group of poets, including Edwin Rolfe, George Elliott, Naomi Replansky, John Ciardi, Don Gordon, William Pillin, Tom McGrath, Gene Frumkin, and Bert Meyers (*Coastlines*, Winter 1956–1957, 39–40).[14] The debate about the potential canon of the "underground" had become vehement before *Howl* even went on trial. The prose argument, in addition, is counterpointed by Weisburd's inclusion, as an editor, of "underground" work neglected by Lipton. In the same issue in which he rebuts Lipton, Weisburd joins with Grover Jacoby in being among the first to publish the gentle anarchy of Philip Whalen's poetry. In the mid-fifties, *Coastlines* could be said to be living up to its name and mapping out one more outlet of the fertile crescent of West Coast poetry.

By September 1957, monthly readings sponsored by Poetry Los Angeles began drawing large crowds, with an "overflow crowd of 300" (*Coastlines*, Winter 1957–1958, 44) attending Kenneth Rexroth's reading in November. Other poets who read that fall included Pillin, Perkoff, Cardona-Hine, Orlovitz, Frumkin, Gershgoren, and Weisburd. KUSC radio began broadcasting a program entitled "Poetry and Talk," hosted by Peter Carr on Tuesdays and Thursdays. In the winter and spring Poetry Los Angeles presented readings at Barnsdall Park by Kenneth Patchen, Bert Meyers, Zack Walsh, Carl Larsen, Thomas McGrath, James Boyer May, Lawrence Spingarn, Josephine Ain, Ann Stanford, and Lawrence Lipton. Another place for readings was Cosmo Alley, where McGrath performed with Ralph Pena, and Rexroth and Perkoff also read. This abundance of activity had begun to get noticed across the nation: the *Beloit Poetry Journal* ran a special West Coast survey issue and Evelyn Thorne's *Epos* magazine in Florida ran an issue loaded with *Coastlines* contributors, calling it "The Los Angeles Movement." Some readers of the tenth issue of *Coastlines* may never have reached the back pages of the magazine where all of this activity was reported. The front cover promises an article on "Lysergic Acid and the Creative Experience," and Mel Weisburd's account of his first LSD trip may well have sent some readers of the magazine off in search of it. Exotic drugs were perhaps easier to score in San Francisco, but the Los Angeles poetry scene was hardly shy about announcing the benefits of chemically assisted visions.

The success of these reading series was marked by the publication of a unique anthology from this period, *Poetry Los Angeles: I* (1958). Although the midcentury marked the emergence of the poetry reading as a performative act capable of defining the boundaries of an artistic community, *Poetry Los Angeles: I* is the only significant collection documenting the participants of a reading series that was unaffiliated with an educational institution. Edited by James Boyer May, Thomas McGrath, and Peter Yates, *Poetry Los Angeles: I* included work by Tom McGrath, William Pillin, Ann Stanford, Gene Frumkin, Bert Meyers, and Gil Orlovitz. Although both Lipton and Perkoff had read in the series, they were omitted in favor of a concentration on the poets whose work fell into the Alan Swallow camp.

One of the editors, James Boyer May, used his own magazine to print a review of *Poetry Los Angeles: I*. May selected Tram Combs, a young poet from San Francisco, whose analysis conferred the same judgment as May and Lipton's assessment that poets had gathered into diverse, mutually respectful assembly that resisted classification: "The book in no way presents a 'school,'" Combs concluded, although he admired the "great variety" in both form and content of the poets (*Trace*, February–March 1959, 49–50). This frequent reiteration of the claim of "no school" suggests that the "great variety" exhibited by the poets in Los Angeles sustained the prolonged, suspended quality that Joseph Harrington proposed as one of a poetry scene's crucial features. Backlit by a nonexistent city, the poets refused to make themselves easily identifiable. In using the elusiveness of an urban omphalos to make the absence of a school ineluctable, they manifestly exuded without any need for the flagrant italics of a poetics their underlying acceptance of each other's rights to participate in contumacious, poignant dialogue. As the editors noted in their introduction to *Poetry Los Angeles: I*, "The poet is one who in company thinks alone and offers his experience as a poem" (*Poetry Los Angeles: I*, 3).

Coastlines's pace of production slowed considerably after 1960, and its survival was in large part due to the editorial energy and fundraising efforts of Alexandra Garrett, who opened up her house to parties that somehow snagged enough donations from the guests to pay a printer's overdue bill. When the magazine finally succumbed in 1964, the accomplishment of its early years was largely forgotten. Robert Kirsch in the *Los Angeles Times* said that "the death of *Coastlines* is sad but not necessarily symptomatic. I don't know whether there is a renaissance here. (Indeed, the term bothers me a little, I am still looking for signs of a naissance.)." A few paragraphs later, though, Kirsch appears to contradict himself: "Is there, in a literary sense, a Southern California culture? I think there is. But I think that it has not yet entered the phase of provincial cultures which crystallize around a time and a setting and a viable center" (August 30, 1964). In *Coastlines*'s first issue, the editors had described Los Angeles as "undergoing a vast social revolution whose shape, although sometimes causing despair, is not yet altogether clear" (*Coastlines*, Spring 1955, 3). As *Coastlines* ceased publishing, part of that revolution was about to make its shape visible in South Central Los Angeles.

The Colorado Connection: Alan Swallow and the Subversive Poets of Los Angeles

While Leslie Woolf Hedley and James Boyer May made crucial contributions as editors, few critics believe their poetry can be favorably compared to other World War II veterans who were poet-editors on the West Coast. Lawrence Ferlinghetti (b. 1919) and Thomas McGrath (b. 1916), on the other hand, not only have large bodies of poetry, but their engagement as editors with the writing of other poets also puts their poems into a dialogic relationship with that imaginary community. In considering the impact of their choices as editors, the similarities and differences between poets in northern and Southern California during the early years of the cold war raise doubts about May's assessment that there are only "intense individualities" at work on the West Coast in a "romantic chaos of creativities." In particular, we can discern a split in the publishing affiliations of each region's poets. The poets living in northern California tended to have their books published by Grove Press or New Directions in New York, while poets in Southern California were most often published by Alan Swallow in Colorado. How the editors at Grove, New Directions, and Swallow found themselves interested in the work of certain poets in a particular region is probably due as much to the happenstance of history as any aesthetic preferences.[15] Before we mull over some of the contingencies behind these choices, let us review the names of poets published by the various publishers. The names in italics here indicate the poet also appeared in *The New American Poetry*.

The list of authors published by both Grove and New Directions was of course considerably longer than the one presented here, which concentrates on American poets that they published during the first two decades of the cold war. Famous for its longstanding support of physician-poet William Carlos Williams and his enigmatic, tragic friend, Ezra Pound, as well as for its very successful edition of Dylan Thomas's *Collected Poems*, New Directions was the elder statesman of this quartet.[16] The extent to which white males dominate these lists provides a stark reminder of how few women managed to get the attention of the most active literary publishing houses. From this chart we can also see the degree to which City Lights and New Directions both promoted many of the same poets. Swallow is the only one of the four not to share any of his authors with the other publishers.

Poets Published by Four Literary Publishers

CITY LIGHTS	GROVE	NEW DIRECTIONS	SWALLOW
Gregory Corso	*Paul Blackburn*	*Gregory Corso*	Edgar Bowers
Robert Duncan	*Edward Field*	*Robert Duncan*	Alvaro Cardona-Hine
Lawrence Ferlinghetti	*LeRoi Jones*	*William Everson*	J. V. Cunningham
		(Brother Antoninus)	
Allen Ginsberg	*Kenneth Koch*	*Lawrence Ferlinghetti*	Gene Frumkin
Bob Kaufman	*Michael McClure*	Bob Kaufman	Don Gordon
Jack Kerouac	*Frank O'Hara*	James Laughlin	Hanson Kellogg
Philip Lamantia	*Charles Olson*	*Michael McClure*	Thomas McGrath
Michael McClure		Kenneth Patchen	Bert Meyers
Frank O'Hara		Kenneth Rexroth	William Pillin
Kenneth Patchen		Muriel Rukeyser	Ann Stanford
Kenneth Rexroth		*Gary Snyder*	Alan Swallow
Philip Whalen			Yvor Winters

No matter who their publishers happened to be, the poets on the above chart were almost unanimously pacifist in their politics. Ironically, three of the four editors served in the military during World War II. Alan Swallow had been born and raised in Wyoming, and went from working in a filling station as a youth to earning a PhD at Louisiana State University. With the assistance of a one hundred dollar loan from his father, Swallow bought a used Kelsey hand press and published his first book, *Signets: An Anthology of Beginnings* in March 1940. He taught briefly at the University of New Mexico and at a college in Colorado before being drafted to serve in the army during World War II. In 1946, he began publishing under several different imprints a variety of books, ranging from travel guides or field books on the Teton Range or Wyoming Mountains to fiction by Janet Lewis and Frank Waters. He resigned from his full-time teaching post at the University of Denver after 1954 in order to work full-time as a publisher. Swallow's other authors and titles included a half-dozen novels by Anais Nin, Edward Loomis's *The Charcoal Horse*, a ten-volume series of novels by Vardis Fisher entitled *Testament of Man*, and many nonfiction books, including several accounts of the Civil War and a history of an American motorcycle manufacturer.

Swallow also published a group of poets, such as Yvor Winters, Edgar Bowers, and J. V. Cunningham, who would appear to fit within the pedagogical standards he encountered when he studied at Louisiana State with Cleanth Brooks and Robert Penn Warren. Swallow's extraordinarily eclectic range as a publisher is his single most distinguishing trait, but he also stands apart in one major way. Although many of the poets published by Allen, Ferlinghetti, and Laughlin took courageous stands, through their selection of authors, on political issues ranging from gay rights to pacifism and ecology, only two of the poets in the publishing chart on page 47, Tom McGrath and Don Gordon, suffered from being blacklisted. Alan Swallow was the *only* publisher in this quartet to defy a blacklist and continue publishing both of these poets after they suffered the loss of their jobs due to the anti-Communist witch-hunts. I am certainly not accusing the other three editors of going along with the blacklist in any way. I am, however, pointing to a singular aspect of Swallow's editorial stance that deserves more credit.[17]

The Only Bomb Shelter Is Psychosis: The Disaffiliation of Don Gordon

The publication in 2004 of the *Collected Poems* of Don Gordon is a major initial step toward establishing his place in the canon of dissident poets. Gordon (1902–1989) published a half-dozen books, beginning with *Statement* in 1943 and concluding with *The Sea of Tranquility* in 1989. Alan Swallow published *Displaced Persons* in 1958, but few reviewers indemnified Swallow's courage or the encouragement provided by Thomas McGrath and his young friends.[18] One-third of the poems that appeared in *Displaced Persons* in 1958 had first been published in either *California Quarterly*, whose best-known editor was Tom McGrath, or in *Coastlines*, founded by two of McGrath's students. Gordon's "At the Station" was the first poem in the first issue of *Coastlines* magazine in the spring of 1955. Its placement opposite the dedication page to Edwin Rolfe should be taken as a primary indication of the editorial predicate of that magazine:

> The landscape has been subtly shifted, it is out of focus or we are:
> Yesterday, manacled to the marshal, I saw the boy I knew at school;
> There were trees where we stand, then the sound of hammers,
> In the morning you will see the scaffolds with their solid arms.
>
> Who has displaced a nation?....
>
> Which way does the big train go?
> Traveler, lost under the station lamp,
> I'm a stranger here myself.
>
> (*Collected Poems* 96)

Gordon's self-portrait, in a metaphorical version of Union Station in Los Angeles, echoes Carey McWilliams's citation of the anonymous quip that "We are all strangers here." Gordon's disclaimer to the traveler's inquiry is in part a defensive strategy by the unnamed narrator, who has already admitted *sotto voce* that she or he has seen a childhood friend within the punitive grasp of the judicial system. The lost traveler may also have seen the hand-cuffed prisoner, and want to know what crime the person has been accused or convicted of; the dissembling statement of the poem's conclusion is meant to head off any expectations of advice or explanation.

Don Gordon was born in 1902 in Bridgeport, Connecticut. His parents moved to Los Angeles in 1912, where his father practiced law and his mother and sister acted in silent films. Gordon graduated from Los Angeles High School in 1919, and finished his college education at Pomona College in 1923. He tried law school, but dropped out, and eventually found work at the movie studios analyzing the potential of popular novels to be adapted into movies. He joined the Communist Party in the early 1930s, and was active in organizing readers at the studio into a union. The title of his second book, *Civilian Poems*, reflects his status as a noncombatant during World War II. In late September 1951, he was subpoenaed to appear before the House on Un-American Activities Committee, but he refused to answer questions, and a few days later lost his job at MGM. For the remaining dozen or so years of his working life, he was mainly employed at a series of outpatient health clinics and at a halfway house.[19]

Gordon is perhaps the most self-effacing political poet of the postwar era. His poems provide very few personal details, and only sporadically allude to the city he lived in for most of his adult life.[20] If his work cannot be found in any anthology published between 1970 and 2000, he still maintained an obstinate belief in an intransigent affirmation with which he countered his assignment to marginality:

> Someone has heard who did not seem to be listening.
> Someone will open the archives on a far-off day of rain,
> Enacting the first law: the conservation of dreams.
> ("Someone Has Heard," *Collected Poems* 194)

While "the archive" for many poets would mean the mounds and mounds of drafts of poems and articles, Gordon's archive is the "obscure tomb" of history:

> Of beliefs and bodies destroyed in the vanguard,
> Of faith that becomes local fact
> In the next generation.
> ("In the Vanguard," *Collected Poems*, 192)

Gordon alone continued to write poetry that refused to consider existence outside the context of atomic or nuclear war. In the three collections of poems he published after *Displaced Persons*, Gordon defines his role as the Cassandra of West Coast poets. Almost twenty years pass between *Displaced Persons* and his next collection, *On the Ward*, but there is no change whatsoever in tone or theme.[21] The final stanza of a poem in *On the Ward*, "The Temporary Man," might serve as a quiet rebuke to the Frankfurt critique of poetry's postwar possibilities:

> My father crouched in the attic
> While the terror swept by
> In the Lithuanian night.
> I learned from him:
> Home is the halfway house to exile,
> We are only on leave from Auschwitz.
>
> (114–115)

Gordon, however, perceived that the entire planet had become a death camp under construction: "The only bomb shelter is psychosis" ("On the Ward, Two," *Collected Poems* 100). Refusing to cower before the overwhelming power of military forces, Gordon's poems do not completely abandon hope, even though "Civilization is a river of refugees / . . . The only river / That never goes dry" ("Refugees," *Collected Poems* 118). A sad yearning permeates his implacable vision: in one of his final poems, Gordon acknowledges that nothing he attempts as an individual will change the plans of "a nation of burghers / Who know where they are." Nevertheless, Gordon writes his poems as his means of taking his place among those he calls "the free-falling ones," those "who believe the parachutes / Will open someday" ("Free Fall," *Collected Poems* 180).

The word "exile" immurs itself repeatedly within Gordon's poems. If old age is configured as a period in one's life in which one enfolds the provisional wisdom of acceptance, Gordon portrays his final years as a period in which he saw the hopes of the "flower generation" of the 1960s utterly quelled, and his neighbors as people who found his stark vision repugnant:

> He seemed the sole survivor
> Of a dead planet,
> [. . . .]
> No one could endure him,
> He said nothing, but they heard:
>   Amnesty, amnesty.
> They were glad when he moved:

They could resume the games.
[...]
They have a compulsion
To talk about him.
They think he had problems
And buried them in public.
They have to decide he was sick
    very sick.

              ("The Neighbor,"
              Collected Poems 128)

One could, I suppose, accuse him of thematic monotony, except that his poems prove that no other genre is capable of allowing an artist the steadfast gaze of prophecy ignored. Gordon mordantly twists one of the best-known aphorisms to remind us of the actual cost of speaking truth to power. "in the country / of the blind / the one-eyed man / is always murdered" ("The Deportee," *Collected Poems* 79). In his final collection, *The Sea of Tranquility* (1989), he portrays the power of civilizations to annihilate themselves as only part of the loss that needs to be addressed.

If we cannot believe in our own end,
How to accept the burial alive
Of the creatures we know,
The loss of the landscape and of birds,
Of the great constrictor,
The tread of pachyderms in the continents
    of fire,
The non-being of generations never to be born.

Now we are on the final plateau
With a view in all directions.
We think we can choose any point
    of the compass
Until we discover we are in Masada,
    besieged by ourselves.

            ("The Missiles," *Collected Poems* 196)

Alan Swallow also published the poetry of William Pillin, who at this point seems to be remembered more on account of his political associations than for the stalwart lyricism of his verse. Midway through *Counter-Revolution of the World: The Conservative Attack on Modern Poetry, 1945–1960*, Al Filreis cites

William Pillin as one of "three well-known communists," the other two being Hugh MacDiarmid and Thomas McGrath, who are mentioned as "models for spoken-word poetry" by Lawrence Lipton in an article in the *Nation* (176).[22] His last major collection, *To the End of Time*, can still be found in an occasional used bookstore, but of all the poets published in *Coastlines* or in *Poetry Los Angeles: I*, Pillin remains the quintessential outsider, despite the fact that he had, not one, but two books published by George Hitchcock's widely respected Kayak Press, *Everything Falling* (1971) and *The Abandoned Music Room* (1975).[23]

Born in 1910 and raised in Ukraine, William Pillin did not speak English until he arrived in the United States at the age of fourteen. He spent the rest of his youth in Chicago, married in late adolescence, and eventually moved to Santa Fe. His painter-wife, Polia Pillin, and he arrived in Los Angeles in 1947, where he self-published his second book of poems, *Theory of Silence*. The poems attracted the attention of James Boyer May, who included Pillin in 1952 in his anthology, *Eight American Poets* along with James Schevill and Harold Witt. Pillin's poetry appeared in over six dozen magazines during the course of his life; one quick sample of his publishing spectrum can be derived from the credits for *Dance without Shoes*: *American Weave, Coastlines, Epos, Essence, Experiment, Flame, Glass Hill, Golden Goose, New Orleans Poetry Journal, The New Republic, Poetry, Sparrow, Tiger's Eye, Voices, Whetstone, Eight American Poets*, and *Pacifica* Records edited by Leslie Hedley.[24] Pillin not only appeared in Yates's anthology in 1958, but also in the special issue of *Coastlines* in 1960 along with a dozen other Los Angeles poets. In 1963 his book, *Pavanne for a Fading Memory*, was published by Alan Swallow. During the last thirty years of his life, his artist wife, Polia, and he eked out a living as ceramicists in a studio on Melrose Avenue.[25]

Pillin's work is much more subtle in its social protest than much of the poetry produced by his cohort on the West Coast. Although he was involved with union organizing struggles in the 1930s, his poems turn away from any oversimplified class analysis and concentrate on the presentation of the processes of work itself. His quietly lyrical accounts of working as a potter are unlike any other poems being written in the late 1940s.

We dug iron-stained
Feldspathic rock
In dew-moist ravine;
Screened in a stream
And loaded barrows
For the damp-bin.
The jungle-damp spot
Had a sweet stink. I was

Muscle-sore witness
To cavernous doings;
Forests of fern
Sunken in swamps
Next to trapped bones
Of pterodactyls.
("Notes on Making Pottery," Part 1, "Clay,"
       Theory of Silence, unpaginated)

A reader might claim to detect overtones of Williams or Rexroth, but neither of these poets would present themselves as actually laboring in the first person while suggesting that their work provided a source of immanent communion with eons of evolution, present in the materials themselves, or with practitioners of his craft in other cultures.

For three hours I sat
Grinding cobalt
In porcelain pestle
For a true lazuli
Such as Egyptians
Tinted eyes of tomb-beetles.
With aching back
And numb hands
I sat grinding
And it pleased me
To imagine myself Chinese
Of the time Hui Tsung
When craftsmen sat grinding
Moon-white celadon
For forty hours
To make a lucent film
In tea-stoneware.
   ("Notes on Making Pottery," Part 3,
"Preparing Glazes," *Theory of Silence*)

The repetition of "sat grinding," varied by the enjambment of the lines, provides a temporal and spatial axis that resists the exotic nostalgia the poem seems to invoke. In emphasizing the much more significant labor ("For forty hours") which earlier masters of his art had to endure to achieve their effects, Pillin undercuts his own self-comparison, and allows the brevity of the lines to do what free verse becomes best at doing: staging the silence that poetry is capable of insisting as being its fundamental component. In this particular poem, in fact, the final two sections contrast the sound of the "raging crucible" of the kiln, in which "dinosaurs captive / in copper pipe / burn, ..." with the concluding revelation of the poem's metaphorical firing.

> For 24 hours of silence
> The big kiln cooled.
> Will they bloom,
> Our vases,
> Tiny monuments
> Of gemlike stone?
> Or will they insult us,
> Cracked and crazed,
> Pin-holed, sulphur-blistered?
> The steel door
> Slowly opens;
> A silver-rimmed majolica
> Bursts
> Into a flowerflame.
>   ("Notes on Making Pottery," Part 6,
>   "Opening the Kiln," *Theory of Silence*)

Pillin's poetics insist that the visionary must be accompanied by patient labor. If William Carlos Williams insisted that "the poet thinks with his poem," Pillin's poems remind us that the poem's thought "slowly opens." The reader is the kiln, Pillin suggests, and many times a poem will not survive its firing.

Echoing Wordsworth's sentiments about the nature of human kindness in "Tintern Abbey," Pillin's political stance turns away from any programmatic solutions:

> That which is good is simply done
> Without the manifesto's noise
> As Francis talking to the birds
>   Or Leo to the peasant boys.

> The socialism of the heart
> Is not in schedules, is in man
> And what is generous on earth
>   Is generous without a plan.
>   ("That Which Is Good Is Simply Done,"
>   *Dance without Shoes* 67)

Pillin shared with Gordon an awareness of the devastating political and military forces that awaited the command of a single person to be unleashed. Pillin's poetry, though, seems to turn to Don Gordon, and yearn to hear him request, as in *Zorba the Greek,* "teach me to dance."

> Death is no medicine to take in small
> Black doses till the dancing limbs are numb
> And sorrow will not silence iron growl
> Of massed frontiers or stop the sunlike bomb.
>
> Dance without shoes until the crimson sun
> Dies at our window in a velvet sweep
>
> We greet with fingertips the morning sun
> ("Dance without Shoes,"
> *Dance without Shoes* 30–31)

Pillin was open to poets from a variety of schools and backgrounds, including Stuart Perkoff, the next chapter's flawed hero, whom Pillin outlived by over a decade. Alan Swallow had died twenty years earlier of a heart attack in his early fifties. If Swallow had lived as long as Pillin, and continued publishing Los Angeles area poets at the same rate, the history of West Coast poetry would be far different. Combined with the loss of Jack Spicer in the same year, and the accident that took Frank O'Hara's life in the following year, Act One of L.A. poetry during the cold war ends with many maybes, including the community of Venice West.

THREE

I Cannot Even Begin to Imagine
the Extent of Their Aloneness

Venice West and The New American Poetry

In analyzing the institutional distribution of space in urban existence, Henri Lefebvre distinguishes between the *near order*, which encapsulates the relations of any loose assemblage of human beings engaged in a recognizable degree of mutual activity, and the *far order*, the cluster of easily identifiable institutions whose codes and rules are defined with imposing specificity. He emphasizes that the inhabitants who constitute the near order can be detected at any given moment by the immediacy and simultaneity marking their endeavors, which confirm the far order's hegemony, even if not always contained within it. This unceasing negotiation of identities, which especially involves the regulation of behavior, is the force that through *paved solitude* drives the cosmopolitan flower.[1] A city, concludes Lefebvre, is an "*oeuvre*, closer to a work of art than to a simple material product. If there is production of the city, and social relations in the city, it is a production and reproduction of human beings by human beings, rather than a production of objects" (Lefebvre 100–101).

In emphasizing human interaction as the prime purpose of the city, Lefebvre awards language the most significant role in the social reproduction of life, and assigns assembly-line labor a subordinate position. A city, as a "*mediation* among mediations" (101), motivates people to test the limits of language, and to acknowledge that the contingency of its uses permeates every possible daily encounter. The importance of language in the perpetuation of a city is perhaps what enables critics to use language and its cultural products as a metaphor for the city. Lefebvre, for instance, construes the city as a book, although he rapidly qualifies this comparison by reminding us that "at best, the city constitutes a sub-system, a subwhole," and that "the whole is not immediately present in this written text, the city" (102). Most probably confined within its momentous scrawl, an obsessively analytical reader of a city will be able to discern larger patterns only after repeated readings, but Lefebvre knows that the context for the book of the city goes far beyond any possible extrapolations of textual margins. The city is an elusive object not because it contains some potential for transcendence, but because the transitions between its morphological basis and the imagined proportions of significance are submerged within the transformations of the ephemeral into the enduring.

The relationship between the near order and the far order in Los Angeles during the second half of the twentieth century is more turbulent than in most cities because of the presence of the culture industries. As played out in the challenges for legitimacy that institutions and communities pose for each other, the development of communities of poets in Los Angeles includes a layer of Beat poets in Venice, California, who renamed their city on the hill Venice West. The contribution of the poets of Venice West to the avant-garde movement of poetry in the United States was at the same time the most provocative challenge to the far order of Los Angeles at the midcentury.[2]

The Holy Barbarians: The Near Disorder of Venice West

"Los Angeles is a graveyard of social relations," observes Philip Ethington in an analysis of its ghost neighborhoods (*Looking for Los Angeles* 29). While the same could be said for the social imaginary, as defined by Norman Klein, of any major city, Ethington notes that the dispersed interments peculiar to Los Angeles are due in part to "one of its central contributions to civilization," the urban freeway. He points to the opening of the world's first four-level interchange (the 101 and 110) near downtown Los Angeles on September 22, 1953, as the impetus of a new set of stratifications in Southern California. Old problems involving culture, however, still awaited solutions. About this time, the most prominent cultural institutions in Los Angeles debated the status of the city within the urban pecking order of the United States. Although the city was synonymous with the glamour of the film industry, and had expanded considerably during World War II due to war material production plants, it lacked the confidence and cultural swagger of older cities.

In late August 1955, Jake Zeitlin, one of the major antiquarian book dealers in Los Angeles, gave a talk at the Huntington Library in San Marino in which he considered the potential of Los Angeles for any "evolution beyond the stages of sustenance and plenitude" (*Small Renaissance, Southern Californian Style* 5). Zeitlin claimed that four major indicators of the cultural development in Los Angeles were libraries, book clubs, printers, and collectors (5).[3] To the far order, the social relationships that Zeitlin described are the most visible elements of cultural development. Their activities do not propose to challenge any value of domestic economy or military ecology. In 1955, however, the near order of communities of poets in Los Angeles would perceive Zeitlin's privileging of manuscript collecting and antiquarian bookstores as being virtually identical with the far order's distribution of cultural capital. If any of these poetic groups could be said to be fundamentally antagonistic to the far order, the community of writers and artists that named itself Venice West had a program that could only be described as *near disorder*. Guilty of every crime from dealing and shooting heroin to incest, the poets in Venice went far beyond failure to take an interest in manuscript collecting. On the contrary, on many occasions three poets in this group, Stuart Perkoff, Frank Rios, and Tony Scibella, would write poems, and then burn them, without making any copies, in honor of "the Lady," the muse that they credited as the source of their inspiration. Other poets in Venice West, such as Bruce Boyd and John Thomas, kept copies of their work, but for years at a stretch would make little or no effort whatsoever to get the work published in book form.

Although by the end of the twentieth century the vast majority of anthologies and accounts of this period either neglected to mention it, or simply cited it in a dependent clause as an other instance of a Beat hangout,[4] Venice West in the late 1950s was regarded as a major thoroughfare of alternative artistic practice. When *Life* magazine decided to give middle-class America a look inside the day-to-day life of Beat artists in its September 21, 1959, issue, the Beat community shown in a six-page photo-essay was Venice West.[5] The selection by *Life*'s editors of an enclave of poets and painters in a dilapidated beach town in Los Angeles to represent "West Coast beats" was probably due to the marketing savvy of Lawrence Lipton, whose book about the poets and artists of Venice West, *The Holy Barbarians*, had been published by Julian Messner at the beginning of summer.[6] Rather than singling out a few individuals as the prime representatives of a generation, Lipton's title was meant to be all-encompassing in its categorization. Replete with transcripts and snippets of conversations between thinly disguised Venice West figures as well as Allen Ginsberg and Gregory Corso, *The Holy Barbarians* was also meant to counter the derogatory overtones suggested by Herb Caen's neologism, "beatnik," a term first launched in his San Francisco newspaper column on April 2, 1958.

Lipton's book differed from the article by emphasizing the poetic community rather than the painters and experimental artists such as George Herms who had been featured in the photographs in *Life*. The article gave the impression that Venice, California, was the latest version of a dadaist beach resort; the photographs depict abundant playfulness, a theme transparent to a high school student quoted as saying, "I'd like to be one (a beatnik) for a week. I'd like to do what I want to do and say what I want to say and have no worries, and know it wouldn't affect me in the future" (36). If the student had had a chance to talk with Arthur Richer, an artist whose wife, Bette, and four children are photographed in a room dominated by his huge abstract canvases, she or he would have found out that being a Beat artist does not mean that you are allowed to do whatever you want to do. Along with poet David Meltzer and future Temple of Man founder Bob Alexander, Richer was present when Los Angeles Police Department vice officers arrested Wallace Berman for exhibiting obscene art in June 1957. Rather than providing this kind of background information, *Life* devoted almost two entire pages at the end of the article to large photographs of high school students putting on a play about being beatniks in which hula hoops and sunglasses are the essential props. This parody at the end of the article was merely the prologue for what *Life* was planning as its follow-up coverage of "The Only Rebellion Around."[7]

Paul O'Neil's diatribe against the Beats slightly over two months later ("Sad But Noisy Rebels" proclaimed *Life*'s cover), acknowledged Lipton's *The Holy Barbarians* as "last summer's best-seller" (116), a mass-market hit that probably spiked the census figures of the Beat population on the West Coast. According to O'Neil, Los Angeles had "no fewer than 2,000 Beats," most of whom he said were living in Venice West, while he estimated the Beat population of San Francisco to be "less than a thousand" (129). Specific poets of Venice West, such as Stuart Perkoff, were left out of both of *Life*'s articles; nevertheless, if even a sliver—say, two-tenths of one percent (.2 percent)—of its weekly readers subsequently looked at *The Holy Barbarians*, over twelve thousand people would have encountered a literate imagination with themes far more ambitious than antic accounts of nonconformity.[8] Along with fragments of poems about standard Beat subjects such as jazz musicians, for instance, Lipton's *The Holy Barbarians* included a subtle meditation on manual labor by Perkoff, though in noting the obvious influence of William Carlos Williams, Lipton neglects the skill with which Perkoff cantilevers "the limits of tensions" to embody the crisis of boundaries provoked by enjambment. If a line of poetry is the basic tool by which a poet destabilizes a sentence, then Perkoff's reconciliation of the mind-body split enables us to savor a brief interlude of propitious balance.

> lifting
> a piece
> of black steel

& carefully
>(conforming to a pattern
>previously set down
>after extensive testing)

>placing it
on a construction
of boards
>extending
certain aspects of bodily structure
to the limits of tensions

>actions taken
within a situation
>once calculated
to destroy all pleasure
>now seem to contain
evocations
>("On Unloading a Boxcar,"
>*The Holy Barbarians* 237)

Perkoff's appearance in Donald Allen's anthology, *The New American Poetry*, the next year as the representative poet of Venice West needed little elaboration on Allen's part.[9] In fact, when Allen mentions Venice West in his brief introduction, he casually cites that scene with the utter confidence that his readers are far more knowledgeable than *Life* magazine's subscribers. General directions to Venice West are no more needed than North Beach would require a parenthetical note about San Francisco. Once again, in retrospect, the success of Allen's anthology is hardly surprising, considering the amount of publicity that his poets received.

Despite two full-length academic studies of Venice West since the publication of *The Holy Barbarians*, many basic details concerning the formation and membership of this community of poets have still not been established. Where does the name of the community itself come from?[10] Lipton never mentions its origins, and according to John Maynard, nobody seems to know who first uttered the term. Stuart Perkoff, however, states that Venice West was first used as the title of a poem by Charley Newman. Perkoff's explanation of the community's name occurred in a long letter that Perkoff wrote Donald Allen in the spring of 1958 in which he recapitulated some of the events that had already caused Venice West to begin disintegrating.

but no one but larry every [*sic*] used the sound as tho it were a title or name
of a "group. or thot of us as a group in that way, that the dadaists were, that
sort of thing. we came together actually quite haphazardly—if you believe in
haphazard arrangements. if you believe in magic, it's a different story. most
of us do. but what I mean is we did not band together in any *principled* or
ideological relationships. altho it is tru [*sic*] that there are enormous areas of
agreement between us on very basic beliefs & attitudes, that is something
that more or less happened, somehow. & was already there, poetentially
(sic). (Allen, Archive, Box 10, Folder 26)

Perkoff names the individuals he considered to be core members of the com-
munity's earliest days, but in subsequent journal entries he made other lists
that provide us with an expanded version of Venice West's primary members
that includes Bruce Boyd, Charles Foster, Eileen Ireland, Maurice Lacy, Law-
rence Lipton, James Ryan Morris, Charles Newman, Julia Newman, Stuart
Perkoff, Suzan Perkoff, Frankie Rios, Tony Scibella, John Thomas, Alexander
Trocchi, and Saul White. Several visual artists were also significant mem-
bers of Venice West, including George Herms, Mad Mike Magdalani, Art
Richer, Jim Shaw, and Ben Talbert, and various jazz musicians also took part
in performances, readings, and private experiments. Because Stuart Perkoff
has generally been regarded as the most significant poet of Venice West, his
journals and letters provide a compelling survey of its core membership.

The prominence of North Beach and City Lights Bookstore in San Fran-
cisco in accounts of Beat poetry has long overshadowed Venice West, despite
the contribution it makes to the complexity of the literary underground on
the West Coast. Primarily generated by their own accounts, the image of Beat
writers radiates palimpsests of constant, exuberant travel. Between 1955 and
1960, for instance, the most famous writers of the Beat generation lived in
Berkeley and San Francisco, Paris, and various points in Mexico and Japan.
Allen Ginsberg, Gary Snyder, Jack Kerouac, Lawrence Ferlinghetti, Gregory
Corso, Diane Di Prima, LeRoi Jones, Michael McClure, Bob Kaufman, Wil-
liam Burroughs, Lew Welch, Joanne Kyger, Philip Whalen, and Neal Cassady
are probably the individuals most often mentioned in discussions of Beat
writing, but how long did a half-dozen of these people live in any kind of prox-
imity with each other? In other words, if one talks about community among
Beat writers, how much was there ever any such thing? *Camerados*, perhaps,
but community? Along with the clusters of poets who gathered around Jack
Spicer and Robert Duncan in northern California, Venice West was as close
to an organic community of artists as the West Coast ever experienced in this
period, though it needs to be noted that Spicer and Duncan were not Beat
poets. Venice West distinguishes itself by more than duration and density,

however. Venice West was unique in its breadth of artistic experimentation and outlaw social behavior on the part of its most significant founding poet, Stuart Perkoff. No other alternative poetic community in the United States between 1955 and 1960 held itself together under the leadership of a writer who engaged and defined his community's identity in all of the following activities at one point or another during these six years: a poetry workshop larger than a dozen people, jazz and poetry events, collage art, founding a coffeehouse named for the community, and poetry readings, all combined with a propensity for drug use that eventually ravaged the community. In Venice West, being an outlaw was not a metaphor, but a spectrum of actual provocations whose literal parts were in subversive symbolic conversation.

What additionally makes it unique as a post-World War II literary community is that all of the above was happening despite the absence, except for one significant exception, of some form of communal publication.[11] This was partially due to the "voluntary poverty" that Lipton promulgated as a point of honor in Venice West, but it is also indicative of the community's extreme ambivalence about publication. The most significant poets of Venice West, Stuart Perkoff, Bruce Boyd, and John Thomas, published together a total of one book (*The Suicide Room* by Perkoff) between 1955 and 1970, and even that was a very slim volume. In the dedication statement to *Howl*, Ginsberg had said of Kerouac's novels that "they were published in Heaven." Much of the writing done in Venice West managed to dodge both this world and the next. Although the poets of Venice West appeared in magazines ranging from *Evergreen Review* to Jack Spicer's *J*, as well as *Yugen* and *Floating Bear*, they seem to have meant it when they scorned the notion of literary success along with social success. For other poets, the underground was a postern to postmodernity. The back door of Los Angeles looked out at a different possibility. Among groups of poets who did achieve some measure of public visibility, Venice West was probably the most oral community of poets in the United States. Public readings and private rehearsals constituted the primary means by which they established a continuity of commitment to their sullen craft.

Although I wish to present some of the writing by the poets of Venice West as material deserving of more critical attention, I am equally interested in examining this material as representative of the kind of dialogue that continues to occur on a daily basis outside of institutional control. If the significance of the poetry that survived the self-imposed winnowing of burned holographs is still open to question, the emergence of Venice West involves an impelling "necessity for inventing that community," to use Lyn Hejinian's formulation for the development of a writer's public life (*The Language of Inquiry* 33). The collapse of Venice West as a community of artists and the fact that much of this deterioration can be attributed to drug addiction should not obscure the value of their distinct combination of social and literary critique or their contribution to the formation of avant-garde poetry. The body of work produced by these poets will not tilt the balance of critical favor away from parallel figures such as Robert Duncan and Jack Spicer, let alone someone as hugely popular as Allen Ginsberg, yet a careful sifting of the documents that survived from this chaotic community reveals a palimpsest of thoughtful poetics underneath the image of spontaneous and improvised activity that intertwines Venice West with other epicenters of social turbulence and cultural resistance.

Feasts of Death, Feasts of Love: Perkoff and the Avant-Garde of *The New American Poetry*

The origins of Venice West in the mid-1950s can be glimpsed in a ten-page letter that Stuart Perkoff wrote Donald Allen at Grove Press, in which he described the group's political situation and its use of drugs as part of the creative process:

> charley newman, julia newman, suzan perkoff, stuart perkoff, bruce boyd.
> all smoking pot. all looking for something. for the same thing, the i-thou,
> the real touching, the real. love. & all ex-radicals, all hip to all the lies, all
> wounded, all fucked up. dug each other, that's all. it was sort of natural. it
> happened. then slowly the pot dissolved the headholes, & the poem began
> to force up. once again. tortuously for me. without giving you every detail,
> anyway, it was bruce & charley pushed me back to writing again. me, I
> pushed them to it. we learned things from each other that enabled us to
> resolve our problems on that particular scene. it was really fabulous. we
> really began to come on, a period began, of productivity, that for quantity &
> quality, I think can match anything done anywhere. but, of course, I think
> that. & that's neither here nor there. (Allen, Archive, Box 10, Folder 26)

Perkoff's description of the group as "ex-radicals" is in part a reference to his youthful days in New York City, where he was one of the first people to resist the imposition of the military draft after World War II. Perkoff's letter to Allen, however, anecdotally reveals that he still maintained some measure of political affiliation with radical groups, though the activities seem to favor personal rather than class liberation:

> after abt a year of running into bruce boyd at socialist partys, I met him
> one nite in a gay bar up the beach. . . . (partying type partys, not Party type.
> dig?) & somehow he told me abt his peyote experience & he was anxious

... to turn people on. . . . now. I had smoked pot. . . . several times. but at the time, not for several months. (this all happened just abt three years ago) so bruce turned me on. at the beach. & we talked, a gas. some time or other when I made it back to his pad, he showed me his poems. some of them. the wittgenstein poem was there, then, tho, & that is something of a masterpiece. I read them he sd: "I don't have any money riding on them." I found out later that he didn't show them to many people at all. (Allen, Archive, Box 10, Folder 26)

Perkoff had moved to Venice sometime in 1952 with his wife, Suzan, and year-old son, Sasha. Other than having very cheap rent, Venice was not a promising place for a young, and according to the estimate of Charles Olson, very good poet. Born in St. Louis in 1930, Perkoff had moved to New York City in 1947, and began publishing poetry before he was twenty years old.[12] Olson noticed his work in *Resistance* magazine, and after a pair of poems appeared in the second issue of Cid Corman's *Origin* magazine, Olson wrote Perkoff that one of them, "The Basket," was "one of the very rare ones, that, so far as my knowing goes, it is standing by itself. . . . (Y)ou and Creeley are the ones I am most glad to run alongside of," Olson stated. "(T)hose two poems of yrs. belong with us, and are something neither of us, or anyone else can visit as you can such another hell . . . that you move me as the clearest speaking of such things I have heard in this half century of the false forwarding of like cause" (*Voices of the Lady* 11). Despite this praise, Olson and Perkoff seem never to have met, though Creeley met Perkoff on several occasions, including at a reading Perkoff gave with Bruce Boyd in San Francisco. Creeley's lines, "Bliss is actual / as hard as / stone," are almost a mantra in Perkoff's writing, appearing in both his poems and journal entries.[13]

At this point, one could consider this cluster of writers as a fragile coterie rather than a community. In any case, both Perkoff and Boyd were included in Donald Allen's *The New American Poetry*, in the preface of which Allen declared that the poets he selected represent "our avant-garde, the true continuers of the modern movement in American poetry," whose antecedents included Williams, Pound, H. D., Kenneth Rexroth, and Louis Zukofsky. His central claim for this new generation is that they all share "one common characteristic: a total rejection of all those qualities typical of academic verse" (xi). While Allen does emphasize the importance of readings as performances in helping to generate an audience for writing that had relatively limited publication, his very brief discussion of the avant-garde status of these poets confines its discourse to their affinity to jazz and the paintings of the abstract expressionist school. Apart from the correlation with other avant-gardes, the question of the experimental status of the work Allen chose is complex and difficult to resolve.[14] A close reading of the contents of *The New American Poetry* reveals that Allen is slightly overstating the case. On the whole, the work that Allen selected is often significantly different from most academic verse at the time; on the other hand, compared with many experiments of modernists, such as W. C. Williams's *Spring & All* and Gertrude Stein's *Tender Buttons*, the poetry in Allen's anthology was hardly audacious in its challenge to formal recombinations of content.

Yet one poem in Allen's anthology stands out in regard to experimentation, so much so that one can only feel bewildered as to why it has been ignored in all commentary about the book. In a landmark volume that has almost no sustained prose passages in any of its poems, consider the following:

> (I hd to get out, once, & push the canoe from behind, my body from the ankles up was hot, sweaty, sun gleaming, my feet cool in the river, lifting & pushing the heavy canoe.
>
> I thought tht others wd get too far ahead & wed be lost, off in the wisconsin woods, where there were neither jews nor cities, a world hot & in winter my feet wd be like encased in the cement of the river, & the canoe wd never be pushed over the flat scrapey sand.)
> [. . .]
> the next year we took a different trip, out lake tomahawk & an adjacent lake, I don't remember which one. In that part of wisconsin the lake lay on the land like a thousand eyes, peering into & thru each other.
> [. . .]
> it wd always be dark by the time the services were over. & secure, in the glass house, lit by the God that shined all our faces, the burning candles of love in our bodies, sharing the glow outward to trees and wind. & the younger kids went to their cabins while the older one had a dance, & carried on intrigues & political arguments & love affairs until 11:30 when the boys walked the joyous road back to their portion of the camp, singing & shouting, clean & alive.
>
> By the time the saturday morning services were over, we were so full & whole that anything was possible. (*The New American Poetry* 300–303)

Published in justified paragraphs, the passages I have just quoted constitute only one-half of the prose that is woven into Stuart Perkoff's four-part poem, "Feasts of Death, Feasts of Love" (hereafter cited as "FDFL").[15] The other half primarily recounts Perkoff's questioning of an older Jewish man about the reason for the eradication of Jews from Europe. The pastoral element of Perkoff's poem is put to a much different use than usually occurs in poems associated with Beat poets. Instead of providing a meditative refuge in which one implicitly rebukes urban materialism, "FDFL" presents its pastoral setting as a metaphor for the survival of religious belief, a renewal of the bond between temporality and eternity.

While contemporary poets and critics have overlooked Perkoff's poem as a continuation of the experiments of twentieth century American poets in combining poetry and prose within a single piece of work, "FDFL" would have been immediately understood within that context by the poets of Venice West. If they were hip, it was not simply because they smoked marijuana, listened to jazz, and lived hand to mouth, or associated with those who lived in that manner. Lipton, with only an eighth-grade education, and Perkoff, with only a high school education, were very familiar with the work of poets who had rearranged the hybrid boundaries of poetry and prose. In *The Holy Barbarians*, Lipton argues that "one tendency" of the writers he is examining is "very marked: the trend towards a combination of poetry and prose." Pointing to Williams' *Paterson*, Patchen's *Journal of Albion Moonlight*, and Louis Zukofsky's "*A*," which at that point, as Lipton mentions, had only been published "sporadically and obscurely," Lipton links up "the oral revolution against the Geneva Code" with the necessity to demolish the line between poetry and prose. "It is not an easy trick to bring off. . . . Charles Olson's *Maximus* poems are a step in that direction and his *The Lordly and Isolate Satyrs* a still longer step. Charles Foster approaches it in *The Troubled Makers*, and Robert Duncan possesses the necessary skills in both media to make a very promising try for it" (Lipton 253–254). Lipton argues that "the line between poetry and prose is very thinly drawn in these circles. Many insist there is no line at all" (231). This argument, however, is being presented in a book that mainly concentrates on a rebuke of the "Disneyfication of a nation" and its adamant theocracy of "Moneytheism."[16] The erasure of genre is more than an aesthetic strategy for Lipton and the poets he is valorizing; the reading lists of Lipton's affiliated writers serve both as an implicit genealogy for both poetic and social alternatives to the "social lie" and as models for further experiments. By 1979, Lipton's reading list would seem familiar, but no one teaching at a college or university in 1959 would have employed his implicit syllabus: Whitman, Baudelaire, Rimbaud, Mallarmé, Jeffers, Crane, Pound, Williams, Fearing, Patchen, and Zukofsky.

In speaking of Perkoff's relationship to the avant-garde, one could begin with the notion that an avant-garde does not react to a crisis, but rather provokes one. Stephen Fredman in *Poet's Prose* points out one problem with this formulation, in that he regards American poetry as being always already in crisis.

When the primary issue in writing poetry shifts from the choice of matter and meter to the decision as to whether poetry, under present conditions, is possible, then that poetry can be truly spoken of as in crisis. . . . There is a legitimate sense in which America can be called the homeland of verse in crisis. This in turn accounts for a characteristic feature of American poetry: Out of this drastic situation arises an often drastic poetry—contentious, overwrought, over- or under-stated, at war with decorum. (4)

Perkoff's "FDFL" is the most drastic poem in Allen's *The New American Poetry* in that it offers a singular response to the convergence of several crises, not the least of which is that Perkoff's poem takes as its subject matter one of the most harrowing acts of genocidal modernity, the eradication of European Jewry. I call Perkoff's poem drastic because the combination of its form and its subject matter seems to have placed it outside the consideration of critical literature. Susan Gubar's comprehensive study, *Poetry After Auschwitz: Remembering What One Never Knew*, neglects to mention it at all, and this can hardly be attributed to the poem's position within the accessible canon. Allen's anthology sold well over two hundred thousand copies, so the poem must have been read. Or was it? Did people simply prefer not to read a poem about the Holocaust? Perhaps it is much easier to read about young people throwing potato salad at CCNY lecturers on dadaism than to consider the complex poetics of a poem that juxtaposes and interweaves the enjambment of free verse with justified paragraphs as it meditates on the genocide of Jews.

In arguing that "poetry reveals more clearly than do other genres both *the occasion and the imperative* of incorporating and foregoing history," Gubar cites at the outset of her book Charles Bernstein's observation about poetry and the Nazi concentration camps: "In contrast to—or is it an extension of?—Adorno's famous remarks about the impossibility of (lyric?) poetry after Auschwitz, I would say poetry is a necessary way to register the unrepresentable loss of the Second World War" (11). In blurring the boundaries of poetry and prose as the "necessary way to register" the Holocaust within what Gubar describes as "the conspiracy in the forties and fifties to nullify the Holocaust," Perkoff establishes the ability of the avant-garde after Auschwitz to engage itself with history even as it deploys an existential poetics.

The musical structure of "FDFL" is impossible to comprehend unless one reads the entire poem. The final section, Part IV of "FDFL" is the shortest section, and yet its repetition of lines that are themselves repeated in parts two and three expands the meaning of the separate sections by compressing their core phrases together. Perkoff's brief, affirmative chant at the end of this long poem seems to hint that he disagreed with Adorno's proclamation that poetry could not be written after Auschwitz. Poetry must acknowledge that calamity, Perkoff argues, but must also affirm the possibility of renewal in Nietzsche's sense of eternal return:

> when the sun dies
> many other suns will still flame
>
> all things contain the seeds
> of their own completion
> all seeds contain the things
> of their own destruction
>
> the sun
> makes a morning
> bright descending on hooded eyes
> the sun's morning
> floods into the sands of war
>
>   wake up
>   hang on
>
> coming together
> coming together
> coming together
>   (306)

The cosmic meditation that concludes the poem suggests a vatic affirmation that is separate from any specific religious tradition in the Common Era, but Perkoff's chiasm of seeds and things is embedded within his search for the meaning of the Holocaust. In his journals in his mid-twenties, Perkoff records his considerations about the relationship between Jewish intellectuals and Western society.

> Freud (?) suggests ("No Ease in Zionism") that the Jews are an international, mobile middle class—both by tradition & force of circumstance. Early Zionists felt that it was necessary for the Jews to return to a working class life—an enlightened one, eased by intellectual & cultural stimulations. Is it possible that this is the answer to some of our problems. What is the relationship of the Jewish intellectual to either of these classes. In western society the intellectual is alienated—a cliche already—but is Jewish society western? To the extent that it is assimilated, of course it is, but in its essence,

its core, it is perhaps unique. If so, there is a chance that once again the specificale jewish poet, critic/academic will function in relation to a society. (Perkoff, Archive, Box 1, Folder 1)

Four pages later in this journal, he comments on Freud's "Totem and Taboo" essay, and then observes: "Now that the USSR follows Hitler's lead, and endangers the lives of 21/2 million more Jews, it grows even blacker. . . . The story of Abraham, which symbolizes the jews refusal to consider any situation absolutely intolerable, absolutely without hope, . . ." These comments indicate that David B. Griffiths's specific classification of Perkoff as a "modern American Jewish poet" rather than simply being assigned to the Beat group has far more evidence than Griffiths presents in *Beach and Temple*. Perkoff's sense of loss in the aftermath of the concentration camps shows up in a short poem that he wrote in his journal several weeks after completing "FDFL":

it's ominously silent.
why is it so silent?
where are the voices of the forefathers?

it's ominously silent.
why is it so silent?

all that I hear are the sounds of the mechanisms,
& the sounds of their flow & their desires.
4.1.57 ("Night Chasm," Box 1, Folder 4)

This poem, which was later folded into "The Venice Poems" along with references to aging Jews living in Venice, was originally the final poem in a table of contents for a manuscript that Perkoff began assembling shortly after writing "Feasts of Death, Feasts of Love." In both the work that was published in *The New American Poetry* and in his journals, we can see a concern about the absence of the voices of the forefathers that makes Perkoff's work distinct from any other young Jewish poet at the time, including Allen Ginsberg.

If Perkoff's contribution to the avant-garde has been neglected, and even suffered the ignominy of being left out of *The Postmoderns* (1980), the revised version of *The New American Poetry*, he is hardly the first street poet of the Beat generation to have his contribution minimized. Bob Kaufman's poetry suffered a similar neglect for a number of years, despite the fact that he had two collections of poetry published by New Directions. Kaufman and Perkoff are probably the two most visible street poets of the Beat generation, although neither was a better artist for their self-inflicted choices.

From Café to Workshop

Perkoff and his companions were viewed by Lawrence Lipton as acolytes to put to use, and Perkoff's letter to Allen provides more than sufficient evidence of Lipton's self-aggrandizement and unwillingness to share the stage. Lipton had invited Kenneth Rexroth to come down from San Francisco and read as part of a jazz-poetry event. Perkoff regarded Rexroth's ability to perform poetry with jazz musicians as verging on ineptitude, and was further infuriated when Lipton tried to exclude Perkoff and his friends from the event. Lipton further disgraced himself by insulting Perkoff's publisher, Jonathan Williams, after a reading by Williams at the Venice West Poetry Center, which was located at 1107 Ocean Front Walk. The wedge that Lipton drove into the community did not dissuade Perkoff from attempting to provide Venice West a visible alternative to Lipton's living room as a gathering place, and along with a friend in the late summer of 1958, he established the Venice West Expresso Café.

As is the case with most small businesses started by young people, the venture was undercapitalized, and would have needed twice the fourteen hundred dollars Perkoff borrowed from his parents to become a viable enterprise. The building that Perkoff and his partner chose had last been used as a bleach factory, and the production process had very efficiently corroded the interior of the building. The bleach, according to Perkoff's journal, "had eaten all the plaster off great portions of the walls and had reduced the floor to the condition of the surface of the moon, pitted, pocked, treacherous" (Perkoff, Archive, Box 2, Folder 7).[17] If the place began as a wreck, Perkoff's plans for the conversion of the structure aligned itself with the improvisatory poetics of the community. It lasted about six months under Perkoff's ownership. December may be the most profitable month for most businesses in America, but a beach town such as Venice tends to hunker down as the winter solstice approaches. Just a few months after opening, customers had dwindled to the point where, in early January 1959, he sold it for a fraction of what he had put into it, little realizing that in about six months the tables at the Venice West Expresso Café would be packed with tourists who were intrigued by the potential *frisson* of a little weekend rebellion. Perkoff's instinct for what kind of business would succeed was absolutely on the mark. His misfortune was that he started too soon, and did not anticipate that his charisma would not be enough to pull the place through its first lean months.

Shortly after the publication of *The Holy Barbarians*, Perkoff looked back on his experience with Venice West Expresso Café and noted that he regarded the café as a "last desperate attempt to come in to the social structure, to function in square society, without *losing* identity, poured all my perceptions & energies into the cafe I didn't write, I didn't paint, I didn't see my family—the sources of my energies" (Perkoff, Archive, Box 2, Folder 7). Perkoff's commitment to this project seems to have registered as an enduring wound. His journal records his self-assessment that he "almost lost sanity. maybe did lose. as it turned out, the experience was a purging of the soul, like I burned out entire areas of myself" (Perkoff, Archive, Box 2, Folder 7). Yet Perkoff was also aware that the Venice West Expresso Café was not just another business that had stumbled badly. If the café suddenly began to thrive about seven months after Perkoff sold it, its popularity was due in part to the series of photographs of the café and its patrons and performers at the end of *The Holy Barbarians.* The first photograph had a notation that was virtually guaranteed to attract customers: "a real Beat generation coffeehouse that tourists haven't discovered yet." When the tourists did discover it, they might have found a completely different place than Perkoff envisioned. In his journals, he explained to himself the aesthetics of his project and how it simultaneously empowered and undermined the café: "the way I originally made it the whole trouble, the reason it didn't, cdnt make it & at the same time the thing it will be remembered for—a kind of inexplicable authenticity—was that I treated the whole thing as a huge 'junk-construction'—& not a business" (Perkoff, Archive, Box 2, Folder 7). The notion of "inexplicable authenticity" being interwoven with the assemblage of the Venice West Expresso Café as a "junk-construction" places Perkoff at about the extreme end of Lefebvre's "near order." At the end of this passage, Perkoff quotes the gist of Olson's aphorism in *The Maximus Poems*, "People don't change. / They only stand / more revealed." Perkoff's attempt to become what he called a "restaurant-owner" was as doomed as his earlier attempt to proletarianize himself. "Like I tried. & thank God I didn't succeed as a restauranteer. Because.... if the cafe had succeeded I wd be—a cafe owner—o image! as it was it drained me completely, reality receded, got farther & further distant, any gesture of mine was either hopelessly inefficient or else childishly, or perhaps, savagely, destructive—" (Perkoff, Archive, Box 2, Folder 7).

Perkoff's life began to resemble a cautionary tale about how soft drugs lead to hard-core addiction. His taste for getting high moved from Tussar, a cough medicine with a strong belt of codeine, to heroin. His response to the birth of a third child, Rachel, was to move out and begin a spree of intoxicated rambling with two young aspiring poets, Frankie Rios and Tony Scibella. Together they roamed the Venice oceanfront, writing poems and then burning them in honor of their muse, "the Lady," a period Perkoff describes in terms of popular culture: "Almost every day frankie & tony & I / three stooge it down the beach into the world." But Venice was more than a setting for a personal circus. By March of 1960, Perkoff had become the leader of the first public poetry workshop in Venice.

Thinking of verse workshop—which has shifted to Wed. nites, . . . I wish
to record the names. Maurice Lacy. Frank Rios. John Thomas. Jim Morris.
Gene Trembleau. Eileen (her last name I don't know, but a fine poet she is!).
Blanche Paul. That many people serious abt, in love with, verse. & they are
good poets, . . . I will, in time, I hope, write more details of each of them for
they deserve serious attention. I wd like very much to edit an anthology of
local poets. Maybe I can for Bob.

well next year" I sd after reading the excerpt from my journal about the
ghetto, meaning maybe next year the poem the ghetto deserves. Next year
in Jerusalem" it says in the seder. Amen. (Perkoff, Archive, Box 2, Folder 3)

So now, workshop over, at Su Berman's alone, she's gone for a few days
to Pasadena. I'm working, teeth out. (ready to blow? O ho Stuart) tonite
John Thomas read some excerpts from his journal, beautiful, beautiful.
Maurice read a poem he's working on, I read the opening part of this jour-
nal * the sound about the ghetto xt. There were about 14 people there tonite.
Which is too many. I don't know what to do about the size. . . . I don't see
how we cd split into 2 groups, I mean, what means of division wd we use?
& wd I take *both*? . . . starting *Film Sense* by SME. What a beautiful mind.
What an eye. Boy that was a hard turd.

John suggested that I get money from Lipton for the magazine. (Perkoff,
Archive, Box 2, Folder 3)

Perkoff's comment on the state of his digestive system was an indication of
more than a lack of salads; Perkoff's drug habits were beginning to take over
his life. Nevertheless, the formation of a large poetry workshop is an indica-
tion that poets living in Venice West saw themselves as more than individual
figures scribbling away in a coffeehouse. As the culmination of the small
group of poets that had begun meeting to smoke pot and share poems back
in the mid-1950s, the workshop and its size reflect problems inherent in any
successful community, especially in terms of accommodating the needs of
new members. Neither the magazine nor the anthology, however, ever man-
aged to make it past the planning stage.[18]

By 1961, however, Perkoff was living in Mexico with a lover, Susan Ber-
man, who gave birth to his fourth child, a daughter named Eva. His ex-wife
and other children had moved to San Francisco. Perkoff returned to the
United States and attempted to get rid of his drug habit. When he returned
to Venice, he was forced to acknowledge that the community he had once led
had completely dispersed.[19]

Morris is in NYC
Tony's in the Valley, working for his father
Frankie's in jail for probation violation
Su B's in Altadena, determined to have naught mas to do with me/wise
decision.

VENICE IS NO MORE
VENICE IS NO MORE.
VENICE IS NO MORE

Something I knew last summer—last fall for sure—isn't & never will be
again—& me still no

(Perkoff, Archive, Journal 28)

During this period, Perkoff continued to publish writing in little magazines, and his appearance in *Yugen*'s seventh issue alongside poets such as Frank O'Hara and Robert Duncan marks the continued respect that his work found outside of the West Coast. *Yugen*, edited by LeRoi Jones and Hettie Cohen, was one of the little magazines listed in Allen's anthology as the core of the underground poetry movement; the issue in which Perkoff appears almost serves as a follow-up mini-anthology to Allen's volume. The disparity between literary recognition and personal circumstances rapidly increased during the next four years. Although Perkoff was not prolific, one could hardly say that he had stopped writing or that he ceased to make distinctions in the quality of his work. The stereotype of the junkie who is unable to function as an intelligent artist is slow to die. When he did return to the United States, he was in physically very bad shape, and even after a period of rehabilitation, he essentially became a street person.

Perkoff was arrested on drug charges in 1966 and was jailed in prisons at Chino and Terminal Island, near San Pedro. He did not return to the streets until the fall of 1970.[20] Upon his release, he lived in northern California as well as briefly in Denver, Colorado, and finally settled back in Venice in 1973; within a year, Perkoff was dying of cancer. He gave his last poetry reading at Papa Bach Bookstore to a full house, but was too weak to read more than a few minutes. Shortly after his death, *Beyond Baroque* magazine ran a picture of him at the reading as the cover of its magazine.

In his final years, he found his continued dedication to poetry acknowledged by his inclusion in two anthologies of Los Angeles poets, including one (*Specimen '73*) that provided him a reading at the Pasadena Art Museum. The one crucial component that might have helped Venice West congeal into a sustainable community seemed to be proliferating. His final period of writing included a book-length poem that was a meditation on the Hebrew alphabet. His published work also reconsidered the Beat poet's social role. "These Are Political Times," for instance, published in *Stooge* magazine in 1972, but not included in his *Collected Poems*, exudes a maturation in Perkoff's anarchist tendencies. If Perkoff had lived even five years longer and remained in Venice, his new work would probably have received abundant attention due to the sudden proliferation of poetry magazines in Los Angeles. This, however, is only wistful speculation: One could say the same of Jack Spicer, whose death in 1965 was recorded in Perkoff's journals. However, even if Perkoff had lived and flourished, one gets a sense that living in Venice would have been difficult for him. In one of his final poems, he imagines one of his favorite poets, Ezra Pound, in Venice, Italy, and the ending of the poem is hard not to read as an explicit comparison between himself and Pound. Their exiles were haunted by ghosts beyond the redemptive scouring of poetry.

> they came as pilgrims to his aging
> in the city of water where overlooked the flow
> past his windows & his mind
>
> they came to receive words
> they hoped for poems
> they wanted to wrap their emptiness
> in his still growing structures
> to receive the brand of his tongue on their flesh & their needs
>
> & they got silence from him
> & they got querulousness & ancient midwestern cackled slang
> or they got only the nothing
> they brought with them
>
> because they cd not overhear
> as he & henry james talked, not of history, or money
> but of the garbage in the canals
> of the city they both so loved.
>
> ("In Pound's Last Years in Venice, Italy,"
> *Voices of the Lady* 450)

The Needs of the Metric: Enjambment and the Poetics of Stuart Perkoff

Although Paul Vangelisti and John McBride published two posthumous volumes of poetry by Perkoff, and Venice West poet Frankie Rios edited another collection that appeared in 1976, Perkoff's poetry has remained difficult to assess because even twenty years after his death, a large portion of it remained in the potential canon. Indeed, even after *Voices of the Lady: Collected Poems* was published in 1998, one could not accurately gauge his growth as a poet because so many of the poems are out of sequence. Poems that were written in the 1950s, for instance, are in a section entitled "Poems written in the 1970s." Perkoff's travails as a street poet and a junkie have contributed to his image as the quintessential Venice West poet, and yet how seriously Perkoff took his craft as a poet! His journals are on occasion indecipherable, but we can often tease out sustained passages in which, even when living in Mexico because of the availability of cheap, but high-quality heroin, Perkoff assiduously strove to develop as a poet. When Paul Vangelisti published Perkoff's posthumous collections of poetry, he commented that enough had been sacrificed to fantasy, yet something close to a fantasy can also infiltrate a poet's life if the details are not checked. The emotional and social chaos of a junkie's life should never be underestimated in its deleterious impact on the addict's life, but in *Utopia and Dissent* (499), Richard Cándida Smith seems to have been caught up in an easy exaggeration of addiction's consequences in claiming that Perkoff was reduced as a writer to "casual diary entries" during this period of his life. When Perkoff wrote and substantially revised a two-page elegy for Gary Cooper that would eventually be anthologized, and then wrote a ten-page play, all within less than forty-eight hours, he was hardly debilitated to the point of stupor that Cándida-Smith suggests.[21]

In fact, even after six years of raw abandon, a journal passage such as the following indicates the seriousness with which Perkoff approached his life as a poet and the importance of poetics to his work:

The morning utters stillness like a prayer.

I don't imagine now that I'll go back to that, but it occurs to me the opening 5 lines cd still open a poem—however it seems kind of a long "introduction"—if it feels like that it's certainly true. That may be the nature of the form itself, which does not excite me particularly today—tho at any time I may again—I certainly hope I do, again many times, O Lady—get the impulse to write a sonnet. I hope I am able to satisfy that impulse more successfully then.

The nagging drive to write a sonnet that this attempt is part of was ultimately satisfied, not by a sonnet, but by the loosely formal structure of "human blood is its own/cartography," tho it is nothing like a sonnet. It seems to me that my poems the past couple months—from "my witch of dance laughter" on—&, yes, even (illegible)—"my mirror shows a human face" & "every dawn of every morning" show many traditional rhythms in the weight of the line & a richer, heavier imagery, a kind of weight that I associate with English iambic metrics—not necessarily Elizabethan, tho it is impossible to use iambics and not echo or deny the Elizabethans—but their language is much richer—even than what we have today—does that somehow go into the area where W. C. Williams searched for the American metric, completely shunning iambics because the meter itself seems to demand either the echoing or denial of a speech m—definitely not ours—& tho it is clean & direct ancestor to our tongue, it is only one such. Altho the exact relationship of the two ain't clear—the differences are becoming more distinct, distances are becoming greater between the parent & the offspring, for the offspring, tho at last part bestow has the vitality, the progenitor has only memories of atavistic reminders of, & this (vitality) is incestuously & surreptitiously devoured by the parent tongue; it infuses the old momma-mouth with anal mess she will not admit to needing.

The uniqueness of the American Speech is not something discovered by 20th century American poets, rather it is something they have formed. No, not the uniqueness—it is what the American metric is being formed in response to. But the clarity of definition which makes possible to verify the distinct uniqueness of the two languages—English & American—is given by the poets, by the metric. Pound, Williams, Cummings, Olson, Patchen, Ginsberg, Perkoff? Creeley. (Yes, I think Perkoff) & others, finding as they gave shape to their work that they were forced to invent a new speech, did & do so in such a way as to rivet the needs of the metric into the living structure of the language—the response becomes a determining factor in the impulse to which it is a response. —ha!!!! October 1965 (Perkoff, Archive, Box 4, Folder 2)

Perkoff's journal essay proposes that the diversion of American poetry from English verse is an act of willed imagination that mingles the desire to be different and the imagined difference as an actual difference resulting in a "living structure" of a new speech. "The needs of the metric" are not what has changed, but rather the desire to make those needs respond to the formation of a distinct language even as that distinctness is not yet visible. The response itself is only part of the shaping that is visible or that can be seen as distinct. These kinds of assertions will be familiar to anyone who has studied the debate about Williams and his variable foot, but I suspect that Perkoff is pointing out something quite different than the variable foot. The "loosely formal" structure he mentions, in reference to a poem that was originally published in *Trace* magazine while he was serving the first year of his prison sentence, is as much about the role of enjambment in twentieth-century American poetry as metrical feet.

human blood is its own
cartography. man knows
the distances, alone
& huge within the flow
islands of purity
great caves of death embraced
by flesh, the map of history
on which all pain is traced.
  ("Untitled," *Voices of the Lady* 123)

The emergence of enjambment as the major consideration in shaping the form of the poem begins with poets such as Perkoff, who use the simultaneous continuity and discontinuity generated by enjambment to rivet the "needs of the metric" to the living structure of the language. In describing the "loosely formal" structure of a poem, "Human blood is its own / cartography," he is hinting at the process through which American poetry is arriving at its own speech. I would argue that, on a formal level, American speech primarily and most effectively gets tested and stretched out in terms of enjambment. "The needs of the metric" are in part a prosody that tests the limits of uncertainty through formations of incomplete perception and response. Enjambment as an always already variant of anacouthala is the waiting that Perkoff is referring to in the following poem:

no one knows
how to wait for the poem. that's
the thing. No one.

all waiting may be
the same, death
is waiting for us, we
wait for it. a simple observation.

if a man cd
wait
the poem, wait
inert & open, I wd
count that a major
craft achievement

bench, beach, bed, any empty
space can be

so filled
if only one knew
know how to
("Untitled," *Voices of the Lady* 156–157)

Bruce Boyd and John Thomas: Venice West and the West Coast

If Stuart Perkoff's poetry is finally becoming part of the accessible canon, other members of Venice West are still waiting for their work to reach even that minimal condition. Bruce Boyd, one of the original members of Venice West and a contributor to Donald Allen's *The New American Poetry*, is perhaps the most elusive poet of the Beat generation. No one seems to know exactly what become of him, not even Donald Allen, who told me in the summer of 1997 that Boyd's royalty checks had started being returned as "not at this address" in the early 1970s. Gary Snyder describes him as a poet who was "seriously interested in Zen practice, in poetics, in ideas . . . an articulate, calm person whom I felt an affinity with right away."[22] My choice of Bruce Boyd as a poet whose work deserves recognition in a canon of minor poets may seem peculiar, especially given that Boyd never had a book of poetry published. Yet if the Beat ethos emphasized an indifference to the mania for success that propelled the "square" world, Bruce Boyd is perhaps the Beat poet for whom that kind of indifference was not a pose, but a genuine outgrowth of his studies of Zen. Other Beat poets may have invoked Zen's stoicism and nonchalance toward material success, but Boyd lived it out. Boyd's indifference was first remarked upon by Perkoff in his letter to Allen. Perkoff said that Boyd showed him some poems, and then commented, "I don't have much money riding on them." One could say that many young poets are indifferent to success at the early stages of their career, but Boyd seems never to have even submitted a manuscript to a publisher. His poetry, though, was acknowledged by his peers to be equivalent to the best work of the period.

He was born in 1928 in San Francisco, and attended the University of California, Berkeley, where he met Jack Spicer. He was a philosophy student, but Spicer pushed him toward poetry, and Spicer eventually published him in his own magazine, *J*. Boyd's work also appeared in the *Evergreen Review*, *Miscellaneous Man*, *Floating Bear*, *Yugen*, and *Adventures in Poetry* as well as another Donald Allen collection, *12 Poets and a Painter* (1964). Obviously it will be difficult to gauge the significance of his poetry until at least one collection is published, but an account by Stan Persky of a reading that Boyd gave in San Francisco in 1959 should suffice to indicate why such a book is needed! According to Persky, Boyd got off to a very bad start with this audience, which included Spicer, by talking at length about his experiences with peyote, but when he read his poem, "Some Apotropeia instead of an Alba," "everybody present recognized that somebody had struck it rich and had written an absolutely authentic poem. This was certainly one of the great poems written during that period" (*Poet Be Like God* 150).

The biographical note in Allen's anthology ("He lives in San Francisco") was true when Allen was assembling that section, but gives no indication that Boyd was a founding member of Venice West, a serious omission given that Perkoff's poems were placed in the fifth non-geographical section of *The New American Poetry*, which only served to dilute the presence of that community within the framework of underground poetry.[23] By the time that *The New American Poetry* was getting its first reviews, Boyd had returned to Los Angeles, where he lived for most of the 1960s. Boyd's oscillation between San Francisco and Venice is yet another piece of the mosaic in which poets on the West Coast are using the entire stretch of the territory to test out the possibilities of parallel communities.

Boyd's relationship of mutual respect with poets such as Jack Spicer, Gary Snyder, and Stuart Perkoff, lends credibility to his assessment of two different poetic communities in his poem, "Venice Recalled," the single best comparative description of West Coast communities of poets in *The New American Poetry*. The poem has received no mention whatsoever in any critical assessment of the period, and given its unfamiliarity, I am going to cite the whole poem, which is dated 1959:

on the salt water streets
that rose & then fell with the ocean
when the fish that were caught in the mud
underneath the wooden footbridge started in to stink,
soon there was always the incoming tide

                there, we were
each his own man

    to speak, the play of sounds, pleasant or
    otherwise, but only open & discursive.

                differently, here, in the language
the oblique sense of a word to stamp one as "in"
                whose dialect (not
dialectic) held
                "right or wrong"
invents a greater crime than just to force the song:

to force it back,
                & closets them wet & huddled together.

   they are fearful in their heads
   of being on the outside looking in
   —to the center of language:

but we who would live openly are its natural peripheries,
& take the unborn where the dead leave it
to grow, at our hand

"always to prefer the common," thus the noble
Heraclitus, in "this world, which is the same for all

   our language is although inductive
   the topology of what we live:
   thus not its substitute but its enlargement.

               there, with us
a new poem always was something
                  the making, something
that asked to be shared at once: seldom a "result"
to praise or blame, & never this only, we mostly looked
behind it for the ways that came together,
between whom, intended, a clearing was being made

in which to discover what, having forgotten
is recovered
     in measure, apart from direction:
   as in accord with old codes,
   codices,
     a kind of law
   of least action in language, or
             taken as return
to the origin,
     a place of actual
welcome, always the nearest
stone path that is watered
          against the coming of guests
      is to say,
        cooler:

& the poem, what it means to say,
for the natural motion of its body, is the clearer
that remarks the wider movement of its actual thought.
(*The New American Poetry* 159–160)

One notices that Boyd is comparing two different communities, one of which he asserts depends on a vocabulary to create a boundary of judgment for who is in or out, and the other in which the act of sharing the work itself becomes the essential process of membership and value in the community. The "natural peripheries" of language are not an artificial zone of imitation by a group dialect, but a magnification of the immediate acceptance of the poem's value as a gift exchange. Within this community the poem can be critiqued, but anyone who aspired to belong to this community would be looked at askance if that "praise or blame" was the primary expectation. The poem may seem like an idealization of a small group of artists before any of them knew that their community would be cited, but such generosity is often a part of the earliest days of any small, intimate group. Given the information in the contributor's note of Allen's anthology, one would assume that he is writing about Venice West from the vantage of San Francisco in saying "differently here." However, the city that is the supposed hub of hipness does not appear to be the lucid community often depicted in the mythology of the period. Boyd's poem points to Venice as a place of "actual welcome" and "actual thought." This echo of Creeley's "as actual as stone" is meant to establish the substantiality of the relationships in Venice, as opposed to the illusion of community in northern California. The scorn for a scene in which the use of jargon established one's membership is palpable and startling, and serves as a bracing reminder of how constrictive some allegedly hip scenes can be in maintaining the strict rubrics of their enfoldment.

Boyd's poem also raises more questions about Allen's initial claim about how the poetry in his volume "totally rejects academic verse." Despite the zig-zag indentations of "Venice Recalled," the poem is closer in its lyric strategy and central theme to Wallace Stevens's "Of Modern Poetry" than to avant-garde experiment. The meditative quality of Boyd's poem is focused on "finding / what will suffice," which will require that one "construct a new stage." For Boyd, the "incoming tide" at the beginning of the poem is not only the movement of the ocean that cleans the canals of Venice, but is also the smaller tide of washing the human walkways to welcome the arrival of poems. The end of the poem circles back to the beginning, and in doing so urges the reader to reinscribe the poem upon the wider path of memory.

The final poet to be considered in this chapter arrived in Venice at the height of its fame. Perhaps, in fact, if John Thomas had not encountered a copy of *The Holy Barbarians*, his curiosity about that scene would never have tempted him to make a detour from the original destination, San Francisco, of his hitchhiking sojourn in 1959. Thomas was a Korean War veteran who walked out on his second wife and children in Texas with no more hesitation than he had shown in leaving behind his first wife and child in Baltimore, Maryland. He immediately attracted attention in Venice West, if only because of the immense physical difference between his stature and a short man like Perkoff. Thomas had a huge barrel chest and a deep voice that could shift effortlessly from sensuousness to disdain in a few syllables. As Perkoff noted in his journal entries, Thomas became one of the leading participants of Venice West almost immediately, and Perkoff recorded his first reading in Venice on May 20, 1960.

> john Thomas—he's a good poet & he reads well & seriously & he's taking a collection. Doesn't in any way mean any compromise on his part. Because he never read before, his own work, til he was satisfied with it himself. Or at least, until he recognized it himself. . . . it still angers me when a scene goes down that treats poetry so—casually! I don't know exactly the word I mean. But when a poet of John Thomas' caliber reads his verse, it isn't just one of the sights & sounds of a Friday nite in Venice, it's an occasion. (Perkoff, Archive, Box 2, Folder 7)

Thomas managed to evade warrants for child support, although this escape necessitated his eventual departure from Venice West to move up north. The search must have subsided after several years, or he managed to negotiate some minimal, token payment, because he returned to Los Angeles in the mid-sixties. He got married again to a woman who worked while he stayed at home, but Thomas was industrious at keeping busy even if he did not hold down a regular job, ordering enough stuff through the mail without paying for it to attract the attention of postal authorities. He also served as the poetry editor of a magazine that John Bryan had started in San Francisco, moved to Los Angeles prior to launching his alternative newspaper, *Open City*. Bryan's *Notes from Underground* included specific directions on how to make drugs, but Thomas was leery of his compatriots' preferences for heroin and various cough medicines. Rather than marijuana, which he disliked because it made him sleepy and unable to read, Thomas indulged in speed, which he was able to keep in steady supply because his third wife's job was at a pharmacy. He became friends with Charles Bukowski, whose poems he typed up off a tape recording of a reading, and thereby managed to save a manuscript that Bukowski had lost.

Thomas arrived in Venice with a certain amount of literary capital. He had gone to visit Ezra Pound while the renegade poet was confined at St. Elizabeths

Hospital in the wake of his trial for treason. In his poem "The Squirrels," Thomas recorded parts of the conversation between Pound, himself, and a young companion of Thomas's who was bird-dogging Pound about twentieth-century writers. In public readings, Thomas was a master at laconically mimicking Pound's rebuke: "When a man gets to be my age / he doesn't have time / to be a walking / encyclopedia of current / lit-er-a-ture" ("The Squirrels," *John Thomas*, unpaginated). Although Paul Vangelisti used the occasion of the publication of *John Thomas* to mark the demise, once and for all, of the myth of Venice West, the book also somberly resurrected the memory of that community for young poets such as Jim Krusoe, Kate Braverman, Harry Northup, and myself, who were gathering at Beyond Baroque in the early to mid-1970s.[24] Thomas's book forestalled any fantasies of being *the* first generation of Los Angeles poets and editors. It also gave younger poets someone to point to when questions about Charles Bukowski and the writing scene in Los Angeles were raised. In general, the poets at Beyond Baroque were indifferent to Bukowski's work and were delighted by the publication of *John Thomas*. It was a book in which it was impossible to read five poems in a row in the same key, though most of them stayed within a stoic and forbearing range. The poems included personal detail, and yet were not at all confessional; they often used collage and had a satiric tone, and were as insistent on the poem's capacity to be a significant gesture, but simultaneously seemed to dismiss public literary efforts as irrelevant exercises for anyone serious about spiritual illumination. The opening lines of the book, spoken by a friend of the narrator as he recalls a long hike to an abandoned, rural cemetery, seem to address any lingering associations with Venice West that readers might bring to this book.

> "The first thing.   to do violence to your own myths /
> To be your own
> Tarquin. . ." said almost without thought, his attention
> on the barbed wire, as I held it up for him
> and he climbed through.
>   ("Tarquin," *John Thomas*, unpaginated)

The opening of "Tarquin" as well as the collage of observations and quotations that fill out the account of their picnic on the gravestone of the "last defender of the Battle of Fort McHenry," echo Olson's strategy in "The Kingfishers," a poem that is often cited as the first postmodern poem. "Tarquin," though, defers any movement either away from the detail or toward the symbolic. As Thomas records his search for the pleasures of memory, he refuses to admit anything but clarity into the presence of the poem. All else, as he twice says, is "merely possible," hinting that whatever else might happen, no similar day or occurrence is likely to happen again. There is nothing as such that will act to prevent revelation from happening, but neither is any propitious sign in the offing, and neither condition is to be desired or rejected through distraction.

Thomas's first book featured writing that belonged neither to the Beats nor to the different strains of academic verse that were emerging. He did not align himself with any school as such. Even when he used subjects such as Zen Buddhism, the poems seemed to be direct warnings against admiring another poet as a model.

> In the portraits he sits cross-legged on a mat,
> fierce eyes glaring from under shaggy brows,
> and his right fist clenched in his lap
> (always reminding me of Jersey Joe Walcott,
> how he could catch them coming in, the young eager ones,
> with that stiff right).
>
> ("The Last Frontier," Field 156)

After living in San Francisco in the early 1960s, and writing many of his best poems there, Thomas had stopped writing. Once again, as with Boyd, to think of Thomas as only a Venice West poet, is to rigidify the West Coast into isolated camps. It was while he was living San Francisco, in fact, that he began publishing his work in magazines such as *Yugen* and *Floating Bear* as well George Hitchcock's *kayak*.

After returning to Los Angeles, Thomas worked on his daybooks, a compendium of his favorite passages from other authors and contributed a piece entitled "Patagonia" to a collaborative book with Paul Vangelisti and Robert Crosson entitled *Abandoned Latitudes*. A large number of the several hundred poems Thomas wrote in the last two decades of his life remain unpublished.[25] His poems did appear in many anthologies, though, as well as some of the best-known magazines of maverick poetics, such as Leland Hickman's *Temblor*. One anthology was entitled *The Outlaw Bible of American Poetry*. In the case of John Thomas, the outlaw aspect involved personal transgressions for which he suffered grievously. Whatever his final travails may have been, the poets of Los Angeles retained great affection for him. Shortly after his death in March 2002, poets gathered to commemorate him at Beyond Baroque in a building on the main east-west boulevard that runs through Venice; the building had undergone a unique transformation in the late 1970s from its original function as a city hall. Perkoff, Boyd, and Thomas must have walked past it many times, but only Thomas lived to read his poetry there.

FOUR

Left-Handed Blows

Beyond Baroque and the Los Angeles Poetry Renaissance

As the Beat generation faded from view, the cold war settled into a grim, high-stakes poker game of dystopic military expenditures. In no other major region of the United States during this period did poets have to confront on a daily basis the cultural and economic repercussions of media enterprises and conglomerates whose hegemony was alleged in its heyday to be so complete that, as Horkheimer and Adorno argued, they no longer felt the need to "justify the rubbish they deliberately produce" (*Dialectic of Enlightenment* 121). While Horkheimer and Adorno's claim that "under monopoly all mass culture is identical" (121), and other aspects of their critique of "the culture industry" overstated their case, perhaps as a deliberate provocation, many poets in Los Angeles did not see such an analysis as much of an exaggeration, even if the studio system did seem to be breaking down by the late 1960s. The need on the part of a new generation of L.A. poets to solidify an artistic identity beyond individual authorship remains an almost constitutive thirst, in large part because the entertainment industry continues to dominate cultural production in Southern California. "Poetry," David James argues, is "of all the arts the least useful to the film industry, and in its recent forms least compatible with its ethos" and "has recognized the impossibility of its profitable marketing by constructing itself in antithesis to everything assumed by Hollywood" (*Power Misses* 195). At least part of the strategy on the part of poets in Los Angeles in choosing to work in a city which embalms itself in the pathos of its own industrial entertainment is to remind those in Hollywood, who assume that everyone has their price, that their home ground serves as an organic site of cultural resistance.[1]

In "Impossible City: A History of Literary Publishing in L.A.," Standard Schaeffer claims that "Los Angeles can only be a temporary residence of serious writers. . . . certainly no serious poets come to L.A. with the intention of staying. In part, this is because staying may be detrimental to their reputation" (*Talisman* 289). Those who do stay seem to fascinate Schaeffer. "The poets here have often gone out of their way to counter Hollywood's corporate power and television's aesthetic of speed, repetition, and surfaces. They have done so by addressing the history of corruption and negation within the region by focusing not only on the historical and material conditions through which their own work has come into existence, but also by recovering older forms that require close attention and a significant investment of time" (295). In invoking "older forms," Schaeffer is referring to "an almost unanimous concern for untimely rhetorical exploration within the formally intricate serial or long poem" (295). He dates this interest in the long poem back to the first issues of *Bachy* magazine in the early 1970s, and says that "a tendency toward book-length poems and novels-in-verse remains to this date and continues to oppose the personality driven art of the city, to counter-act it, to demand longer attention spans and to embrace historical themes which are constantly being glossed over by the community-at-large" (295).

The contrast goes deeper than Hollywood, however. Persisting in their craft in the belly of the beast, the poets Schaeffer considers to be the most important in Southern California have had to develop different strategies than poets elsewhere in order to sustain their projects. "Time and time again, poets in Los Angeles have expressed that their very presence here seems to require their isolation from whatever poetic trend might be dominant elsewhere in the country. Merely celebrating 'the surface of language' or mimicking the talky, clubby style so dominant in New York or resorting to the overly ironic and self-referential strands of the Language School seem beside the point if not outright inappropriate to many of Los Angeles' most serious poets" (294). Schaeffer seems skeptical of the likelihood that critics will examine how their strategies differ, since "otherwise perceptive commentators" have not up to now been "aware of the connection between the long poem" and Los Angeles-based poets, leading them "to overlook the poetry of the region as being derivative of the Stuart Z. Perkoff-Charles Bukowski Beat aesthetic" (295).

The central gathering place for many of the poets that Schaeffer refers to in his article has been Beyond Baroque, a literary arts organization established in a storefront building in Venice, California, in 1968 that nourished the development of several communities of poets in Los Angeles as they were interwoven with several other subcultures. As we examine the poets associated with Beyond Baroque during the past four decades, we will see that a strict division between Hollywood and poetry cannot sustain itself, either in theory or daily life. Some poets in Los Angeles have been professionally involved with the movie or music industries as part of making a living, and included that experience as part of their poems.[2] The division between poets and what Murphet calls the "vision machine" is a permeable border. In focusing on these variegated communities and on their practical, quotidian address to the contestation over canon formation long before it became a crucial matter of debate in the academy, one possible question concerns how much these poets' proximity to the film and music industries contributed to their self-imposed peripheral autonomy within American poetry. A substantial contingent were less interested in how editors elsewhere evaluated their writing than in how their activities as poets served to confront the city with a community that preferred to keep the definition of that term as open and "empty" as possible. If moguls of the multiplexes were puzzled by the renitent, zigzag prosody of community emerging in Southern California, the poets at Beyond Baroque's workshop, as well as workshops spinning off from it, also took pride in not being easily classified by poets elsewhere. The antinomian streak in American poetry constantly tempered whatever desire poets in Los Angeles might have felt to supplicate editors elsewhere for acceptance on any terms other than their own deeply grooved interstices of a canon self-constructed out of prolonged reading and sagacious dispute with immediately accessible peers.

Many alternative literary arts organizations have flourished at various points in the past half century in the United States: St Mark's Poetry Project in New York City; the Loft in St. Paul, Minnesota; and the now-defunct Intersection in San Francisco are some of the main ones. All of these are known or remembered for their workshops and reading series, and St. Mark's became famous for its production of mimeographed publications, but only Beyond Baroque brought together a multitude of complementary literary activities as a means of generating community during its development into a poetic cynosure in Southern California. When Beyond Baroque shifted in 1979 from its original site to its current location, the task involved moving a small press library of several thousand titles, Compugraphic typesetting and paste-up equipment, and a stockpile of back issues of its own publications as well as more than a hundred metal folding chairs that served as the basic seating infrastructure for its workshop and reading audiences. A literary bookstore was soon added to the new premises.

Although Beyond Baroque's reading series and workshops continue to serve as its most publicly visible means of attracting poets, its distinctiveness among alternative literary organizations derives from its early emphasis on incorporating as many aspects of literary production as possible at one site.

From 1975 to 1985, Beyond Baroque provided the poets in the region with the opportunity to have a poem critiqued on Wednesday night, test the revision out loud at an open reading before the featured poet on Friday, type and paste it up for publication during the following week, and subsequently bring it back from the printer to be shelved at the library and sold at the bookstore. Each poet's decision on what facilities of Beyond Baroque she or he wanted to take advantage of offered continual opportunities to new members of the community to observe older poets, and to learn from their progress as well as their errors. Beyond Baroque presented very little in the way of impediments to an artist's decision about how mature she or he was as an artist, and its institutional projection into the development of the community continually favored potential rather than enactment. Perhaps most importantly, poets minimized the notion of institution even as their accumulated palimpsests of place reinforced their community.

Beyond Baroque: The Early Years

In the years after the dissolution of Venice West, the neighborhood maintained its reputation as one of the more disreputable, if not tougher parts of Los Angeles. It is easy to forget that Venice was much more isolated from Los Angeles in the mid- to late sixties than it is today. Marina del Rey, the world's largest man-made small craft harbor, was still on the Los Angeles County Board of Supervisors' drawing boards; the southern edges of Venice meandered into the open lots and fields dotted with wild mustard which eventually reached the Ballona Wetlands. Its northern border was marked by a defunct amusement park on a pier that was frequently set on fire by transients and amateur arsonists. The community adjacent to the north, Ocean Park, was not in fact that distinguishable from Venice even in the early 1970s, when Ocean Park's main street had at least four rescue-mission type operations. But Venice also distinguished itself from the other nearby coastal communities in that it was also home to the most substantial neighborhood of African Americans and Latinos on the West Side of Los Angeles. With the exception of Long Beach, the Oakwood section of Venice, in fact, currently remains the only minority neighborhood that exists in close proximity to beachfront property in all of Southern California.

In early 1968, George Drury Smith's life gave only the slightest hints that he would find himself becoming the genesis for a literary renaissance in a community known for its bohemian tolerance of artists and cultural castoffs. Smith, who was born in 1927 near Dayton, Ohio, had spent very little time in Venice up to that point. He had occasionally visited Venice on weekends while he was working as a district training supervisor for Pan Am Airlines in Los Angeles between 1955 and 1957, but lived in Chicago, Dallas, and San Francisco for the next six years. In 1965 he got a teaching credential and began working as a language instructor in the Santa Monica Unified School District, mainly teaching French, Spanish, and English as a Second language, as well as working on a master's degree in languages at UCLA.[3]

When Smith was forty, his grandmother and mother died, and he decided to use his inheritance to launch an experimental literary magazine, a project he had seriously considered as early as 1964, when he even went so far as to do a mock-up of a cover and a title page accompanied by an editorial introduction. His second attempt began at offices at 73 Market Street in Venice, but in July he chose to establish permanent headquarters by purchasing a lot with two buildings on West Washington Boulevard just north of its intersection with Venice Boulevard. Real estate speculators were not exactly converging with frantic bids for this spot, which was being sold for back taxes. Across the street was a lesbian bar and a junkyard called Ma Klein's Appliances; down the street was Brandelli's Brig, a bar frequented by pool-playing bikers: an elongated rectangle depicting a slightly crouched, solitary boxer still juts from the side of the building above the front entrance.

Beyond Baroque's front building was three stories high; in the rear was a one-story "pagoda style" building which had once served as an old railroad station on Venice Boulevard. The larger building was in total disrepair, "a wreck," according to Smith. "It had no running water, and all of the windows were broken." Smith steadily worked to fix the building, a task which proved far easier than launching a commercially successful, experimental literary magazine. The initial issue of *Beyond Baroque*, a name Smith says came to him in a dream, failed to make much of an impact, especially in terms of subscriptions. Needing to generate some revenue, Smith started up a prepublication service called Bayrock Publications, which included an IBM compositor. He also decided he would open up the western half of the first floor of the front building once a week to the public, which in Venice at that moment included everyone from aspiring musicians and drug addicts (not necessarily distinct categories) to individuals so removed from any identifiable classification that they could only be described as dropouts from the hippie culture. Every Thursday evening was devoted to "Happenstance": "There is no format and there are no rules. This is conceived as a poetry reading and rap session where anything can happen. Why not come, relax, chat, do your thing, while drinking coffee. You don't have to read anything, but most people do sooner or later" (*The Newsletter*).

Relaxing and chatting were not priorities for some of the poets who soon showed up and were reassigned Wednesday evenings as their weekly slot. Joseph Hansen, a concise, ironic poet and fiction writer who went on to write the David Brandstetter mystery series, and John Harris, a poet who had been born in China and spent part of his childhood there with his missionary parents, revived a poetry workshop that Hansen had led at Frank Souza's The Bridge on Kenmore Avenue (*Echo 681* 136–138).[4] Hansen and Harris were soon joined by two young poets, Jim Krusoe and Lynn Shoemaker, who had recently finished college and were living in Venice. Having dropped out of a PhD program at the University of California, Davis, in part because of disenchantment with academic poetry, Shoemaker was both involved in the resistance against the draft and the Vietnam War, and had also joined the all-volunteer staff of the *Free Venice Beachhead*, a monthly newspaper devoted to revoking the annexation of Venice by Los Angeles over a half century earlier, and the establishment of a counterculture city. The secession movement never reached fruition, but the local neighborhood's desire for Venice's original autonomy reinforced the artistic groundswell of the community throughout the seventies. Shoemaker became the managing editor of the third issue of *Beyond Baroque*, which was guest-edited by Hansen and Harris, and focused on the "New Venice Poets," which included not just Beyond Baroque's workshop, but Jack Hirschman, who was living on Quarterdeck in Venice, and who had recently lost his job teaching at UCLA, in addition to featuring community organizers such as John Haag.

A year later Shoemaker edited a follow-up workshop anthology, *Venice 13*, which did focus only on work from the Beyond Baroque workshop. Smith served as the printer for this book, but was not himself the publisher. The major addition to the poetic lineup was Harry Northup, an actor born in Kansas in 1940 who had moved to Los Angeles in 1968 after several years of working as an actor in New York, and who eventually acted in many films directed by Martin Scorcese and Jonathan Demme.[5] Smith was diligent about mailing out press releases for all of Beyond Baroque's activities. Northup's inclusion in *Venice 13* and the announcement in a newspaper of his participation in its publication reading caught the attention of Leland Hickman, a poet and actor who had also recently moved to Los Angeles. Northup and Hickman had known each other in New York, but had lost touch with each other; Hickman surprised Northup by showing up at the reading.[6] By late 1971, Hickman, too, began attending the Wednesday workshop and sharing portions of his long poem, "Tiresias," which quickly became recognized in the workshop as a major work-in-progress about a personal journey as harrowing as anything in the plays of Eugene O'Neil or Sam Shepard.

Far more sexually explicit than Ginsberg's "Howl," Hickman's long poem-in-progress, "Tiresias," provided Beyond Baroque's Wednesday night workshop with a chance to assert itself as a public group when many of its members attended Hickman's first sustained reading of portions of the poem at Papa Bach Bookstore in October of 1971. The attendance of the Beyond Baroque workshop community at that reading, in fact, signaled the beginning of many links between the workshop with Papa Bach, a site primarily known at the time for its double feature of draft counseling and the best selection of Marxist literature in Los Angeles. The workshop and the store went on to become far more involved with each other's fate. Workshop leader John Harris eventually owned the store and expanded the size and scope of the store's new magazine, *Bachy*. Leland Hickman would become the editor of that magazine for almost ten issues, and would build on the experience he gained at that magazine in handling a large page publication when he began his own magazines, *Boxcar* and *Temblor*.

New issues of *Beyond Baroque* were slow to be assembled, and Smith chose to publish small pamphlets of mainly local literary news, together with a few poems, which he called *NewLetters*. Unlike the first perfect-bound issue of *Beyond Baroque*, *NewLetters* was saddle-stitched. By 1972 Beyond Baroque had incorporated as a nonprofit foundation, and was using bulk-rate postage to distribute a significant chunk of *NewLetter*'s print run of fifteen hundred copies. These issues served not only to publicize events at Beyond Baroque as well as at independent bookstores such as Papa Bach and Chatterton's, but also to give detailed directions on how to get to Beyond Baroque (vol. 2, no. 4, Winter 1972–1973, 3). It wasn't exactly a secret location, but as noted before, Venice was hardly as familiar an icon as it became after MTV in the mid-1980s broadcast images of the Venice Boardwalk around the world, transforming that public performance venue into an arena almost as famous as Disneyland.

The Friday night poetry reading series for which Beyond Baroque has become most famous was quite sporadic in its early years, and attendance was unpredictable. Jim Krusoe remembers six people showing up to listen to Kenward Elmslie, and "three of them left at intermission." Other events, however, were more indicative of the future: Jack Hirschman's readings on September 25 and October 24, 1972, brought a heavy response and this galvanized attention so much that a few months later Smith noted in *NewLetters* that "(r)ecent presentations at the Center have found people crouched in the doorway, hoping to hear a note or a word, and perhaps gain entrance after intermission" (vol. 2, no. 4, 5). Audiences proved so indefatigable that speakers had to be placed outside the building so that the crowd on the sidewalk could hear the poems being read inside. Of course, the phrase, "hoping to hear a note," reminds us that Beyond Baroque's early programming was not simply literary, or restricted to the contemporary. A music series directed by Smith focused on performances of Early Modern compositions, and attracted an audience quite distinct from the poetry crowd. In addition, Smith curated the exhibitions of visual art which rotated in tandem with the seasonal reading series.[7]

Smith managed to accomplish all this while working at other jobs to support himself, jobs which fortunately brought him into contact with individuals who supported Beyond Baroque at critical moments. One of Smith's jobs was production and editorial work for a local weekly newspaper, the *Argonaut*, whose publisher, David Asper Johnson, allowed Smith to use its photo-typesetting equipment to set issues of *NewLetters*. Although the National Endowment for the Arts was eventually to have a major impact on arts funding in the United States, it must be emphasized how little grant support was given to Beyond Baroque during its first five years, and how distinct that makes its genesis and survival from other community-oriented literary projects at the same time. The Poetry Project at St. Mark's-in-the-Bowery, for instance, was *begun* with federal money, in part because its original impetus fixed itself at a site that was already feasible for expansion as a community center.[8] In contrast, Beyond Baroque was begun in a converted storefront, and its total assistance from government agencies in its first five years was less than a thousand dollars.[9] One can only wonder how the Poetry Project would have fared if it had had similarly thin rations. The survival of Beyond Baroque during these early years largely happened because of the devotion of volunteers such as Alexandra Garrett, a reticent poet who had been the only woman in Tom McGrath's poetry workshop in Los Angeles during the 1950s, and who had worked as an editor and major fundraiser for *California Quarterly* in its final years. Garrett contributed thousands of hours of work to Beyond Baroque and was the founder of Beyond Baroque's small press library, which developed into the largest such public, non-university collection on the West Coast.

In 1974 Smith applied for, and received, an Expansion Arts grant from the National Endowment for the Arts, and this grant in part enabled him to open up the larger back room of Beyond Baroque's first floor to accommodate the larger audiences for readings. If grant money was becoming available, it might well in part have been due to a recession between 1973 and 1975 so severe that the federal government finally attempted to ameliorate its effects by employing individuals in arts activities for the first time since the Works Progress Administration. Smith's transformation of Beyond Baroque from a for-profit publishing venture to a non-profit arts center enabled him to snag some funds from CETA (Comprehensive Employment and Training Act) and use them to hire several people for tasks such as typesetting. One of them was a young poet from Florida, Exene Cervenka, who recalls that when she arrived in Los Angeles in 1976, "The workshops were *the* place where you could have your stuff read and commented on honestly. No pretense—people either liked it or they didn't, and they told you *why*" (*Los Angeles Reader* 8).[10]

The workshop also contributed to the development of how poets read their poems out loud. James Krusoe recalls an evening where Wanda Coleman read a poem at the Wednesday night workshop: "(She) would come down and read like a 'bat out of hell' and knock everybody out in a certain way, but then I could never tell what she was doing because it was so animated and so rhythmical and I couldn't hear the words. So, after one of her readings, I said something like, 'Wanda, would you do me a favor and read this poem really slow?' and, Wanda just like 'Drop dead!' looked at me, and then picked it up and read it and it felt like ten minutes between each word and it was the most amazing, most powerful reading that she had ever done. I was really amazed. And everyone was really amazed, no kidding, and from that on, in my mind, Wanda read slowly. And that power was able to come through. Because, (before) she would read it like 'skat' when she first started."[11]

By the mid-seventies, the publication projects of Beyond Baroque had diverged: one publication retained the eponymous title, while *NewLetters* evolved into *NEW* magazine. *NEW* also changed its appearance; instead of a thirty-two-page issue which was erratically pasted-up, it was printed on newsprint in runs of sixteen thousand copies in 1976, and its circulation eventually peaked at twenty-five thousand. Made available for free, bundles of *NEW* were dispersed around the city at the entrances or near the check-out counters of restaurants, bookstores, and record stores. When Beyond Baroque received a grant to produce full-length poetry books, the same strategy was adopted, though the paper was of slightly higher quality. Although many literary organizations develop a reputation for concentrating on their own, the startling thing about the six writers chosen in a free, open competition was that none of them were closely associated with Beyond Baroque. These poets included Watts Writers Workshop member K. Curtis Lyle (*15 Predestination Weather Reports*), Eloise Klein Healy (*Building Some Changes*), and Maxine Chernoff (*A Vegetable Emergency*). The variety of work chosen by Krusoe gives some indication of the writers and forms that were beginning to influence Los Angeles poets in the mid-1970s. Lyle's writing reflected the surrealist influence of Bob Kaufman and Aime Cesaire; Chernoff's prose poems appealed to a widespread interest in Los Angeles in the prose poem; and Healy's sly lyrics showed the first stirrings of her feminist commitment.[12]

The Linocomp typesetting equipment that Cervenka worked on had been acquired by Beyond Baroque through a grant from the National Endowment for the Arts in 1975, and the machine was in constant use by poets such as Jack Grapes and Michael Andrews, whose Alley Cat Reading Series in Hermosa Beach included a series of books that anthologized the featured poets. Throughout the 1970s, the reading series under Jim Krusoe continued to attract larger and larger audiences, as well as new members, such as Alicia Ostriker, to its workshop. The small amount of space for all these events, though, continued to pose a major problem. The need for Beyond Baroque to find a single building that could house all of its activities and accommodate the increasing audiences propelled the search for another location. The passage of Proposition 13 in 1977, which devastated school budgets and led to the eventual decline and virtual demise of the Southern California region's Poets-in-the-Schools program, also provided Beyond Baroque with an alternative plan for expansion. The shortage in city government revenues forced the closing of various city agencies and structures, including the Old Venice City Hall, which had been built around 1907 and served Venice until it was annexed by Los Angeles in 1927. Councilperson Pat Russell had to vacate her offices there, and she recommended that the site be used for a new library in Venice. However, the lack of funding made such a project impossible for several years, and by late August 1978, the city administrative board recommended that Beyond Baroque's application to use and maintain the space be accepted.

The move was made during the following summer, and an official "gala opening" occurred on Friday, October 26, 1979, with a weekend that included poetry readings by Kate Braverman and Wanda Coleman, and a Renaissance music concert on Sunday evening.[13] The transition to the Old Venice City Hall was marked by several major organizational shifts. On September 30, George Drury Smith resigned as president and chairman of the board of trustees, and James Krusoe resigned as vice president. After ten years of unceasing struggle, Beyond Baroque had found a home which could provide enough space under one roof for all of its activities, and Smith felt his task was complete. Although this new space was less than a half-mile away from the original site in Venice, the move marked a major shift in the social and poetic emphasis of Beyond Baroque.

A large number of the poets in attendance at the Old Venice City Hall festivities also had their poetry calendar marked for the following evening. On Saturday, October 27, dozens of poets read at a fundraiser, "Flores Para Nicaragua: A Gift of Poetry and Sharing from the People of Los Angeles," at KPFK radio studios in North Hollywood. All proceeds from the reading, which was broadcast live from 1:30 PM to midnight, went to NICASO, the Nicaragua Solidarity Organization for Medical Supplies. This event represented a convergence not only of poets such as Lee Hickman, Wanda Coleman, Peter Levitt, Jim Krusoe, Manazar Gamboa, Jack Grapes, Dennis Phillips, Harry Northup, and myself, who were significantly associated with Beyond Baroque or Papa Bach's *Bachy* magazine, but also of a contingent from the Woman's Building. While poets such as Eloise Klein Healy, Holly Prado, Deena Metzger, Aleida Rodríguez, Jean Samuels, and Martha (Lifson) Ronk were hardly exclusively affiliated with the Woman's Building, their participation in the event, along with newly emerging poets such as Laurel Ann Bogen, Charles Webb, and Austin Straus indicated that poets in Los Angeles were fully engaged in both the maturation of their base institutions as well as interweaving their voices into international issues. Nor was this reading the end of such protests: Julia Stein, who also served as an editor of *Electrum* magazine for several issues, organized an "Artists Call Against U.S. Intervention" in January 1984 that she called *Flores para Centro America*; the series of seven readings, which included Manazar Gamboa, Laurel Ann Bogen, Max Benavidez, Michelle T. Clinton, Ivan Roth, Bill Oandasan, and Naomi Quinonez, concluded with yet another half-hour broadcast from KPFK.

Ten years later, Eliot Weinberger acerbically inveighed against what he regarded as the political passivity of American poets: "In the disaster of Reagan America, were there five of the five thousand poets who spoke publicly against it, except when the NEA budget was cut? Few are engaged in what was once routine service to the poetry community: translation, book reviews, editing magazines, essays on poetry, poetry readings where one reads the work of others: any sort of literary context in which to locate themselves" (*Works on Paper* 122–123). The figure of five thousand poets cited by Weinberger refers to the listings in a Poets & Writers Directory. Two weeks before Reagan was elected as the next president, a large number of Los Angeles poets were already speaking up in support and defense of those who would become the next major targets of a terrorist campaign affiliated with the Central Intelligence Agency, nor would they cease speaking after Reagan was inaugurated and then reelected; other poets and editors in Los Angeles, such as Clayton Eshleman and Doren Robbins, would join the chorus of condemnation at readings at such places as the Church in Ocean Park, whose minister, Jim Conn, encouraged poetry readings and theater performances in the large open space of his congregation's Sunday meeting area. Eshleman and Robbins read there with Denise Levertov, a reading to which I walked from my apartment three blocks away; for a decade and a half, the apartment served as the headquarters for my own publishing project, Momentum Press. I had started my adventure as an editor, though, at other intersections in Los Angeles; whatever degree of success Momentum Press achieved has its origins in the generosity of those who entrusted my judgment despite my youthfulness. I was far more confident than I had any right to be, though how could I not but feel the passion of those much older than I was, who still stand before me as embodiments of poetic integrity.

The Momentum Workshop: A Golden Age of Los Angeles Poetry

For two years in the early 1970s, I had a job as a blueprint machine operator at an architectural and house building company called Larwin, that paid

Independent "Little" Magazines in California with a Special Emphasis on Poetry, 1968–1985

NORTHERN CALIFORNIA	SOUTHERN CALIFORNIA	CENTRAL CALIFORNIA
Alcatraz	Bachy	Café Solo
Aldebaran Review	Barney	Kaldron
Back Roads	Beyond Baroque	
Bastard Angel	Big Boulevard	
Beatitude	Cafeteria	
Big Sky	Chismearte	
The Fault	Chrysalis	
Floating Island	Con Safos	
Foot	Crawl Out Your . . .	
Gallimaufry	Earth Rose	
Heirs	Electrum	
Hills	Fuse	
Hyperion	Intermedia*	
Isthmus	Invisible City*	
Juice	Laugh Literary . . .	
kayak	Little Caesar	
Loon	Little Square	
Mango	Maize	
Manroot	Marilyn	
Miam	Matrix	
Panjandrum	Momentum	
Phantasm	Mudborn	
Poetry Now	Nausea	
Second Coming	NeWorld	
Stooge	Pearl	
This	Poetry LA	
Tottel's	rara avis	
Tractor	Scree	
Wormwood Review	Stonecloud	
Yardbird Reader	Sulfur	
	Sunset Palms Hotel	
	Third Rail	
	Willmore City	

*magazines that had offices in both northern and southern California

$2.25 an hour, but I frequently worked ten to twelve hours of overtime per week; by the time Larwin laid me off in the spring of 1974, I had managed to save a couple thousand dollars and I was able to get by on unemployment. While working at Larwin, I had served as the poetry editor of *Bachy* magazine, published by Papa Bach Bookstore, for its first two issues, and had attended Beyond Baroque's Wednesday night workshop assiduously in order to encourage submissions. The handsome (too handsome, in fact, in its desire to be taken seriously) first issue had impressed the workshop participants enough so that Leland Hickman submitted the first five sections of his long poem, "Tiresias," to the second issue. I was chafing under the limited amount of poetry I could publish in *Bachy*, however, and there had been complaints, according to Ted Reidel, about my choice of poets. I managed to get John Harris installed as the next poetry editor, thereby leaving that responsibility in trustworthy hands, and decided to start my own publication, which I decided to call *Momentum*, perhaps as my comment on how I hoped to contribute to and sustain the proliferating small press movement, especially on the West Coast.

Living in California as a young poet in the early 1970s made little magazine editing the rite of passage into a community. One aspect of this ritual involved the mechanical assemblage of the magazine or chapbook, all of which seemed like a foreign language to me. The prepress production work of typesetting and paste-up had been taken care of by other people on the staff of *Bachy*, and I knew nothing about the actual process of transforming typewritten manuscripts into typeset galleys. I did not know what point size was, let alone what ratio of point size to leading worked best for poems, nor had I even heard the term "bullet" in regard to type, or that a thing such as small caps existed. I also had to find a printer I could afford. Once again, Paul Vangelisti saved me an immense amount of time calling around for quotations for printing estimates. In the course of bringing out his first half-dozen issues of *Invisible City*, he had found a printer, Gemini Graphics, in Marina del Rey, about a half-mile away from Beyond Baroque. The two sisters, Myrt and Eileen Ferrer, who owned the business were not only willing to print whatever we brought to them without any questions about the contents, but once we got established, were willing to accept payments on the jobs spread out over a couple of months. They always retained a copy of whatever they printed, and by the end of the century Gemini Graphics had more than a few choice, rare items squeezed into the bookshelves in front of Myrt's front office. In starting, therefore, I had to figure out how to accomplish all of the other tasks involved in transforming a stack of manuscripts into the first issue of a magazine.

"Poetry does not arise and exist in a vacuum," observed Louis Zukofsky in *A Test of Poetry*. "It is one of the arts—sometimes individual, sometimes collective in origin—and reflects economic and social status of peoples" (99). I saw no reason to pretend that my magazine was not dependent on my labor, and so the cover of my first issue reprinted a blueprint order form from my job. I didn't necessarily expect readers to understand why it was there, but I chose it as a deliberate marker of what had made the magazine possible. This was not a magazine coming out of the middle class and its abundant cultural capital, a point I reiterated by using for the cover of the fourth issue an unemployment claim form I had to fill out every other week. At this point, I hope it's safe to confess that my search for employment in 1974 was less than eager—not that there were many jobs to be found. The American economy was having its first sustained downturn in over a decade, and Southern California workers were especially hurt.

In starting my magazine, I was very fortunate to meet up with another aspiring editor, Harley Lond, a bearded, stocky fellow who was close friends with one of the actresses, Becky Goldstein, in the Burbage Theater Ensemble, with which I was associated as an actor for two years. Lond, who had dropped out of college in the mid-1960s to wander around the West Coast for a couple of years, had settled back in his hometown in the early seventies. Lond had undertaken the challenge of being the theater's administrative director, and after guiding the group into a nonprofit status, started his own publication, *Intermedia*, which ran for a total of seven issues. Although we had some contributors in common, such as Richard Kostelanetz, *Intermedia* favored much more experimental work than my magazine. Its format, too, was distinct: one issue had all of its materials enclosed in a box, which led to the problems at the post office. The items included a loose fish hook, which the post office claimed could prove dangerous to a mail delivery carrier. When outright censorship faltered as a means to deter cultural work, the anti-imaginative currents within the public sphere of the state apparatus found other obstructions to pose to the distribution of any alternative art. In sharing the same umbrella organization, Lond and I were not consciously copying Beyond Baroque's policy of alternating issues of literary experiment with issues devoted to more conventional poetry; in retrospect, however, it is interesting that at least two organizations in Los Angeles were simultaneously committed to an inclusive program of unaffiliated artists. Lond brought in jazz musicians to jam on Sunday nights at the theater and started up a film program. The Burbage also sponsored a workshop by the actresses which specifically developed a feminist play called *A Woman's Evolution* and offered the east side of the brick wall behind the theater to be used for a mural by Judith Hernandez. (The mural was later covered over by a wall constructed by the adjacent property owners.) The nonprofit status of the organization, which used the playhouse's name as its title, enabled both Lond and me to apply for small grants after we had produced a couple of issues of our magazines.[14]

The first issue, in the spring of 1974, was in many ways simply a continuation of my editorial inclinations at *Bachy*, which were attuned to my favorite poets at that time: Weldon Kees, Denise Levertov, Kenneth Patchen, Roger McGough, Adrian Mitchell, and Philip Levine. The fourth issue of *Momentum*, which appeared in the spring of 1975, was the first to demonstrate any serious growth as an editor. The issue opened up with a five-page, double-columned section of *Tiresias (I:9:A)*, which Hickman had written several years earlier but had been unable to find anybody willing to publish it. The next piece, Harry Northup's eight-page poem "I Cut My Mind Open in an Esso Station" was almost as candid as Hickman's in its surreal sensual turbulence. The real star of the issue, however, was Holly Prado, whose prose poems had begun attracting national attention the year before.[15] This was the last issue to be typeset and pasted-up by a paid professional. By the time the next issue's contents had been assembled, Beyond Baroque had started NewComp Graphics, which permitted me to acquire some minimal production literacy.[16]

Technological self-empowerment impels an individual to reconsider his or her relationship to a potential community, but it can also be an emotionally challenging definition. I remember sitting at the machine at Beyond Baroque, and simmering with frustration at how much time it was taking to get the material out. Whereas the average computer in use in 2010 can change typesize from 11 point to 10.5 or 11.5 with a few keystrokes and quick clicks on the mouse, the first typesetting machine that Beyond Baroque owned as part of NewComp Graphics Center had only a capacity to use five of a total of seven different type sizes at one time. The person before me may have been working on flyers, and the machine might have had 72 point, 48 point, 36 point, 24 point, 14 point, and 6 point. If I was going to use 12 point, 10 point, and 8 point to convert typewritten material into galleys, then I had to lift the machine's lid, reach in, give a four-inch tube a gentle twist, set it in its container, take out the 10 point lens, reach back in, ease it into its armature, close the lid, sit down, begin to type, and watch the words appear on a tiny screen less than one inch high and four inches wide. Trying to produce narrow columns of type on a machine on which one could not see the columns made me feel like an airplane pilot without radar on a foggy night. This machine had no memory whatsoever. If one were typing prose, one could hear the machine begin to generate impressions on photosensitive paper as soon as the line length had been reached. If one were typesetting poetry, one had to tap the hard return in order to launch the machine's internal print mechanism. Regardless of genre, the words were temporarily recorded on film-sensitive paper that then had to be run through a developer. First, though, one had to press the paper advance button to feed sufficient lead paper into the developer canister, and one had to hope that the paper feed process went smoothly, because if the light-sensitive paper crimped against the entry point of the canister, one would have to type the entire text all over again. The same was true of the developing process. One fed a leading edge of paper from the canister into the first rollers of a developing machine and slammed a lid shut to keep the unfurling scroll unexposed. Whether the subsequent set of rollers inside the machine decided to pass the paper safely through the developing chemicals, or to wrap an hour's worth of typesetting into a thick rind around rubber cylinders seemed a matter of mechanical whim. If the paper jammed in the developer, one went back to the keyboard and typed it all out for the second time. Or the third time. Or the fourth time, or until the canister and developer stopped taking turns at betraying one's unsubstantiated efforts. Even after coming out of the initial developer, the sheets had to be soaked in a tub of chemicals for a half hour, and then shifted to a small basin of water to rinse off. This was the work of making the work of poets visible. One can turn to Paul Hoover's anthology and read the work of Wanda Coleman, and it sits there on the page, ready for a teacher in Texas or Illinois or Michigan or Pennsylvania to use, but it was this obstreperous machinery that helped that poem arrive on that distant page. As Barrett Watten pointed out in his interview about the West Coast Print Center, the typesetting for Hanna Wiener's poem in Paul Hoover's *Postmodern American Poetry* makes use of his original typesetting of that text.

Shortly after the fifth issue of *Momentum* came out, a coterie of poets who had appeared in my magazine at least twice, if not three times, gathered at our mutual instigation in Kate Braverman's apartment and discussed forming a workshop. Though Harry Northup, Lee Hickman, Dennis Ellman, Peter Levitt, Braverman, and myself never named the group, I suppose one could call it the Momentum workshop. Given how often we met at Braverman's apartment, however, the West Washington Boulevard workshop might be appropriate, too. Ironically enough, after the workshop started, this group of poets—as a group—never appeared together in an issue again. It was as if the magazine had brought us together for the purpose of pushing each other to write longer poems or to change our work in a way that perplexed the other members of the group. Often publishing projects come out of a workshop, but in this case, my publishing project brought us together.[17]

The poets who comprised the workshop also provided most of the initial manuscripts I turned into books. Levitt, Krusoe, Northup, and Ellman were among the first poets I published, and each title I published added to the attention that the magazine was beginning to attract. I made plans to publish

Braverman and Hickman, but both were reluctant to release a manuscript until I had established myself as a publisher. Fortunately, Beyond Baroque was hardly the only alternative cultural center in Los Angeles. Less than a year and a half after the Woman's Building had opened in November 1973, a week-long festival attracted writers, artists, and performers from around the country to lead workshops entitled "Women in Design," "Women and Words," and "The Performance Conference" between March 20 and March 27, 1975.[18] Journal writing received a significant amount of attention at the "Women and Words" conference, and Prado used her own writing about this conference as the central focus of *Feasts,* a book of autobiographical fiction. Prado's willingness to use unusual arrangements of lineated prose, some-times in double columns on a page, attracted my attention for the way that it made the distinction between prose and poetry almost impossible to detect. I still regard *Feasts* as one of the most intriguing pieces of writing by a mav-erick feminist writer of the twentieth century. Her subtle, lapidary mosaic of feminist social life contained the kind of wisdom that one hoped to find in personal writing. Prado's protagonist, Claire, provides the women writers from out of town a place to sleep, and in recounting the background of this conference, manages to blend the quotidian life of writers with a public event in a way that is both more intimate and generous than the transformation of such materials in Beat literature. "To turn our gold into ordinary ground, the best possible solution," she advises, and the ordinary ground of literary labor seemed to be best possible complementary alchemy (26).

Prado had begun to take herself seriously as a writer about the same time as I started editing *Bachy.* I had spotted what proved to be her first published poem in one of the last issues of *Apple,* an Illinois-based magazine sold at Either/Or Bookstore in Hermosa Beach. The same poem also appeared in the *Anthology of L.A. Poets* edited by Vangelisti, Bukowski, and Neeli Cherry. It wasn't until 1974 that she quit her job as a high school English teacher and devoted herself to her own writing. Her willingness to discard economic security impressed poets such as Deena Metzger, who herself had been the target of censorship at a college in the 1960s. "In 1975, when I first met Deena (Metzger), she asked me if I would help organize a conference at the Wom-an's Building for women writers to come to—a weekend conference to which writers from all over the country would come—and a lot was talked about our own journals," Prado remembers.[19] The journal form contributed to the overall tone of *Feasts* as well as some of its content, but the willingness to shape the story on the page into parallel columns of abbreviated, elliptical language was the breakthrough that made the book stand out.

Despite a lack of reviews, *Feasts* was my first successful book. Prado gave several readings that enabled the book to reach an audience yearning for empowerment associated with what Eloise Klein Healy has described as "communities of intention."[20] Looking back on it, I should have charged more for every book. Of course the average paperback was $1.95, but that was a price based on mass marketing. Although Prado's *Feasts* was the fifth title I published, it was my first substantial accomplishment as a publisher and its success encouraged Kate Braverman to entrust her first book of poems to my press. Brimming with an audacious, quasi-feminist impunity, *Milk Run* received much more critical attention, not only because of its achievement as a collection of poems but because the press had achieved a critical mass of back titles.[21] The more visible profile enabled me to begin taking chances in terms of book design, and I could do so because the number of stores willing to carry poetry books was increasing rapidly. George Sand Bookstore had joined Chatterton's, Papa Bach, and Either/Or as reliable outlets for poets. I stocked and restocked these stores with Braverman's book.

The books were strictly paperback editions, and there was no standardized format. My struggles as a book designer were due, in part, to the typesetting equipment itself. It was impossible to control the quality of the type coming out of the machine at Beyond Baroque. Sometimes it was light and almost faded, other times the type came out as though it were in boldface. In addition, the cardboard plates used by Gemini Graphics compounded the variations in type. All in all, the production portion of publishing was not a situation that allowed one to concentrate on achieving an aesthetic object. When I began assembling manuscripts for my first anthology of Los Angeles poets, *The Streets Inside: Ten Los Angeles Poets,* I decided to use Bodoni typeface as a way to compensate for the inconsistencies I confronted. Other typefaces such as Garamond seemed to career between pale silhouettes and scorched blots on any given session, but Bodoni hit the same plodding but effective density week after week. Bodoni has all the sprightliness of scuffed, high-top work boots. If one would tend to call it robust instead of graceful, at least the words felt palpable on the page, and reading did not feel like a squinting contest. The virtual necessity of using Bodoni proved to be one of the book's dismaying flaws, according to one reviewer, the poet and publisher Stephen Kessler.[22]

The official publication date was the middle of the last week of December 1978, when I picked up copies of the book from Gemini Graphics, and I held a New Year's Eve party in my house to celebrate its arrival. Although the book has a copyright date of 1978, it is a book that more properly belongs to the next year, and it was throughout 1979 that *The Streets Inside* established itself as the final major volume of a trilogy of Los Angeles anthologies in the 1970s. Despite the very narrow representation of a complex scene, the anthology was fortunate enough to receive some serious reviews, better than the book in itself deserved. Robert Kirsch's review on mid-April did not mention the other two books, but it would have been impossible, I believe, for my book to be acclaimed without those books having set up a context for *The Streets Inside* to distinguish itself from. Not the least of the distinctions was that Charles Bukowski was nowhere in sight; what was almost deliciously appreciated by the poets in my volume was that his absence was not perceived as so remarkable as to be worth remarking on. Robert Kirsch was effusive in his praise: "If Los Angeles were San Francisco, this would be a golden age for poetry," he wrote, and book orders poured in.[23] I began to regret that I had priced the book at five dollars when it should have cost at least seven and a half, if not ten.

By the time I decided to fold my magazine, Hickman had moved from workshop leader to being the paid editor of *Bachy* magazine and began interviewing pairs of poets for each issue, concentrating on the poets who had been featured in the anthology.[24] Hickman took the opportunity of editing *Bachy* to push the long poem that both Vangelisti and I had emphasized in our magazines and presses. One of the poets Hickman admired was Dennis Phillips, who also lived in Ocean Park. Phillips's poems were almost always long series, and when Lee published them, he was forced to cram them onto the page. One had the sense of paintings hanging on walls so close together that the viewer could not avoid the impinging overflow of color from the neighboring paintings. Vangelisti and Phillips seemed to be the poets in Los Angeles who were attempting to purge any remnants of the personal or autobiographical from their writing, and their poems need to be inserted into a prominent position of any account of avant-garde writing in the 1970s.

In the introductory essay to *In the American Tree*, Ron Silliman acknowledged that feminist and gay poetry were also important components of the changes in American poetry between 1970 and 1985. My press was hardly the only one to publish an integrated list of feminist, gay, and straight poets, and by failing to name these presses, he missed an opportunity to remind his avant-garde audience of how much cultural work was being accomplished by the small press movement which Language writing emerged out of, and how writers such as the ones I published were contributing to the development of the still-continuing civil rights debate regarding matters such as gay marriage. When I look back at my archives, I find a copy of *Alternate: The International Magazine of Sexual Politics*, and in its "Special California Issue" of 1980 are reviews of *The Dog and other stories* by Joseph Hansen, which I published in 1979 and which went into a second printing, as well as a review of issue number 10 of Dennis Cooper's *Little Caesar*. That issue of *Alternate* also contained a three-page article on Hansen's out-of-the-closet detective, David Brandstetter, as well as a review of Judy Grahn's *The Work of an Uncommon* Woman.[25] Gay critics elsewhere took note not only of Hansen's book of poems, *One Foot in the Boat*, which I published in 1979, but of one of the most overlooked first books of poems in this period, Jack Thomas's *Waking the Waters*. Thomas had grown up in San Diego, and Dennis Ellman and I had met him in a poetry class taught by Glover Davis at San Diego State. After graduating with an MA, Thomas lived in Spain and Canada, and would eventually return to San Diego, California, where he would die of AIDS in the mid-1980s. He was living in Toronto, Canada, when he first sent me a manuscript. In a review of *Waking the Waters*, gay critic Rudy Kikel said that "(Thomas's) raptures are not come to easily. As betrothed to reality as he is to Rapture, it is only after submission to Experience of this world (in the Blakeian sense) that Thomas entertains romantic notions. And after all, only after evidence of 'disenchantment' is any symbol worth its salt—or our credulity—arrived at."[26] In publishing Hansen's and Thomas's books, I sent the audience for my publications an unmistakable signal that I was not interested in tokenism, and I reassured Hickman that as a publisher I was providing him with authorial comrades.

I had first seen Lee Hickman read at Papa Bach Bookstore in October 1971, and the response to his performance had been sensational within the small, but growing community of Los Angeles poets. The critical response eight years later to Hickman's poems in *The Streets Inside* convinced me that his book was destined to become one of the defining productions of Momentum Press.[27] I ordered the best possible paper I could afford, and decided that I would use Peace Press as the printer rather than Gemini Graphics. Since NEA grant money largely ended up in the hands of printers, I wanted in part to spread the wealth around and to support a combination print shop/publisher aligned with my publishing poetics.[28] When Peace Press had a proof copy for me to read, I rode my old motorcycle over to Culver City and ran my hand over the huge uncut sheets, each containing eight pages of text. The paper felt more like cloth that had just been ironed. I stood there for a few minutes, gently rubbing the paper, almost caressing it. I was on the verge of a triumph by a friend and mentor, and for once in my life, I savored a plenitude of possibility. Indeed, *Tiresias I:9:B: Great Slave Lake Suite* went on to receive over a dozen reviews, and it was nominated by the *Los Angeles Times Book Review* as one of the five best books of poems published in 1980. The other books competing for the prize had been published by Black Sparrow and Knopf, and I had hopes that this nomination would help call enough attention to Hickman's project to justify support for the publication of the entire poem. Unfortunately, *Great*

Slave Lake Suite turned out to be the only volume of his poetry published in his lifetime. A posthumous volume, *Lee Sr Falls to the Floor*, was published shortly after his death in May 1991 by Martin Nakell's Jahbone Press.

The publication of *Tiresias: The Collected Poems of Leland Hickman* by Nightboat Books/Otis Seismicity Editions in 2009 has revived interest in Hickman's poetry and in his unfinished long poem, which he had originally intended to be six books.[29] Scrupulously edited by Stephen Motika, *Tiresias* provides a chance for readers to compare and contrast his first prize-winning elegy for his father with the longer, more formally complex version that comprises one of the "Elements" of *Great Slave Lake Suite*. Selecting a representative passage from "Tiresias" is almost inherently a frustrating assignment in that there is no way to convey how interwoven repetitions of phrases, such as "blue sun breath door," recoil their counterpointing affirmations throughout the often harrowing narrative. The musical effect of the incremental stanza structure of "The Hidden," for instance, as it grows from nine lines in the first stanza to fifteen lines in the sixth stanza and then decreases at the same rate, with every stanza opening and closing with an apostrophic "o," would require citing the entire four-page poem to demonstrate its modulated convocation of bereaved wisdom. Out of the necessity to compress, therefore, I offer these passages from the "Elements" of *Great Slave Lake Suite* as brief glimpses of Hickman's obsessive, incantatory vision:

    this song or segment of song for that flawd song Leland at
        26 in 61 tongue out dripping for
        balm in the corrupt
    land bereft angry hungry weeping
    male snake of that time in my dark those pale hard headlights wove
        over my dusty ceiling from
    cars beneath my window, wide open on selma my
        gay young hustlers
    lust bereft angry hungry weeping where
    Beckett Faulkner at a loss glare down that my
        strong song's urge
        hoist me higher in my malign
    fire this song or fragment of song for that snarld song Leland at
        26 in 61 isolate rubble down gutters shuffler in
    our thick spit pool of absolute freedoms against the law to be
        legal, heritage bilge trash, out still for
    balm in glutton land policemen to kneel to to pray to, mostly a
        lone in Los Angeles aching

all down selma vine to highland hardon bared icy in drizzle shouting
    four a.m. hank cinq at lung top get a guy
fuck me in azaleas spit on my face slap me by the church at las palmas
    way we slay the blue temple/ weird
wanderings of my subtle body

                             ("O Blue Temple" lines 1–23)

It is interesting to note that this recollection of his youth (age twenty-six in 1961) in Los Angeles does not seem to reflect any interaction with the Beat rebellion in general or with Venice West in particular. If the enforcers of social authority ("policemen to kneel to to pray to") demand abject obedience, Hickman pushes back in his poem with a masochistic rhapsody. His deployment of Tiresias as a prophetic figure who discerns his own complicity in the self-deceptions of desire and power appears in the poem's opening lines, in which he blends his own primal associations of sexual ambiguity and role-playing by invoking the blind Greek prophet's encounter with snakes.

RAIN RAIN TIRESIAS BLIND WORD RAIN
inside   clouds black wrap me rain
Tiresias   witchman   shapeshifter   shaman
    slurp up
wordpour   scare up your lifesong   out
from your god-dead birdgut vision Tiresian,   blow-
job-grum Tiresias word-rain/   up, rise
up/ your snakesplitting stick erect
high over memory snakebed

                        (*Tiresias* I:1)

Hickman's snakebed of memories includes a childhood warped by a period of deprivation and minimal sustenance in Bakersfield, sexual encounters with older men (one of whom appears to have gone to prison as a result, several arrests, and periods of incarceration. Coiling and uncoiling in a "rooming-house cell/selma at macadden // place/parking lot now," Hickman summons the "male snake of that time" to re-create the flailing chaos and abjection of his youth. (Hickman's portrait of self-debasement as well as his capacity to subject others to a ravenous id is entrenched in the harrowing decades before the Stonewall rebellion; West Hollywood as a potential social and political haven was too remote a prospect to be anything other than science fiction.) Anguish and remorse palpitate throughout "Tiresias"; "how can I go on" the narrator reproaches himself, in "Picasso Deathday Night," in the aftermath of having bullied a weak, hunchbacked drifter until the man begs for his life.

slow motion explosion lone grebe on the beach.
please don't kill me sir please don't kill me sir.
sick to my self hard work working inward.
(four colors azalea—don't forget it—distinct tart aftertastes.
    so then under what acid glare sequester my squalor-born
    deformed song body please sir don't
    kill me don't kill me sir please.
    w/just enough razor-slatch in levis crotch (now it's caught me/I cut
        wild left melrose blood surges turgid thru steel
        cockringd tight-thongd testes pufft-up high mass purple
        and early already danger-queen cruel   ripping
thru my sharkskinnd night don't like shark skinnd but ripping, ripping

    manzanita manzanita sycamore locoweed creosote oak lone gray
        grebe grebe grebe grebe grebe grebe grebe grebe

Although most of "Tiresias," including a long twenty-five-page account of his childhood and early adolescence, consists of passages from his life that seem to be almost cauterized from the kind of daily detail that assuages the poems of poets such as Frank O'Hara and James Schuyler, "Tiresias" at one point does manage to surmount Hickman's self-inflicted wounds and break free into the potential reconciliation of the poem itself as mediating companion:

I'm on my skates, Anacapa st. sidewalk, front of my aunt's house,
    in Santa Barbara,
    & I wd like to tell you what the sun felt then she felt cold.
I wd like to tell you what the moon felt like then he felt nothing
    & what can a song feel?
    spiders in the palmtrees, rattlers in the outhouse, something
    deep underneath the sidewalk when you put yr ear down, yeah.
poem, I drive without insurance for you I wash my socks for you I smoke
    to death.
mother dont die dont die I want to be near you as soon as I can, mother.
& poem, I am going to be to you what a man wd be to a man who wd
    love him: I swear.

Even as Hickman's topology makes frequent use of streets in Los Angeles, one of the poets he most frequently published as an editor also uses the city as an extension of her inner cartography. If Hickman's poems suggest a blend of Gerard Manley Hopkins and John Rechy, Wanda Coleman's poetry embeds itself in a fluent hybrid of Charles Bukowski, Gwendolyn Brooks, and James

Baldwin. Ultimately, like Hickman, Coleman's work defies easy categorization. The speaker in "Canned Fury" who claims "I am an outlaw, they assert / there's a ten-digit number stamped on my frontal lobe" is a familiar figure in her depictions of life in South Central Los Angeles. While the streets might not be named as the anaphora of "Where I live" rolls through an implicit urban cartography, the gaze of authority appears within the opening lines ("see that helicopter up there? Like / god's eye looking down on his children") and concludes in its seventh iteration with an image of a sexualized economy of subjugation:

> where I live
> at the lip of a big black vagina
> birthing nappy-headed pickaninnies every hour on the hour
> the county is her pimp and she can turn a trick
> swifter than any bitch that graced this earth
> she's the baddest piece of ass on the west coast
> named black los angeles

Successful pimps are never reluctant at imposing their will; the unpunished violence of the police force is annotated in Coleman's long poem, "South Central Los Angeles Death Trip 1982":

> without evidence to support the supposition
> they swore the twenty-one-year-old
> consumer was involved in the robbery of the
> popular Manchester Avenue chicken shack,
> [. . .]
>   they say an officer
> yelled freeze and this inexperienced
> young black hoodlum being unfamiliar with the
> procedure of how one freezes while being held face down
> on the sidewalk, hands cuffed behind one's back
> could not do so. therefore the inability to freeze
> under these conditions cost him his life.
> *(Mercurochrome* 146–147)

While Coleman as a poet might best be known for themes primarily concerned with the relentless oppression of her community, her poems also testify to the burden imposed on all those who confront the grueling redundancy of office labor and thereby retaliate as testimony against those who claim that the system of work and rewards is not suffering from its own version of "chronic renal failure." Coleman speaks for more than her own limited employment opportunities, but for all of those confined by systematic exclusion from professional training and equitable dignity:

> i am a clerk
> i am a medical billing clerk
> i sit here all day and type
> the same type of things all day long
> insurance claim forms
> for people who suffer chronic renal failure
> [. . .]
> for this service i am paid a subsistence salary
> i come in here each morning
> and bill the government for the people by the people
> for these patients
> i sit here and type
> is what i do and that's very important
> day after day/adrift in the river of forms
> that flows between my desk and the computer that
> prints out the checks
> there are few problems here. I am a very good clerk.
> i sit here all day and type
> i am a medical billing clerk
> i am a clerk
> i clerk
>
> ("Drone," *African Sleeping Sickness* 101–102)

Coleman's adamant gaze at the day job that yields a subsistence salary remits a cautionary note; the trimming down of the final three lines to a sentence in which the nominative category ("a clerk") switches to predicative agency suggests that something other than submissive abjection or deferential obedience is at work in this poem. The object in the predicate of the final sentence is withheld, hinting that those who expedite oppression are not escaping notice, even if for the time being they go unnamed, nor will she be passive in the face of aggression. Unlike the typist in "The Love Song of J. Alfred Prufrock," Coleman understands that the performative aspects of her daily life are intimately intertwined with the nature of language itself, which when delineated as poetry can allow its agent to disguise her plans for retaliation. If, as Julian Murphet observes, Coleman's poetry "registers a sense of the black body as the site of everyday violence in Los Angeles," he also acknowledges that her "corporeality is more versatile than most contemporary black aesthetics" (McNamara 106). Murphet attributes her adept thematic range to her willingness to engage in a profound medita-tion about the relationship of language to power and cites a portion of Cole-man's multi-part poem, "Essay on Language," as an example of the poetics at work in her self-portraits of communal and shared grievances. In a similar self-examination in an italicized poem at the beginning of her full-length collection, *Mercurochrome*, Coleman lifts her hands from the keyboard and extends them toward the reader's vulnerability:

> *thus you hold me*
> *frozen in your doubtful vision*
> *in your study of my brownness. believe*
> *my curious fingers. trust my*
> *daring fingers*
> *as they probe your opened wound*
> *to find a roundness*
> ("The Language Behind the Language" 15)

In the prison-house of language and ceaseless labor, Coleman's poems set up a field hospital in which she performs triage on those who most need succor and healing.

Hickman's success in being ranked with poets published by Knopf and Black Sparrow, the latter outfit having added Coleman to its list of authors, complemented the respect accorded my publication of Alicia Ostriker's *The Mother/Child Papers,* which was also achieving a modest amount of praise on the East Coast. Ostriker had lived in Los Angeles for a year while her husband, Jeremy Ostriker, worked in Pasadena at the Jet Propulsion Labora-tory. She began attending Beyond Baroque's poetry workshops, and her writ-ing immediately caught Krusoe's attention.[30] He told her to send me some poems, and I accepted them for issue number 9–10 of *Momentum.* In cor-responding with her, I learned that she had a work-in-progress about the birth of her third child during the Cambodian invasion launched by Rich-ard Nixon. The chance of publishing a book that would concentrate on a feminist analysis of motherhood impelled me to guarantee her that if she finished the manuscript, I would publish it. With that commitment in mind, Ostriker devoted herself to finishing the book, which combines both prose and poetry. As with Hickman's book, Ostriker's poetics provided a startling contrast with the kind of poetry that had been advocated by Daniel Halpern in his anthology *Young American Poets* or would be championed in Silliman's *In the American Tree.*

Ostriker was not the only poet outside of Los Angeles whose books I published. I had reviewed Jim Moore's first book, *The New Body*, in an issue of *Beyond Baroque New* and though like Ostriker, we had never met, decided to invite him to submit a manuscript, which included a long poem in the voice of an old female translator living in Prague. *What the Bird Sees* came out in 1978, and Moore traveled from Minnesota to Beyond Baroque to give a reading hosted by Jim Krusoe, whose second book, *Small Pianos*, I would also publish that year. While Kate Braverman's poetry in the 1970s showed the influence of Hickman's supercharged metabolism, Krusoe used the Momentum workshop as a testing ground in which he confronted Hickman's hypotactic privations by writing in an almost completely opposite manner. If Krusoe's first full-length book of poems, *History of the World*, favored a working-class persona with a strong dollop of understated humor, the poems in *Small Pianos* seemed to call upon the stark rhetoric and unflinching logic of Eastern European poetry in mulling over the fate of the human condition. Krusoe was exemplary as a poet and editor; not only did he guide Ostriker my way, but he also recommended the work of Len Roberts (1947–2007), whose first book, *Cohoes Theater*, was a finalist for the Elliston Prize after I published it in 1980. Roberts, who lived in Pennsylvania, went on to publish a total of ten full-length collections of his own poetry in addition to volumes of his translations of the Hungarian poet, Sándor Csoóri.

Distribution remained a nagging, almost overriding problem. Although an attempt to form a Los Angeles Poets' Co-op quickly floundered in the mid-seventies, the magazines and presses were eventually able to unite in an effort called the Literary Publishers of Southern California, which was headed up by Harley Lond of *Intermedia* magazine and Dan Ilves of *Stone-cloud*.[31] Over two dozen presses and little magazines contributed to a catalog and participated in a major book fair in downtown Los Angeles as a way of getting the word out, all of which encouraged other poets to begin their publishing. Literary Publishers of Southern California ended up as the starting point for other collaborations. Dennis Koran's Panjandrum Press had moved down to Los Angeles from San Francisco in the mid-1970s, and published several successful books, including one on cooking with garlic that helped balance with the economic zero-sum game of publishing poetry. I had admired both the book production and quality of Mudborn Press for several years. Judyl Mudfoot and Sasha Newborn had founded Mudborn in Santa Barbara, which was developing its own subdivision of the West Coast renaissance. John Martin was on the verge of moving Black Sparrow there, and Capra Press had developed an estimable position in the small press world. (See Clare Rabe's *Sicily Enough* and Ann Nietzche's *Windowlight* as novellas from this period that deserve more critical attention.) Not only were poets such as John Thomas, Bruce Boyd, and Jack Hirschman oscillating up and down the coast, but presses, too, were swimming up and downstream.

In the fall of 1979, Panjandrum, Mudborn, and Momentum put together a joint catalog that listed our forthcoming titles and backlist and provided an order sheet at the back. Mudfoot handset the type and printed it herself, and it remains one of my favorite souvenirs. As a document, it reinforces the larger cultural work we were all doing. Panjandrum devotes facing pages to promoting an anthology of gay poetry and an anthology of women's writing: *Angels of the Lyre,* edited by Winston Leyland was on the right hand side and *This Is Women's Work*, edited by Susan Efros, on the left. Panjandrum's other titles were by Robert Gluck, Madeline Gleason, David Gitin, Nanos Valaoritis, Edward Mycue, and Hunce Voelcker.

Among these presses, the most important was Little Caesar Press, and even though Dennis Cooper had a great deal more cultural and economic capital than I did, he was not spared the drudgery of operating an independent publishing project. On a daily basis he, too, faced the tedious labor of packaging books up to take to the post office and standing in line. My technique was to help myself to several extra paper bags every time I went to the grocery store, and whenever I was tired of reading manuscripts or typesetting or pasting up galleys or proofreading, I would relax a moment with the gratifying monotony of taking a pair of scissors and cutting along the seams of the grocery bag, cutting out the bottom, and then wrapping a half-dozen copies of a book up so that they would be somewhat protected when I shipped them fourth-class, book rate to a store in Philadelphia.[32] Cooper, perhaps, was less tired than I was when he tackled a stack of orders for books, but Little Caesar absorbed an extraordinary amount of his energy, and his willingness to speak up for a wide range of poets provided a sustaining camaraderie.

Coming Attractions: Beyond Baroque and the "Little Caesar" Generation

Perhaps the youngest, and most ambitious, poet to show up at Beyond Baroque in the 1970s was Dennis Cooper, who was born in Los Angeles in 1954, and had grown up in a wealthy part of Los Angeles. He had attended Pitzer, a private college near Pomona, where he studied with Bert Meyers and met Amy Gerstler. Meyers told him that if he wanted to be a poet, he should drop out of school and concentrate on poetry. Cooper took his advice, and went to Europe, and then came back to Los Angeles and studied with Ron Koertge at Pasadena City College. Cooper started his own poetry magazine, *Little Caesar*, in 1977, and it quickly gained a vociferous readership because of his eclectic editorial blend of articles on punk and popular music, film criticism, and a huge swath of casually deft poetry. He also caught the attention of older poets because of his unabashed but thoughtful enthusiasm for how lively the scene was in the late 1970s and for his willingness to be specific about his favorite local poets.

A friend of Cooper's named Terry Cannon was publishing a monthly arts newspaper named *GOSH!* in Pasadena. Cannon published a series of articles on Los Angeles poetry by Cooper, including an article that described in detail the poetry reading that celebrated the publication of *The Streets Inside* on January 14, 1979.

> All ten poets in the collection read for twelve to fifteen minutes each . . . The very large crowd, which spilled out onto the sidewalk in front of Intellectuals & Liars, was in rapt attention throughout. The richness of the event was moving in a true and undeniable way, being a fine reflection of the wealth of talent and ideas in the Los Angeles poetry scene. . . . This reading is one of the finest defenses for the power of the vocalization of poetry and for the amount of talent among Los Angeles poets that I've ever witnessed. There is a feeling among many local authors now that there is a renaissance of some sort on the rise in this city, both in literary quality and interest. ("The Poetry Reading," *GOSH!*, February 1979)

Cooper plunged into the scene and took it to another level of accomplishment. Under the imprint of Little Caesar Press, he began publishing books by poets who had been living elsewhere, but had decided that Los Angeles now offered possibilities for non-university poets not available elsewhere, which of course included "the Industry." Michael Lally, for instance, had recently moved to Los Angeles in hopes of developing an acting career, and he managed to get some roles on shows such as *N.Y.P.D. Blue*. In addition to Lally's *Hollywood Magic*, Little Caesar Press published large, handsome collections of poems by art critic Peter Schjeldahl and Tim Dlugos as well as Lewis MacAdams who had moved to Los Angeles from Bolinas, yet one more instance of the fluidity of the West Coast as the headwaters of the revisionist canon. Although he first gained notice as a poet on the St. Mark's scene, by the 1970s MacAdams was primarily associated with the West Coast, where he became involved with a variety of ecological causes, including the founding of the Los Angeles River Project.

In 1980 Cooper brought together the best of a younger group of poets from across the country into an anthology entitled *Coming Attractions*. This was not the first anthology to use Los Angeles poets as the epicenter for its table of contents, but it was the most effective in making a case for how the city's poets were becoming representative of an emergence in other cities, such as Chicago, of a post-Vietnam generation of poets. In Cooper's anthology, poets elsewhere were not cast as the lead actors in the drama of contemporary canonization of "the next generation"; rather, in Cooper's estimate, Los Angeles poets were every bit as deserving of serious attention. By juxtaposing the work of Elaine Equi and Jerome Sala, both of whom at that time lived in Chicago, with younger Los Angeles poets such as Jack Skelley, Bob Flanagan, and David Trinidad, *Coming Attractions* suggested that a tipping point had been attained in integrating a new generation of poets. The anthology shimmered with youthfulness; Cooper was more than happy to inform others that another underground was in a hurry, and readers who wanted to be in the know had better not waste any time in learning about the most promising new poets.[33]

Flanagan and Skelley had formed a band, *Planet of Toys*, that played around town at the various clubs that proliferated during post-punk/new wave scene of the late 1980s. Flanagan's lyrics addressed his slowly deteriorating medical condition with mock irony: "It's fun to be dead" was the chorus of one song that had an upbeat melody. Flanagan had actually surpassed everybody's expectations: the average life span of a person with cystic fibrosis was less than a quarter century; his sister had died of it at the age of twenty-two. In his early thirties, Flanagan managed to write and play music and keep his sense of humor with a self-deprecating grace that inspired the community. His work became more and more autobiographical, and he eventually became known as a performance artist influenced by Chris Burden. However, Flanagan was also one of the best poetry teachers in Los Angeles. He led the Beyond Baroque workshop for many years in the 1980s, keeping it going when there was declining support for the institution. When he finally died in the mid-1990s, he had nearly established a world record for longevity for a person with cystic fibrosis.

Cooper's success with *Little Caesar* inspired several poets in his group to begin their own magazines. Jack Skelley had become the head of New-Comp Graphics at Beyond Baroque and was in charge of booking time for the several dozen poets and presses that used those facilities. Skelley started his own magazine, *Barney*, which featured the work of numerous Los Angeles poets, including Amy Gerstler, whose work was not included in *Coming Attractions*, though even at that early point the very fine balance of tone in her voice marked her as someone far too mature to be condescended to as an ingénue. Cooper had met her when they were both students at Pitzer College, and he published her first chapbook, *Yonder*. As we all expected, her work continued to gain widespread attention and respect, including a much-deserved National Book Award in 1991. In any future critical book that focuses on Los Angeles poetry between 1968 and 2008, her poetry will merit at least as much space as I have devoted to Don Gordon or William Pillin.

The sustained importance of the poets associated with Little Caesar to her literary development can be noted in her inclusion of Cooper, David Trinidad, and Tim Dlugos in the 2010 edition of *Best Poems of the Year* anthology series, which she co-edited with David Lehman. This culmination of a lifetime of closely reading the work of her peers reflects a process that began when she co-edited a literary magazine called *Snap* in the early 1980s, whose contributors overlapped with Skelley's *Barney*.

Although Cooper had financial resources in personal family money far surpassing any other Los Angeles poetry editor, he still had to do an immense amount of the production labor himself. At that time, Cooper was probably the fastest one-fingered typist on the West Coast, and he poured extraordinary amounts of time into typesetting issues and books at NewComp Graphics Center. Distribution also required a substantial commitment of time. On one hand, many independent bookstores in Los Angeles, such as George Sand, Chatterton's, and Intellectuals & Liars in Santa Monica, stocked and sold small press publications and held poetry readings. On the other hand, each of these stores required constant stocking, which only happened because editors such as Cooper drove from store to store with their stock.

Cooper's gregarious acuity and taste enabled him to inherit the Friday night reading series from Jim Krusoe, who had managed to nurture it to a vibrant pitch without any budgetary support whatsoever. Cooper, on the other hand, was able to guarantee poets from out of town the remuneration of a specific reading fee, although the need for Beyond Baroque to show income from their events in order to apply for grants required that the institution relinquish its policy of free admission. The ticket price was still low, however, and few people in the audience seemed to mind paying. Ironically, the poets ended up often getting less money under the new policy, since the previous practice of passing the hat would often yield more than fifty dollars. The influx of out-of-town poets accelerated. Sometimes they would read at one of the bookstores, and also at Beyond Baroque, and other times they would read at a store and then return to read at Beyond Baroque. Ted Greenwald's first reading in Los Angeles, for instance, was at Intellectuals & Liars bookstore, where he was paired with Kate Braverman. He then came back in the early 1980s to read at Beyond Baroque at Cooper's invitation, as did several Language poets based in San Francisco, including Barrett Watten, Carla Harryman, Kit Robinson, Steve Benson, and Ron Silliman, the last of whom stayed over at my apartment after a memorable talk and reading in 1981.

Cooper's own work was beginning to attract major critical attention. His second large collection of poems, *The Tenderness of the Wolves*, was published by Crossing Press in 1982, and he became the second Los Angeles poet to be nominated for the Los Angeles Times Book Award for poetry. As with

Hickman's *Great Slave Lake Suite*, Cooper did not win, but a second nomination for a Los Angeles area poet against a field of nationally recognized poets indicated that the recognition of Hickman's book was not a fluke. The question in the community seemed to be not "Are we as good as . . . ?" but why the National Endowment for the Arts seemed to rig the panels with writers who year after year passed over the applications of Los Angeles-based writers. Theoretically, the readings were blind to the names and locations of the writers. By 1982, though, none of the poets in *The Streets Inside*, who went on to appear in my next anthology, *"Poetry Loves Poetry,"* had won a creative writing fellowship, despite repeated applications, and it was extraordinarily difficult to believe that our work was getting a fair reading; many poets in Los Angeles regarded the NEA's literature program as an antidemocratic bureaucracy, and the agency's failure to address the damage done by the notoriously contentious panel of 1979 only reinforced those suspicions.

Other poets in Los Angeles who were not part of what appeared to be a new inner circle at Beyond Baroque began to grumble at their reduced stature at Beyond Baroque. After years of building a scene into prominence, they felt they were being relegated to supporting roles and walk-on parts. In some ways, it was impossible to tell exactly who belonged to what group any longer. The Wednesday night workshop split into two groups, each claiming the title of "Venice Poetry Workshop." One group, which included poets such as Frances Dean Smith (a.k.a. "Franceye") who had participated in the Wednesday night workshop for many years, moved less than fifty yards away, to meet in a room at the old Venice jail, which had been converted into a visual arts center (S.P.A.R.C., Social and Public Art Resource Center). They published two saddle-stitched anthologies, *Net Weight* and *Rhyme Scheme*, each one informing the reader that they constituted the Venice Poetry Workshop. Their split with Beyond Baroque, however, was not complete. Each chapbook was typeset at Beyond Baroque.

The rift in the Wednesday night workshop was in part a result of a change in the administrative side of Beyond Baroque, which was also to have serious consequences for Beyond Baroque's relationship with third-world and minority communities in Los Angeles. In 1977 Manual "Manazar" Gamboa, a poet on parole from San Quentin showed up at Beyond Baroque, working as a volunteer. By 1979 he had become administrative vice president, and when Smith resigned as president, Gamboa took over and immediately made several significant changes. *NEW* magazine became *Obras*, and the reading series concentrated on third-world readers. Unfortunately, attendance declined precipitously, but even more foreboding was Gamboa's lack of action in applying for grants. The board of directors decided to replace Gamboa with Jocelyn Fisher, who had been working as the Beyond Baroque librarian.

Fisher started another publication, *Poetry News,* which lasted for almost twenty issues. One of the most controversial articles was a piece by Cooper, "The New Factionalism," in which he remonstrated with the "first generation" of Los Angeles poets for being unwilling to be more publicly assertive about their literary ambitions. Much of the acrimony that arose after Cooper's article on "The New Factionalism" appeared to involve different estimates of the value of publishing in "local" magazines. Many poets in Los Angeles believed that appearing in *Bachy* was as commendable as having a poem in *Epoch* or *Paris Review.* If a poet such as Kate Braverman appeared in the *Paris Review* and *Bachy,* as well as *Momentum,* the local consensus was that these were all equally commendable feats. If this equivalency were to be perceived elsewhere in the country as West Coast arrogance, we regarded such a reaction as proof that the East Coast was in no mood to grant Los Angeles poets a seat at the table as equals. Their motive seemed plain enough: L.A. was already in charge of popular culture, and it simply wouldn't do to allow them any more power. Indeed, the lack of anything but the most token representation by Los Angeles-based poets on NEA peer panels for creative writing grants during the past forty years has been an egregious example of unwillingness to accept Southern California as full colleagues.

Beyond Baroque continued to struggle financially. It did acquire a new typesetting machine, a Compugraphic 7500 that made preprint work a great deal easier since everything that was keyboarded was recorded on a floppy disk, but the number of typefaces did not especially increase. The building itself deteriorated. The smell of mildew permeated the entrance hall. Mice ran with impunity across the workshop floor and hopped into trash cans in daylight in search of crumbs from discarded chip bags. Two young cats, Oops and Boots, were brought in by Alexandra Garrett, and they eventually stemmed the tide. Other infestations were more determined. Beyond Baroque attempted to organize a poetry component for the 1984 Olympic Arts Festival, but United States Secretary of State George Schultz led an attack on UNESCO, which would have provided a large chunk of the festival's funding. When the United States withdrew its funding of that sponsoring organization, poetry became the only major art form not included in the Olympic Arts Festival. Compared with the horror that Schultz and his associates, such as Negroponte, unleashed in Central America, the cancellation of a poetry festival is hardly a criminal act, yet the connection between the two is not negligible.

When Cooper departed for New York in 1984, no one involved with Beyond Baroque realized that the next quarter century would be far more of a struggle. The budgets at Beyond Baroque may not have seemed abundant during Krusoe's and Cooper's tenure as directors of the reading series, but in retrospect they came to be viewed as rivers of milk and honey. In 1985 the Literature Program of the National Endowment for the Arts chose to award the Poetry Project at St. Mark's in New York a grant and reject Beyond Baroque's application. Rumors circulated in Los Angeles of displeasure of NEA officials at the sight of political posters at Beyond Baroque concerning antinuclear weapon demonstrations. Regardless of the reason, Beyond Baroque faced the most severe crisis of its existence. The band *X* gave a benefit concert, which cleared over ten thousand dollars. The concert kept the organization going, though it was in a rather dilapidated condition. When news arrived of the NEA decision not to fund Beyond Baroque, poet Jim Cushing wrote an article in which he described Fisher's office: ". . . a square area of plaster the size of a bulletin board has fallen off the wall, exposing the boards. Beneath this ruin is a green plastic wastebasket full of rainwater. A sign over her desk reads, 'Metaphors be with you'" (*Reader* 8).[34]

Having rallied disparate communities of poets behind Beyond Baroque and led it back from the verge of collapse, Fisher decided to attend graduate school and started to scout for a replacement. Her eventual successor, Dennis Phillips, was an unlikely candidate, in part because he had not been particularly involved with Beyond Baroque until the mid-1980s crisis. Phillips, born in Los Angeles in 1954, grew up in the city and attended Cal Arts in the early 1970s, where he very briefly studied with Clayton Eshleman. Until he returned in 1976 from graduate school at New York University, however, Phillips had never attended any events whatsoever at Beyond Baroque, and he initially came into contact with the organization only when he unsuccessfully submitted a manuscript to its book contest in 1976. Although Hickman serialized his long poem, "The Frontier," in several issues of *Bachy* magazine, Phillips did not regard the region's poets as hospitable to his post-Eliot poetics, and he only sporadically attended readings at Beyond Baroque. At various points he had met poets such as Amy Gerstler, and knew Benjamin Weissman, the new reading series director, although that acquaintance was mainly because of their shared matriculation from California Institute of the Arts. When Phillips accepted the post, his first book, *The Hero Is Nothing*, had just been published by Kajun Press in San Francisco.

Despite the expectation of a difficult tenure, Phillips accepted Fisher's offer, although he recounts that it was contingent on the willingness of Amy Gerstler to serve as assistant director. Over the years Gerstler made many contributions to Beyond Baroque, not all of which I am free to recount, but certainly part of her assistance was to provide some advice to Weissman about which poets to select for the reading series. Weissman's knowledge about contemporary poetry was extremely limited, and he depended on poets such as Gerstler, Vangelisti, and Phillips to keep the series abreast of developments.

Phillips maintains that Weissman's tenure as the reading series director actually marked a maturation of the series in a national and international sense. Although Weissman at that time lacked Cooper's onstage star power and charisma, he was similarly adept offstage in bolstering Beyond Baroque's national presence by securing readings by poets such as John Ashbery and Philip Levine and fiction writers such as Ann Beattie, Charles Baxter, and Raymond Carver, who gave readings to standing-room-only audiences. Weissman certainly did not exclude local poets from his series, but appearances by the oldest members of Beyond Baroque's poetic community did become more infrequent and their introductions were often perfunctory. The grousing of the region's poets, however, was the least of Phillips's problems.

"The first day on the job, I was sitting in the office and our bookkeeper, Nancy Krusoe, comes in and says, 'We don't have any money.'" Phillips went to work on applying for the next possible NEA grant and flew to Washington, D.C., not so much in hopes of lobbying directly, but with the intention of making Beyond Baroque visible to arts administrators. Phillips believed it was important that the NEA understand that Beyond Baroque was a more complicated site of poetics than the image of Venice, as portrayed on MTV video clips, might suggest. Beyond Baroque won back its funding, but NEA grant money was only sufficient enough to enable Phillips to play an incredibly stressful month-to-month game of paying bills.[35]

One example of the problems that confronted Phillips is the bookstore, which served as an outlet for small presses. In mid-December 1986, Phillips wrote Hickman and asked him to be patient in terms of past due payments for sales of *Temblor*, which by then had four issues out. "I think I've solved the bookstore's problems without having to close the thing down. There is someone who will run the bookstore (not just do the books once a month) on a voluntary basis until the $3000 debt is paid off . . . please be patient for a few more weeks until David Smith gets used to the whole thing."[36] The bookstore worked on the same 60-40 split that was the common arrangement of publishers and bookstores, which would indicate that the store in the mid-1980s was managing to serve its audience. The forbearance of small presses in collecting payment, and still providing the store with deliveries to restock the shelves, also would serve as an indirect contribution to Beyond Baroque during the crisis period when the loss of NEA funding had nearly led to Beyond Baroque ceasing operations.

The primary challenge that ended up absorbing the bulk of Phillips's attention was control of the building that housed Beyond Baroque. The original lease with the city permitted Beyond Baroque to sublet a portion of the building, and Manazar Gamboa had signed an agreement with Los Angeles Theater Works (LATW), giving them some space on the western side of the second floor. When Phillips took over, Fisher had mentioned to him that Susan Lowenberg coveted the entire building, and Fisher's warning proved prophetic. As LATW achieved a well-deserved reputation in the early 1950s for producing award-winning plays in Los Angeles, such as *Greek* by Stephen Berkoff, it began lobbying for the performance space on the first floor, and when the lease came up for renewal, it launched an all-out campaign to become equal tenants of the building. LATW viewed the performance room as space that should be available to them as cotenants of the building; Lowenberg referred to that space as the "community room" whenever she talked with Phillips, and Phillips constantly had to correct her: "No, that's Beyond Baroque's performance space." The conflict eventually involved a legal battle, and fortunately, Phillips was able to secure the assistance of a major downtown legal firm on a pro bono basis. After losing its funding, Beyond Baroque had seemed vulnerable and without major allies, while Los Angeles Theater Works was enjoying its high-profile connections with the film and theater industry in Los Angeles.[37] The arrival of a legal challenge in response to LATW's incursions under the letterhead of an important law firm underscored that Beyond Baroque was not without resources, and finally the matter was settled, if not to their mutual satisfaction. One might best describe their truce as a zero-sum game. Both organizations remained in place, and this skirmish resulted in reaffirming Beyond Baroque's control of the building as the master tenant. Phillips managed to stymie LATW's expansion at the Old Venice City Hall, but it absorbed an enormous amount of energy at a time when Beyond Baroque was on a month-to-month financial basis.

The performance space itself began to alter. Phillips shared with a number of other Los Angeles poets, including Hickman and myself, an affinity for theater and music, and he brought in a playwright, Wayne Linberg, who set about making the space for the readings also capable of being used for theater. He painted all the interior walls black and obtained a set of theatrical lights. The seating was still a set of metal folding chairs that ranked as the most uncomfortable seating for any long-running arts organization on the West Coast, but the performance space itself was slowly being altered.

Other shifts were also taking place in the organization. NewComp Graphics Center began to fade as a production resource for local poets, although it made an important contribution to the survival of Clayton Eshleman's *Sulfur* magazine in the mid-1980s. Eshleman had already logged some time in Los Angeles when he taught at California Institute of the Arts in the late 1960s and early 1970s, and he returned to Los Angeles to teach at Cal Tech in the 1980s, where with institutional backing he launched a successor to his earlier magazine, *Caterpillar*, which remains one of the great literary magazines of the twentieth century. *Sulfur*, though, quickly ran into censorship problems and lost its funding. Eshleman was on record as not having much respect for the poets who had labored to develop a local infrastructure. "Los Angeles poets want to be known as a school in order to increase their visibility," Eshleman once told a journalist, "to have an identity larger than any one of them could possibly have individually. . . . There is no Los Angeles poetry. Los Angeles is a suitcase city. I just happen to live here." When Eshleman needed a cheap means of getting his next issues produced, however, Beyond Baroque's NewComp Graphics Center provided *Sulfur* with the assistance it needed to endure and eventually flourish after Eshleman moved the magazine to Michigan. Eshleman is a poet whom very few readers or critics of American poetry remain neutral about. Phillips worked as a book review editor of *Sulfur*, and says that he learned a great deal from him. No doubt Eshleman will be the subject of a biography some day. He has produced a major body of work, and there are more than enough lively anecdotes to keep the narrative interesting. "Clayton's a master bridge-builder," observed Dennis Phillips in a conversation with me one afternoon, "and a master bridge-burner." In my case, the bridge never got built, let alone incinerated.[38]

Eshleman was one of the few poets in Los Angeles who declined to contribute to my second anthology, *"Poetry Loves Poetry,"* which serves as a repository for the multitude of communities of poets in Los Angeles at the time. In addition to the poets featured in my first anthology, I added poets such as Bob Flanagan, Jack Skelley, Peter Cashorali, and David Trinidad, who had been featured in Dennis Cooper's *Coming Attractions*. *"Poetry Loves Poetry"* also gave a number of Los Angeles poets their anthological debuts. Wanda Coleman, Amy Gerstler, Martha (Lifson) Ronk, Suzanne Lummis, Charles Webb, Aleida Rodríguez, and Doren Robbins have all gone on to achieve significant acclaim. In joining ranks with Charles Bukowski, Gerald Locklin, Jack Grapes, and Ron Koertge—as well as recent arrivals such as Lewis MacAdams, Michael Lally, and Peter Schjeldahl, a vivid "multicentricity" began to be visible to readers in Los Angeles as well as elsewhere on the West Coast.[39] MacAdams, who remains a resident of Los Angeles, has contributed to the emergence of an ecological poetry in Los Angeles through his advocacy of the Los Angeles River Project.

"Poetry Loves Poetry" came out in the summer of 1985, shortly after Phillips had taken over Beyond Baroque. I chose to use the dedication page of *"Poetry Loves Poetry"* to acknowledge George Drury Smith for the gift of affiliation with dozens of poets throughout the city. Although local reviewers pounced on that dedication as evidence of cliquishness, the anthology presented poets from all over the region, many of whom had ambivalent relationships with Beyond Baroque. The enormous variety of poetry was, in fact, the book's most intriguing feature to David St. John, who arrived in Los Angeles two years

after it appeared and found it to be best guide to a scene that had seemed much more one-dimensional from a distance. Unlike his colleague at USC, Carol Muske-Dukes, St. John regarded Beyond Baroque as an integral part of the maturation of contemporary poetry. In part, his level of comfort with Beyond Baroque as a contact zone probably could be attributed to his roots in California. He had grown up in Fresno, and as a young man made trips to San Francisco, and admired the music coming out of the canyons of Los Angeles. He moved to Los Angeles knowing of Beyond Baroque and found in *"Poetry Loves Poetry"* a repository of the layers and interstices of poetry in Los Angeles, which upon direct contact proved to be intriguingly convoluted.[40]

If one were to compare *"Poetry Loves Poetry"* with an anthology such as *The Morrow Anthology of Younger Poets*, which was also published in 1985, the difference in the diversity of the work would be an immediate distinguishing aspect. By diversity, I am referring to more than rhythmic variations or the tonal connotations of imagery, but to the willingness of the poets to take on subjects outside obvious, particular themes with which they might be associated as a result of identity politics. One critic, who was on the whole favorable in her judgment of the book, claimed that she was unable to find any lesbian poetry in *"Poetry Loves Poetry."* It remains unclear to me why it was important to make certain that the poets I included could have their gender preferences extrapolated by readers through imagery that corresponded with a social identity. It was much more important to me to have poets represented by the dialogue within the various communities. My decision to select poems by lesbian poets such as Eloise Klein Healy and Aleida Rodríguez that focused on overtly political themes reflected my desire to insert a layer of the community's history of protest into the anthology. Healy's poem, "El Playon de Chanmico," for instance, invoked that evening the poets of Los Angeles had gathered to protest the undeclared war in Central America.

Although the acceleration of my publication projects into the ranks of Knopf and Black Sparrow as a book prize contestant would not have been possible if Beyond Baroque had not, in both the first and last instance, been there as a workshop and as a production facility in order to make these books more than the manuscripts of a passionate coterie, other sites of literary activism were also contributing to a discourse of resistance to neocolonialist agendas aligned with the nuclear weapons industry. *"Poetry Loves Poetry,"* the last major project of my brief, if intense, enterprise, more than quintupled the number of contributors to *The Streets Inside* and implicitly acknowledged the contribution of other cultural projects such as the Woman's Building. In looking back at this volume, which is now a quarter-century old, I am pleased by how poems that were first published in *"Poetry Loves Poetry"* have remained present and available to contemporary readers. Suzanne Lummis's

"Letter to my Assailant," for instance, can be found in Charles Webb's *Stand Up Poetry*. Lummis's poem is a model of the Stand Up in how it manages to treat a grim subject with passionate irony.

> On such occasions
> one comes to know someone spectacularly fast.
> Even with your unfriendly arm at my throat
> you could hide nothing from me.
> [. . .]
> "I can't breathe," I gasped,
> and you loosened your hold.
> I suppose I should have been grateful,
> instead I left impatient with men,
> with their small favors.
> I suppose you felt the same about me.
> You'd no sooner reached through my torn blouse
> when my screams made you bolt.
> We leapt from each other
> like two hares released from a trap. Oh, oh,
> something's not right between men and women.
> Perhaps we talked too much,
> or did we leave too much unsaid?
> When you ripped my shirt mumbling
> "I don't want to hurt you,"
> I replied, "That's what they all say."
> I'll admit I was glib if you'll admit
> you were insensitive. Look,
> the world is brimming with happy couples,
> benign marriages, with men and women
> who've adjusted to each other's defects.
> Couldn't we adjust to each other's defects?
> I'll begin by trying harder not to forget you,
> to remember more clearly
> your approximate height, your brown shirt,
> which I described to the police.
> Our encounter must stand out in our minds,
> distinct from all others.
> I never intended
> all this to become blurred in my memory,
> to confuse you with other men.
>
>   (*In Danger* 42–43)

A quarter century after I first published this poem, I do not necessarily expect readers to correlate this poem with the activism of Suzanne Lacy, a performance artist associated with the Woman's Building, who staged a major protest about the endemic violence women are subjected to on a daily basis, regardless of whether one characterizes this period as postmodern.

Phillips voluntarily cut short his term as director of Beyond Baroque, which cannot be said of his successor. He had been working simultaneously as an instructor at a local art college and decided that he needed more time to write. In choosing the next administrator, Phillips focused on addressing the organization's perennial need for fiscal stability and decided to recruit someone who had been successful as a fund-raiser for arts organizations. The candidate who was selected, D. B. Finnegan, received a rave review from Margaret Jenkins in San Francisco, but Finnegan proved to be "a disaster" in Phillips's estimate. "Part of the problem was that nobody respected her because she didn't know poetry or literature. She had run a dance company."[41] Finnegan left about the same time that Weissman resigned as reading series director. In general, no one remembers this period as one in which Beyond Baroque managed to distinguish itself. "The oscillations at Beyond Baroque have always had an impact on the community. As a centerpiece, Beyond Baroque has always been a point of reference, and a point of reaction," David St. John observed, and Finnegan's period as director was mostly a point of reaction.[42]

Suzanne Lummis, for instance, had studied with Philip Levine at CSU Fresno, and moved to Los Angeles in the late 1970s with hopes of an acting career. While she did write and also perform in award-winning plays, her vision of Los Angeles poetry coincided with a demand by many of her peers in the city for an exceptionally literate performance of texts. Beginning in 1989, Lummis provided the faltering scene with a splendid series of annual poetry festivals that took place throughout the city and displaced if not quite replaced Beyond Baroque as the center of poetic self-definition in Los Angeles. After the fifth festival, she co-edited an anthology with Charles Webb that in Southern California resulted in a pair of anthologies that further shifted the epicenter away from Venice.

In between "Poetry Loves Poetry" and Grand Passion, however, two other anthologies contributed to the scenes to the move around from Venice. Blair Allen's two-volume anthology, Snow Summits in the Sun, received virtually no critical attention, even in Los Angeles, and yet Allen's vision as an editor deserves belated acknowledgment as being among the better underground efforts of that decade. In a certain sense, Allen turns the tables on what might be thought of as a typical East Coast editorial approach, i.e., pick out a core group of New York-based poets and select poets from elsewhere to fit that model. Allen instead focuses on Southern California poets and performance artists: Guillermo Gomez-Pena, Juan Felipe Herrera, Wanda Coleman, Julia Stein, Sesshu Foster, Kate Braverman, and Mark Salerno, and then adds other poets, such as Ivan Arguelles, Jon Davis, Miriam Sagan, A. D. Winans, and Laurel Speer to provide a sense of headlands beyond the coast. Two of the poets included by Allen, a Korean War veteran, Sesshu Foster and Michelle T. Clinton, the latter of whose work I had included in *"Poetry Loves Poetry,"* in turn edited their own anthology, along with Naomi Quinonez, *Invocation L.A.: Multicultural Poetry in Los Angeles.*[43]

Tosh Berman, the son of Wallace Berman, took over Beyond Baroque after Finnegan's resignation, and became not only its administrative director, but its simultaneous artistic director, a conflation of roles that eventually influenced the organization's return to its emphasis on a center for poetic activity. First, though, Beyond Baroque had to crawl yet again out of a crisis in the mid-1990s that was not so much a case of a wolf at the door as that the sheep did not care whether Beyond Baroque existed as a refuge. One of the members of the board of directors, Fred Dewey, kept the doors open on the basis of sheer willpower, and slowly the word got out that poets were back in favor. Dewey, born and raised on the Upper East Side of New York City, had attended Brown University and is not a poet himself, but is passionately devoted to the art and its social possibilities.

Dewey believed that the best chance for Beyond Baroque's survival required that Berman's compression of the leadership roles be maintained as a practical necessity.[44] Funding for arts organizations continued to decrease, and money to pay two people was simply not available. In being the single individual most associated with Beyond Baroque during the past fifteen years, Dewey has restored a sense of continuity and stability that probably proved to be the deciding factor in enabling the organization to have its lease on the building renewed for another twenty-five years. The challenges to getting this lease extended were extraordinarily formidable. The original situation that allowed Beyond Baroque to begin its occupancy of public space was directly related to a fiscal crisis. Capitalism's self-indulgent privileging of greed as a civic virtue returned with a hurricane-cycle vengeance at the end of the first decade of the twenty-first century. In addition to yet another obstinate effort by Los Angeles Theater Works to acquire the building for itself, Dewey had to negotiate with individuals at Los Angeles City Hall who had other ideas for how city property might be used.[45] Dewey's accomplishment deserves as much detailed acknowledgment as Stuart Perkoff's foray into establishing a Beat coffeehouse, but it will fall to some other writer to undertake this account. In the meantime, suffice it to say that Dewey's retention of the Old

Venice City Hall for Beyond Baroque so that it can hold poetry events and workshops on any day of the week it chooses stands in contrast to the unfortunate situation at the St. Mark's Poetry Project, which for all of its much deserved legendary status, must still accommodate itself to a reading schedule of Monday and Wednesday. Both Beyond Baroque and the Poetry Project face demographic challenges in the future. The local population within walking distance of both venues has transformed during the past forty years from a built-in audience of young people primarily interested in alternative culture to post-gentrification neighborhoods dominated by individual commitment to portfolios of property values. Although Los Angeles has the reputation of being the city difficult to traverse, New York City is far from being a zone of instantaneous journeys: the non-Manhattan boroughs have increasingly valorized their own arts centers. Dewey has faced similar problems in terms of coordinating programming and potential audiences.

One of Dewey's first projects was to embed Beyond Baroque into the history of Venice by having walls with brief excerpts of poems by poets associated with the neighborhood included as part of a project to rebuild the facilities such as public showers for beachgoers. Dewey's choice of poets reflects the actual history of the area and defies the prediction made by John Maynard on the first page of his book about Venice West: "If there are no plaques dedicated to the poets and artists who made it famous as an enclave of the Beat Generation in the late fifties . . . , it is because if they were still around in force, respectable people would undoubtedly be making plans to chase them away." The desire to exclude an active community such as Perkoff, Boyd, Thomas, Rios, and Lipton from Venice is evident in its lack of public housing for artists, but Dewey's commitment to a collage of poetic fragments as a public genealogy of Venice coteries serves both a didactic purpose as well as aesthetic judgments. The poetry of Manazar Gamboa, who remains the only person of color to have held a director position at Beyond Baroque, is alongside the work of Exene Cervenka, who worked at Beyond Baroque as a typesetter and librarian, as well as the poetry of Linda Albertano and Jim Morrison on one wall; Stuart Perkoff, John Thomas, Bruce Boyd, Frank Rios abut another part of what Dewey calls the "oral history" of the neighborhood glyphed into the plasticity of solemn congelation.

The dedication of this public memorial remains a fond memory for Dewey, whose first years in charge of Beyond Baroque are fraught with what he characterizes as self-inflicted turmoil. He had been asked to join Beyond Baroque's board of directors in 1994 by Richard Grossman and Luis Alfaro, and within a few months they asked him to consider being board president. His lack of experience led to a joint appointment of two artistic directors, which proved to be so rambunctious a period that the board of directors ended up "in complete melt-down." Dewey ended up having to put the organization back together piece by piece, working without any salary for two and a half years.⁴⁶

The other major project was a collaboration between Dewey and Michael Datcher, who was the director of the World Stage at Leimert Park, in which they set up a series of events in an art festival that involved exchanges between each of the organizations at the turn of the century. "The World Beyond" proved successful enough that it managed to get some funding for a second go-round, but the brunt of finding financial support for these collaborations fell almost entirely on Dewey. Barely holding on itself, Beyond Baroque found itself in the position of not only competing on a national level for scarce support, but having to share what little it could get with other equally needy collectives. "Every single penny of the grants went to the authors (who read) in the festivals," Dewey said. "There was no administrative money whatsoever. But nevertheless, it started dialogues between institutions at a moment when nothing was happening in terms of political or cultural innovation."⁴⁷

Dewey expects to continue booking the reading series so that poets as diverse as Will Alexander, Robert Grenier, Rae Armantrout, Stephen Rodefer, Patti Smith, Laurel Ann Bogen, Charles Webb, and Michael C. Ford feel welcome and appreciated. If sufficient funding could be found, he would like to continue publishing *Beyond Baroque*, the last number of which appeared in 2004. He managed to publish books by Ammiel Alcalay and Simone Forti, but many hoped-for collections of poetry continue to languish far beyond the initially proposed publication dates. In the meantime, he has concentrated on expanding and cataloging Beyond Baroque's small press library and the chapbook archive, which is certainly the largest such collection in the United States outside of academic collections. The most important aspect of his future commitment to Beyond Baroque, however, is his desire to keep the space as open as possible to the development of coteries as they transform their intersubjectivity into the agency of self-empowered public space.

FIVE

Fault-Line Communities

Multiculturalism, Stand Up, Spoken Word, and the Maverick Avant-Garde in Los Angeles

Beyond Baroque may seem the cynosure of Los Angeles poetry in recent decades, but for many poets in Southern California, it served only as intermittent headquarters or point of cultural engagement. Numerous artistic collectives and projects gained some measure of social traction in Los Angeles, especially after 1970, and poets also sought outlets at some distance inland as well as along the coast. Dolores Hayden's epilogue to *The Power of Place* points to "the urban places that house ordinary working people" as the first place one should look to find "ethnic and women's history as the missing mainstream experience" (244). One book that addresses at least a portion of Hayden's suggestion is *The Sons and Daughters of Los: Culture and Community in L.A.*, a collection of essays edited by David James. The Woman's Building, Highways Performance Space, the World Stage in Leimert Park, and Self-Help Graphics in East Los Angeles are just a few of the artistic organizations whose histories reveal the diversity that Hayden espouses. Indeed, the contrast between the center and the margin—and the difficulty that the narcissistic panopticon of literary theory has in perceiving beyond its immediate radius of critique—can be illuminated by a juxtaposition of Jameson's famous analysis of the Westin Bonaventure Hotel, in the first chapter of *Postmodernism, or, the Cultural Logic of Late Capitalism*, and the history of the Woman's Building, which existed for most of its history a mere three miles away from the Westin Bonaventure. One would never suspect from reading Jameson's essay that an alternative to the whirligig of postmodern entrapment had its doors wide open to those who yearned to engage in radical critique.

The Woman's Building was initially a project of visual artists. According to Laura Meyer's "The Los Angeles Woman's Building and the Feminist

Art Community 1973–1991," the Woman's Building was an outgrowth of the Fresno Feminist Art Program, which was founded by Judy Chicago. In the fall of 1971, Chicago returned to the Los Angeles area, where she had worked as an artist in the 1960s, and began teaching at California Institute of the Arts in Valencia. A pair of feminist faculty members, Arlene Raven and Sheila de Bretteville, joined together with Chicago to start an alternative arts school for women. Originally opened in November 1973 at the former Chouinard Art Institute, the Woman's Building relocated in the summer of 1975 to a warehouse district in downtown Los Angeles that was north of the Los Angeles Union Train Station. Its programming included writing workshops, poetry readings, performance art, and art exhibits (*The Sons and Daughters of Los* 39–62). As was the case with Beyond Baroque, the struggle to survive, especially in the 1980s, required heroic effort on the part of many individuals, including poets such as Terry Wolverton, who sacrificed much of her own writing time in order to serve as a leader at the organization. Wolverton's superb memoir, *Insurgent Muse: Life and Art at the Woman's Building*, portrays the tensions between the commitment to one's needs as a writer and the demands of a community struggling to maintain its contribution to imaginative consciousness in Los Angeles.

The Woman's Building had its own in-house literary production facilities, which were better than Beyond Baroque's in that the Woman's Building also had printing equipment, including letter press, that permitted its membership to take their projects straight from manuscript to finished book. Susan King, a poet who lived in Venice, used these facilities to publish her books through the imprint of Paradise Press. As was noted in a tenth anniversary retrospective catalog, the Woman's Building also included a graphic arts center and printing facilities, which were all put to work in designing and publishing *Life in L.A.*, an anthology of poems by women associated with the building. The Woman's Building was also responsible for a feminist magazine entitled *Chrysalis*, which contained surprisingly little poetry by poets in Los Angeles. In contrast, poet Aleida Rodríguez and prose writer Jacqueline DeAngelis focused on Los Angeles-based writers in the seven issues of their magazine, *rara avis*, which was first edited out of their apartment in Venice, but came to be more associated with the Woman's Building because of their feminist activism of contributors such as Eloise Klein Healy.[1]

The World Stage, founded by Kamau Da'aood and Billy Higgins in 1989 at Leimert Park, emerged after the insurrection of 1992 as the most prominent center in Los Angeles for African American writers to gather, perform, and critique each other's work. Although its major development falls outside the time frame of the cold war, it deserves to be cited as an example of how previous models can revive themselves even after a long absence. In attaining its twentieth anniversary, The World Stage has become the first sustained setting for African American writers since the founding of Watts Writers Workshop in 1966 by Budd Schulberg. The Watts Writers Workshop, in comparison, lasted less than five years.

According to Eric Gordon's article in *The Sons and Daughters* (63–84), Da'aood regards The World Stage as a direct outgrowth of his experience in the Watts Writers Workshop, which involved many genres and was not limited to poetry. But it is also, in the largest sense, a conscious replication of the identity achieved by a community when its cultural activities first became known outside of its area. In part, this continuity between Leimert Park and the renowned jazz scene on Central Avenue in Los Angeles decades earlier occurred because of a literal connection: Horace Tapscott, the founder of the Pan Africkan People's Arkestra, began his music career on Central Avenue and finished it with regular performances at Leimert Park. Nor have poetry and music been the only art forms present at Leimert Park: Ben Caldwell's KOAS Network made video technology available to the neighborhood youth.[2]

South Central was not the only portion of Los Angeles to undergo the havoc and repercussions of the mid-century civil rights movement. In the first half of the 1950s, for instance, East Los Angeles was undergoing a spatial assault far more ominous in its ultimate ramifications than anything experienced by the poets in Venice West. In making use of Venice as an urban base for their critique of American social life, Stuart Perkoff did not have to face the unrelenting ambitions of developers intent on bringing a professional sports franchise to Los Angeles, no matter how much suffering might be imposed on those whose neighborhood was being demolished. The crisis in the community addressed in Perkoff's letter to Donald Allen, for instance, pales in comparison to the pressures exerted by business interests intent on evicting families from Chavez Ravine. Unfortunately, a text such as the late Manazar Gamboa's collection of poems, *Memories Around a Bulldozed Barrio*, which might properly belong to a study such as this one, is very firmly in the ranks of the potential canon. Although it is listed in the bibliography of Raúl Homero Villa's *Barrio-logos*, not a single line is actually cited in the book itself. I do possess a copy of this spiral-bound book and I published some of his poetry in my own magazine, *Momentum*, in 1978, but until Gamboa is fortunate enough to have the edition of collected poems or selected poems he deserves, his work will remain representative of the obstacles confronting those interested in this region's poets. Gamboa was not only a poet, but also worked at Beyond Baroque in a number of capacities, ranging from librarian to president of the board of directors.

If cultural geographers such as Mike Davis have worked in public media, Chicano literature has also had the advantage of a writer who works both sides of the avenue. Victor Valle is not only a poet whose work began appearing in the 1970s in Los Angeles, but a critic and historian whose projects have interrogated the assumptions behind the social imaginary of the Anglo establishment. His simultaneous commitment to poetics and journalism has led to what has been described by Raúl Homero Villa in *Barrio-logos* as "a practical discursive legacy." One outgrowth of the celebration of the bicentennial of Los Angeles was the founding of the Los Angeles Latino Writers Workshop, which culminated a half-dozen years later with an anthology, *201: Homenaje a la Ciudad de Los Angeles*. In the introduction, which is not credited to Valle, though primarily written by him, a challenge is presented not only to the hegemonic institutions but also to those in the community who might be tempted to assimilate, and in doing so, collaborate with those who would erase the place-rights earned by the labor of cultural workers: "The cultural heritage of this city's more than two million Spanish-speaking people who have stubbornly thrived like the nopal of our desert hillside, can no longer be ignored" (*Barrio-logos* 108).[3]

Probably the best-known poet and playwright to have grown up in Los Angeles is Cher'rie Moraga, who had her first poem published in *rara avis*. Naomi Quinonez and Marisela Norte have also achieved significant recognition, although Norte is the only one of these three to still live in Los Angeles. Gloria Enedina Alvarez, Ruben Martinez, and the late Gil Cuadros have also distinguished themselves as poets in Los Angeles, but none of the above named writers were associated with *Con Safos*, which was published between 1968 and 1972, and briefly revived in the early 1990s. The magazine that deserves more attention within this context is *Chismearte*, which was founded by Victor Valle in 1976, and vigorously pursued a dialogue with visual representation in its issues. In fact, on the whole, Chicano visual artists in Los Angeles such as Gronk and Willie Herron, have had much more success than their strictly literary counterparts in escaping from what Octavio Paz described as a "labyrinth of solitude." Other poets have worked in a cross-disciplinary manner to recover or articulate the recent insurgency in cultural poetics. Max Benavidez, whose first book of poems I published in 1984, has also written about visual art. Harry Gamboa, Jr. is a playwright, video and performance artist, and poet who has collaborated with visual artists such as Gronk in public performances, and Luis Alfaro has won considerable acclaim for his performances since the early 1990s.[4]

Charles Bukowski and the Stand Up School

Charles Bukowski (1920–1994), the poet most often associated with Los Angeles, never read at Beyond Baroque, nor to my knowledge was he ever asked to.[5] On the other hand, poets frequently aligned with Bukowski's poetics or whose lives intersected with Bukowski's picaresque predilections, such as Ron Koertge, John Thomas, and Gerald Locklin, all occasionally read at Beyond Baroque. Bukowski's role in the maturation of various scenes in Los Angeles involves far more than the patina of literary credibility derived from his stature as an internationally recognized poet and fiction writer. One of his central contributions was a relatively brief stint as an editor, which yielded both a literary magazine and an anthology he co-edited and for which he wrote a memorable introduction.

Bukowski was born in Germany in 1920 and brought to America at the age of two. He grew up in Los Angeles and attended City College, after which he hurled himself at stupor, and (to paraphrase John Berryman) stupor stared straight back. As a young man, Bukowski wandered the United States, taking on a series of low-paying jobs and living in boarding houses, not so much a *poete maudit* as a man who was both self-destructive and a cunning survivor. An issue of *Matrix* magazine, which was published in Philadelphia in 1952, for instance, had a contributor's note for Bukowski that simply observed it had been awhile since the editors had last heard from him. Bukowski's long alcoholic spree concluded with him on the verge of death in a public hospital in Los Angeles. When he finally recovered, he rededicated himself to writing poetry, and undeterred by his close call, drinking. The two activities kept him going for close to another forty years. Although John Martin's Black Sparrow Press became known as Bukowski's main publisher for the last quarter-century of his life, his reputation as a poet in the late 1960s was primarily built upon several collections that had been published by presses located around the country, ranging from E. V. Griffith's Hearse Press in Eureka, California, to Loujon Press in New Orleans. Of the ten collections of poetry that Doug Blazek listed in his *A Bukowski Sampler* in 1969 as providing the source of his selections, only one, in fact, was published by Black Sparrow Press. Martin often claims that he discovered Bukowski, but Martin benefited immensely from the small presses that had provided Bukowski with a stage for his sardonic monologues between 1955 and when Martin began publishing Bukowski in the late 1960s.[6]

Bukowski's emergence from the small press publishing underground was a tortuous process for him compared to the slightly younger set of poets comprising the most frequently cited members of the Beat generation. Bukowski's work appeared more than once alongside poets such as Ginsberg, Corso, and Ferlinghetti, but Bukowski's poetry seemed more doggedly existential in his alienation than the Beats, who were notorious for their scorn of work. Bukowski had a job; maybe he was surly about it, but he went to work. In the end, this proved to be the basis for his way out of drudgery, when Martin gambled on Bukowski's capacity for generating mounds of poems in hopes that he could be equally prolific as a fiction writer and offered to subsidize him while he produced a novel. *Post Office*, a fulminating account of Bukowksi's only sustained job, appeared in 1971, and in 1972 Bukowski won a creative writing grant from the National Endowment for the Arts. Martin went on to reprint his first two major collections of poetry, *It Catches My Heart in Its Hands* (1963) and *Crucifix in a Deathhand* (1965) in *Burning in Water, Drowning in Flame* (Poems: 1955-1968). Anyone with access to a special collections library that has copies of the books published by Loujon Press owes a visit to the reading room; Martin's edition of these books in no way does justice to the impact these early books by Bukowski had on its original audience.

Although poet Robert Peters would eventually label Bukowski's style as "gab poetry," he was also among the few critics working at a university willing to praise Bukowski's work for its ellipses of blunt lyricism.[7] Peters was also the first to point to the difference in quality in the work that Bukowski did before he met John Martin. Bukowski's poems from the late 1950s onward show the flagrant melodrama that often dominates the narratives of Beat writing at its most popular. To a certain extent, the Beats and Bukowski are brothers-in-arms reflecting each other's defiance of easy respectability and conventional prosody, but they also diverge in these matters. Though the apparent ease with which his poetry can be read masks the bittersweet layers of its ironic, profane sincerity, Bukowski's free verse seems almost impertinent in its casual approach to line breaks. The Beats, on the other hand, were often much more consciously concerned with craft. In contrast to the Beats, Bukowski's poetry did not celebrate the pleasures and enlightening terrors of pharmaceutical consciousness. Unlike the Beats, Bukowski loathed giving readings or making public appearances, and his reputation for what few performances he gave was that they usually dissolved into inebriated antagonism between the audience and himself. This was not about community formation: None of the listeners were meant to leave the reading hall with any sense of an altered social relationship with each other as a result of hearing Bukowksi's poems. Through its very divergence and contrast in poetics and subject matter, therefore, Bukowski's writing demarcates one poetic boundary of the Beat spectrum.

Bukowski began *Laugh Literary* with Neeli Cherry, a young poet from San Bernardino who would eventually change his last name to Cherkovski and write a biography of Bukowski. As an editor, Bukowski emphasized poets who had a peripheral relationship with the Beat generation, such as Harold Norse, Jack Micheline, and John Thomas, or Los Angeles area poets who were even less identifiable with a movement or generation, such as Gerda Penfold and the late Steve Richmond. *Laugh Literary* lasted only three issues, but its demise was not the end of Bukowski's editorial journey. If Perkoff had first considered the possibility of an anthology of poets associated with Los Angeles, Bukowski, Cherry, and a young poet, Paul Vangelisti, whose poetry had appeared in the final issue, decided that they shared enough enthusiasm about a variety of poets in Los Angeles to gather them in a book. Published in early 1972, with nothing more on the front of the plain brown cover than the simple title, *Anthology of L.A. Poets,* this collection was a comparatively thin volume. While one might argue that economy of production led to a decision to have all the poets appear in a single photograph rather than the traditional headshot that accompanies a poet's work in anthologies, the photograph perhaps says more than we might expect. First of all, it is a group photograph, implicitly asserting that these individuals at the very least consent to be recorded in each other's company. In the photograph, the poets, unidentified, are gathered together on an outdoor staircase, standing and sitting in no particular order. The book included William Pillin, Jack Hirschman, Holly Prado, Alvaro Cardona-Hine, Barbara Hughes, Gerald Locklin, Ron Koertge, Linda King, Rosella Pace, John Thomas, Stuart Perkoff, and the editors themselves. The *Coastlines* and Venice West poets were having a reunion of sorts, and women poets were beginning to claim their place in the city, too.

Anthology of L.A. Poets

"I think it has long been needed. This town has been smeared long enough both as a place to live and a place to create," Bukowski wrote to his publisher in mid-March 1972 (*Living on Luck* 148). Almost a month later, he sat down and pounded out a forward to the anthology in which he made a point of praising Los Angeles as a place to live.

> It is important to know that a man or woman, writer or not, can find more isolation in Los Angeles than in Boise, Idaho. Or, all things being fair, he can with a telephone (if he has a telephone) have 19 people over drinking and talking with him in an hour and a half. I have bummed the great cities and I know this—the great facility of Los Angeles is that one can be alone if he wishes or he can be in a crowd if he wishes. No other city seems to allow this easy double choice as well. This is a fairly wonderful miracle, especially if one is a writer. (*Anthology of L.A. Poets,* "A Foreword to These Poems," unpaginated)

Whether this double choice remains as easy in Los Angeles after the turn of a century is doubtful, and yet Bukowski's choice of poets for his anthology is a double one, for this slim volume juxtaposes both the earliest members of the Stand Up school of poets and some of the primary figures in the first wave of communities of poets in Los Angeles associated with *Coastlines* or Venice West.

Unlike the Language movement which started almost exactly at the same time, but which had already begun announcing itself with that term in a major poetry directory as early as 1973, the "Stand Up" movement of poetry began almost entirely as practice, and still has yet to have even a monograph devoted to its history.[8] In focusing on a simultaneous requirement that the poem come alive on the page with the same precise verve as it plays to a crowd in a coffeehouse, Stand Up poetry distinguishes itself from performance poetry and slam contests, which are often judged and valued based on the poet's ability to project a beguiling demeanor or hip insouciance. In addition, Stand Up poetry, despite a casual prosody that makes W. C. Williams's variable foot look Miltonic by comparison, expects its practitioners to be well-read in the traditions. Nevertheless, the publication of *Stand Up Poetry* by the University of Iowa Press signals that Southern California's major school of poetry achieved its first formal step toward recognition outside of its communities and institutions, and if theoretical appreciation and analysis has lagged, it has not affected the accelerating popularity of the school. The long journey toward this recognition began with the anthology which Bukowski co-edited, choosing a pair of poets, Ron Koertge and Gerald Locklin, whose work went on to define a style of prose poetry that refused to abandon line breaks, while at the same time winking at the culture industries and using the imagery of popular culture to contextualize the bonds of coterie affiliations.

> because i knew i would be walking her
> through some of the meaner night streets
> of downtown l.a., i reached in my glove compartment
> and slipped a fold-back knife in my pocket.
> and we did run the gamut of some fairly unsavory
> concentrations of humanity, but as each potentially
> tense encounter approached, i patted my pocket
> and felt a little less naked.
>
> safely back in the car
> i extracted the weapon from my pocket
> and found us both gazing at
> a b-flat harmonic accidentally filched,
> years ago, from one of fred voss's
> dodecaphonic parties.
> (Gerald Locklin, "Do you remember the scene in *The Godfather* . . .")

The fundamentally chatty tone of Locklin's narrator epitomizes the development of the conversational tone in the Los Angeles Stand Up school. The New York school of poets who gained attention in the late sixties and early seventies certainly worked hard on generating a sense of immediate auditory compatibility between the writer and audience, but the Los Angeles bar and horse track talk scenarios were far less self-conscious about their hipness. Whereas the New York school appeared to be addressing an audience largely consisting of other poets, the first wave of Los Angeles Stand Up poets seemed to be indifferent to the makeup of the audience.

Although *Anthology of L.A. Poets* contains the first stirrings of the Stand Up movement, the collection largely serves to sketch the disparate kinds of writing that appeared in one of the decade's most significant poetry magazines, *Invisible City*. Unlike the brief three-issue run of *Laugh Literary*, which was an average flurry of a life span for hundreds of such magazines, *Invisible City* lasted twenty-eight issues during a ten-year run. During that time, coeditors Vangelisti and John McBride repeatedly featured many of the poets who appeared in *Anthology of L.A. Poets* as well as publishing full-length books by them through their Red Hill imprint. The range of poets in *Anthology of L.A. Poets* goes from the meditative work of Holly Prado to the deadpan satire of Gertrude Penfold. The first poem in Bukowski's final issue (February 1971) was by a young poet, Paul Vangelisti, who had recently moved to Los Angeles from San Francisco. If Vangelisti's poem opened the final issue of Bukowski's magazine, then Bukowski initiated *Invisible City*'s first issue, also published in February 1971, with a set of ten poems, and he continued to be a featured writer in its first half-dozen issues.

Two years after Bukowski's editorial collaboration with Vangelisti and Cherry, a long, two-part article appeared in the *Los Angeles Times* about the intensifying rumors of a significant revival of poetry in Los Angeles. Wary of sounding like a provincial booster, Bukowski initially dismissed claims that a renaissance of any sort was in motion. "Listen, man, I'm always overjoyed when I read good writing," he told the reporter. "If someone can write better than I can, it's great. It fills me. It doesn't make me feel bad. It makes me feel good. I don't feel so good lately." As the conversation continued—"Another smile. Another frown. Another beer."—Bukowski conceded, "I said there's not much going on. But when I think about it, there is a stir. Not a gigantic flame, but it's a good, workmanlike stir." At another point, though, Bukowski emphasized "Not a scene. Not yet, man."[9]

In the course of the interview, Bukowski pointed to three poets who became associated with the Stand Up school of poets, Gerald Locklin, Ron Koertge, and Charles Stetler. Seven years later, Bukowski had dropped two of those from his personal roster of favorite contemporary poets. Locklin alone remained as the only poet in Southern California whose work he deemed worth reading.[10] By that point, though, a series of other editors had turned a "workmanlike stir" into a flame that did not seek to draw upon his approval or disapproval to gauge its efficiency.

The anthology that Vangelisti co-edited with Bukowski was the basis for a reading series that Vangelisti organized at the Pasadena Museum of Modern Art, which in turn provided the focus for a larger sequel to *Anthology of L.A. Poets*. On a white front cover as bright as a drive-in movie screen on a hot August afternoon, the poets are clustered like the points of a constellation, each separately standing on a separate invisible stage with their arms raised not in surrender but in praise of hard-won imaginative radiance. The front cover has no words whatsoever. The back, instead, contains the title, *Specimen '73*, stenciled in large type. Once again, the lack of any editorial assertion on the front or back cover is rather unusual; in fact, the book mentions no credits detailing previous publication whatsoever, which becomes almost a demand that the work be dealt with by the reader on its merits. Contemporary poetry, especially in the academic world, partially generates and reinforces its hierarchy by emphasizing where one's work has been published. The page listing the provenance of the poems serves as the major means of claiming instant valorization and eligibility to draw upon one's cultural capital. The refusal to acknowledge or provide such information is implicitly a subversion of the normal means of social, literary identity. This is all the more an emphatic disavowal of participation in the literary game given that anthologies by their very definition are supposed to be collections of work previously published. In addition to most of the poets published in *Anthology of L.A. Poets, Specime '73* contained work by Robert Peters and Charles Wright.

Invisible City was perhaps one of the most political poetry magazines of the seventies, though the word political does not mean that the editors subscribed to any programmatic interpretation of history or social formations. Wasting no space or time in announcing its social coordinates, Paul Vangelisti's brief essay, "Why I Am a Socialist," started on the cover of the first issue, unhesitatingly denying comfort to ideologues of any persuasion. The first of Vangelisti's own seven poems in that first issue was dialectically entitled, "The Revolution, The Revolution"; a direct reference in the poem to the events at Kent State the previous year emphasized the unwillingness of the editors to let recent turbulence become subsumed in the rituals of corporately mediated obliteration.[11] Both Vangelisti and McBride contributed several essays to the magazine during the course of its existence and typical of their analysis is a comment by Vangelisti in issue no. 13/14: "If we are to derange the egocentric, expansionist course of U.S. poetry, nothing less is indicated than a resistance to the self, an ideological and aesthetic vulnerability to what surrounds us." If the combination of left-wing politics and animosity toward the confessional school's glorification of individual angst seems to indicate a course of emergent poetics parallel with the Language school of the early to mid-1970s, one would find that suspicion confirmed in Vangelisti's own poetry as well as in the work he translated and published. Of all the poets in this period whose work could be said to belong to the kind of canonical reformulation mounted by the Language school, Vangelisti remains the poet and editor least able to be absorbed by this movement, at least by the accounts written by its participants.[12] The singularity of his vision developed directly out of his ability to include a wide range of voices within his publishing projects.

McBride and Vangelisti had met in 1966 while undergraduates at the University of San Francisco. Vangelisti, who was born in 1945, was four years older than McBride, and by 1968 had moved to Los Angeles to study for a Ph.D. at the University of Southern California. By the summer of 1970 McBride had graduated from college and was working on the assembly line of American Can Co., fulfilling Bob Dylan's acerbic comment in "Subterranean Homesick Blues" about the reward for two decades of toil at the brain factory. Vangelisti was working as a recreation director for the San Francisco parks. "One bright and windy July day, John called in sick and visited me at the playground. We decided then & there that a magazine should take place— the name did not come until a few weeks later, scribbling it on a postcard to a friend in Los Angeles" (*Invisible City*, November 1977, unpaginated).[13] McBride decided not to go to graduate school, and although he would soon pass his qualifying examination, Vangelisti decided by late 1971 that he would concentrate on writing his own poetry and editing *Invisible City* and publishing books. Vangelisti's time at USC, however, proved crucial for his formative encounter with English poet and critic, Donald Davie, whose teaching inspired Vangelisti to link several disparate figures into his editorial foray and introduced Vangelisti to the work of George Oppen, whom Vangelisti contacted. Oppen immediately recognized his talent, writing an introduction to his first published book, *Communion* (1971). Davie also encouraged Vangelisti to consider translation as a means of expanding one's knowledge of poetry's social potential. He had spoken only Italian until the age of five. He once mentioned to me that he was unable to ask for directions when he arrived at his first elementary school, and initially ended up in the second-grade classroom. "I was tall for my age, and no one else there spoke Italian, so I just followed the kids who were my size," Vangelisti recalls. He eventually used his knowledge of Italian to translate the most experimental poets in the language, providing himself with a model of avant-garde activity completely ignored by poets more commonly associated with Language writing.

Vangelisti's own preference for translation and experimentation was increasingly inspired by another maverick West Coast poet, Jack Hirschman, whose willingness to "translate" from languages that he could barely read was matched only by the audacity of his ferocious commitment to a poetic vocation. Hirschman had a PhD, and taught at the University of California, Los Angeles for a few years, but by the late 1960s had lost his job and was living in Venice. Although he never attended the nascent Beyond Baroque poetry workshop, he provided a model of alternative poetics for many of the young poets who were beginning to gather around Beyond Baroque during its first five years. In particular, Jim Krusoe regarded Hirschman as an exemplary figure for what the role of the poet required. With interests ranging from Jewish mysticism to Caribbean surrealism, Hirschman's eclectic poetics made him an unpredictable poet. He translated Rene Depestre's *A Rainbow for the Christian West*, which Vangelisti published in 1972, while Papa Bach Bookstore published his translation of Ait Djafer's *Wail for the Arab Beggars of the Casbah* (1971). Hirschman then turned toward Artaud and performed his translations at readings around Los Angeles with an intensity that bordered on hallucinogenic suspension of disbelief. I witnessed one such reading at the Century City Playhouse in 1974. Shortly afterward, Hirschman made his move to San Francisco permanent, where his poetry grew increasingly didactic in its Marxist admonitions of the working class. Once again, along with John Thomas and Bruce Boyd, Jack Hirschman's maturation reminds us that a permeable boundary between northern and Southern California is an essential feature of the West Coast Poetry Renaissance.

As the Language movement began to gain more and more attention in the 1970s, its best-known members emphasized their alignment with similar movements and methods such as the post-1917 Russian constructivists and *zaum*, but neglected to integrate contemporary avant-garde poets in other countries whose writings had preceded Language writing by at least a decade. Vangelisti's anthology *Italian Poetry, 1960–1980: from Neo to Post Avant-garde* reminds us of how much poetry from the recent past needs to be accounted for to comprise any global account of poetic audacity during the cold war. If one widens a textual framework to imagine a more complete picture of avant-garde activity within poetry after World War II, then the emergence of editors and poets in Los Angeles between 1971 and 1991 committed to an investigation of a maverick poetics will have a more accurate context. If one fixes the limits of contemporary American experimentation in the 1970s to the core group of Language writers, then the poets in Los Angeles will always be perceived as playing a game of follow-the-leader, whereas Vangelisti's work as a poet and editor provided a model not only for avant-garde work, but of recovery of past texts and a generosity toward other forms of work that challenged the conventional lyric.

During the first half of the 1970s, Vangelisti claimed that "a commitment to the kind of clarity" required when one wishes "to embody in verse the material reality of one's age" necessitates an emphasis on what he called "a strong concentration on the subject. . . . This explains the preponderance, in the first ten issues, of poets who dealt with immediate subject matter in a straightforward manner. . . . Many of these writers lived, as I did, in Los Angeles" (*Invisible City*, November 1977, unpaginated). Under the rubric of Red Hill Press Vangelisti and McBride rapidly expanded their editorial presence with a barrage of book titles in which they embraced and affirmed the past in Los Angeles (Perkoff, Thomas, Bukowski, and Frumkin) while being among the first to publish individuals such as Gerald Locklin and Ron Koertge with titles which established them in the forefront of the Stand Up school of poetry. Simultaneously, Vangelisti and McBride confronted both groups with books of poems by experimental Italian poets. Such an eclectic catalog was not as disparate as might first appear. As McBride pointed out in an introduction to an anthology of Italian poets, it was an emphasis on attacking "mass language" that linked these books; indeed, imbued with a profound skepticism toward the poem as a "cultural press release" for bourgeois discourse, Vangelisti and McBride published the "idiosyntactic" and the colloquial with the same enthusiasm.

> We had the idea that we were involved in a perpetual avant-garde, not an avant-garde of a given period, not an avant-garde that has any particular program in any sense exclusive of other programs, but a program that was essentially radical in the sense of a program that is open-ended, unfinished and perhaps to follow our title, Invisible City, unrealizable. So I guess my editor and I, in our personal as well as our public lives have been fascinated by the unrealizable.[14]

Invisible City ran for a total of twenty-eight issues, the last of which was a huge "triple" issue that languished without any critical notice until Robert Peters decided to risk charges of "nepotism" and write a review of this particular issue in order to call attention to "its iconoclasm, which remains as vigorous as ever" (231). Peters first commented on the staging of the textual material: "to encourage readers to see each large tabloid page as an entity in itself, the pages are unnumbered . . . The theory—and there is a theory— is that the magazine is composed by page and not by 'field.' What precedes or follows individual pieces relates to and amplifies those individual pieces.

The editorial statement, which one would normally expect following the title page, is buried deep within . . . How refreshing to find editors with a rationale behind what they are doing—the construction of *Invisible City* reaches towards being an art form."[15] Vangelisti and McBride's magazine expanded the capacity of Los Angeles poets to represent their interests as readers of contemporary poetry. If a poet such as Ray DiPalma first caught my attention in an anthology entitled *Quickly Aging Here* in the late 1960s, it was *Invisible City* that seemed most forthright about delineating the interstices between his poetry and the work emerging in Los Angeles neighborhoods.

The Rage of Talent: Leland Hickman's Editorial Journey

At a conference in 1999 on postmodern women writers, editors, and publishers entitled "Page Mothers," Marjorie Perloff asserted that Leland Hickman deserved consideration as a member of this category of cultural workers along with Lyn Hejinian and Kathleen Fraser. Specifically pointing to the almost excruciating care which Hickman devoted to presenting a text in *Temblor* in a manner as close as possible to the writer's configuration, Perloff broached the issue of the labor required to maintain a magazine when the editor had no institutional base to provide him with financial or intellectual equity. "How did he do it?" Perloff asked at one point in a slightly astonished tone of voice. One could ask the same about many individuals who worked as poet-editor-publishers during the small press movement, but Hickman's effort is a singular case in part because the magazine he is best known for focused on poetry which was extraordinarily different from his own. To understand how he did it is to attempt to reconcile the poetics of his own writing with his editorial choices, for there is no instance in post-World War II American poetry of a poet-editor of a major magazine with such an incommensurate disparity.

If, as I suggested earlier, Donald Allen's anthology served as a pathbreaking text for the gay literary underground, it also allowed its editor to remain secreted within a diving bell; Leland Hickman, on the other hand, wrote with candid, and occasionally harrowing, lyricism about his sexual chaos, and yet his poetry remained in another kind of closet, since as an editor he focused on poets whose writing provided few clues as to how to understand Hickman's own work. Even if the majority of poets Hickman published between 1982 and 1990 were not core members of the Language group, their influence was such that the ambiance of the magazine overwhelmed the few poems in *Temblor* in which the first person lyric peeked out in any way whatsoever. While Hickman's "Tiresias" was adamantly first person, the Language poets were engaged in a struggle reminiscent in its comprehensiveness of the

Protestant campaign in the Renaissance to scour all images from churches: their desire to renew or initiate a contestation with the dominant ideology demanded that everything familiar be stripped from the delivery systems of the hegemonic apparatus, and this especially included unmediated narratives in the first person. Hickman's baroque imagery would seem to make him the most unlikely candidate to work on behalf of the relatively few members of this insurgent movement, which with the assistance of post-structuralist theory delivered a resounding challenge to the complacency of much academic poetry, and yet his willingness to do so most likely derives from and extends out of his earlier association with—and advocacy of—a group of poets in Los Angeles who shared, in their own idiosyncratic way, an aggressive skepticism about the lyric models popular in the academy.

Although Leland Hickman first met several of the poets to whom he would dedicate portions of his long poem-in-progress, "Tiresias," at Beyond Baroque, and he did a considerable amount of typesetting at its facilities, his editorial journey properly begins at Papa Bach Bookstore in West Los Angeles. While Venice certainly has earned its substantial position within any account of Los Angeles poetry, it will probably find its role in future studies of Los Angeles poetry somewhat reduced by the necessity to compress the period between 1948 and 1968 in order to give the poets and editors between 1968 and the end of the century more sustained attention. As that occurs, one will find the intermingled scenes of L.A. poets rippling inland. If a longitudinal equator is drawn in this future map, it will probably extend from Long Beach north to Universal City. In passing through Watts and Hollywood, the cultural contribution of bookstores such as Sisterhood Bookstore and Charlotte Gusay's George Sand, both located on Westwood Boulevard, will become part of a larger unfolding that emphasizes magazines such as *Chismearte* as well as *Invisible City* and intermingled communities of performance artists and poets with the development of gay enclaves such as West Hollywood. In citing non-coastal bookstores as a colligating axis of informal interpretative communities in Los Angeles, the publishing imprint of Black Sparrow Press will also be accounted for in a manner that befits its enormous accomplishment.

As an initial gesture toward redrawing the map, one could hardly do better than to start with Leland Hickman's apprenticeship as an editor at Papa Bach Bookstore, which was not fully appreciated by the poets of Los Angeles until it went out of business in the mid-1980s. The building that housed Papa Bach Bookstore on Santa Monica Boulevard in West Los Angeles was demolished toward the end of the century to allow a car dealership to have a showroom and lot, so anyone wishing to visit the site of many memorable readings will have to settle for crossing the street and standing at the Nu Art movie theater box office, which was a favored habitat of Los Angeles poets, along with the Fox Venice and the Los Feliz. Papa Bach Bookstore was a large, two-story high brick building with a tin roof that needed repair. In the rear of the store, a thirty-foot deep loft the width of the store had been constructed. As one walked into the entrance, an L-shaped counter with a cash register was to your right and a large magazine rack was to your left. Directly in front of you were shelves that featured the current titles that were the most likely to be bought by Papa Bach's customers; casual customers who were looking for the latest self-help guide on the best-seller list quickly left empty-handed. Against the left wall were shelves of Marxist literature; to the right as one walked to the rear were novels and psychology, anthropology, and history. Underneath the loft, the poetry section was well stocked and maintained. Its position in the rear was less a reflection of its economic contribution to the store than a providential allocation of social space to those who wanted to talk about what they found on the shelves without worrying about being told to lower their voices.

In my original plan for this book, I set aside some pages for a short account of Leland Hickman's life, but fortunately Stephen Motika of Nightboat Books in New York City collaborated with Paul Vangelisti's and Guy Bennett's Seismicity Editions at Otis Art Institute to publish *Tiresias: The Collected Poems of Leland Hickman*; Dennis Phillips and I contributed essays to the book that will inform readers about his life. After Kate Braverman served as a poetry editor at *Bachy*, Hickman became the editor for a total of ten issues; his own creative focus on the long poem showed up in his choices as an editor, with long serial poems by Dennis Phillips being featured in several of the issues as well as poems which were several pages in length by Peter Levitt and Kate Braverman. Hickman also began to interview the poets he regarded as the leading figures in Los Angeles, including Holly Prado, Deena Metzger, Eloise Klein Healy, and James Krusoe. Hickman was primarily interested in poetry, and *Bachy* from its first issue onward had published fiction and photographs. Despite not being especially interested in a general literary magazine, Hickman managed to organize each issue so that the poetry, fiction, and photographs seemed proportional and well distributed in their sequencing. It should be emphasized that it was never simply a local magazine, and Hickman from the start kept its pages open to contributors such as Ron Schreiber from the East Coast or Garrett Hongo, whose work Hickman had encouraged me in 1974 to publish in *Momentum* magazine when Hongo was a completely unpublished poet.

While Hickman continued to publish poets associated with the Beyond Baroque workshop, a perusal of *Bachy*'s issues during the second half of its existence reveals other organizations and sites for poetry and cultural work that acknowledge the sites elsewhere in the region where poetry was thriving. Issue number 15, for instance, ran a portfolio of Bob Flanagan's collaged fliers for poetry readings at Chelsea Bookstore in Long Beach. In successive issues, Hickman ran the complete script of a feminist collaborative dramatic project that had been composed in a writing workshop led by Jean Samuels at the Woman's Building. In the same issue in which he published the first act of "Dark and Bright Fires," billed in its subtitle as "Women's Collective Autobiographies," Hickman also published a "collaborative interview" between D. E. Stewart and Suzanne Lacy, the latter of whom had her picture on the cover of the first issue (1978) of *High Performance* magazine. Both magazines included Lacy discussing her project, "Three Weeks in May," in which she had set up a twenty-five-foot map of Los Angeles on the steps of City Hall and recorded the sites of reported rapes in the city. *High Performance* continued publishing for almost twenty years and its issues are replete with the vital and flourishing performance art scenes that helped define Los Angeles in the 1980s as an art center. One task awaiting some other scholar is to compare the issues of Hickman's editorial projects in the 1980s with *High Performance*. Restricting the poets he published in those magazines to a literary environment, as if it were not in concurrent dialogue with an equally prominent underground arts magazine, serves only to empower those whose canonical preferences for strict artistic boundaries infect all too many syllabi and books of criticism.

In the early 1980s, Hickman appears to have decided that he would make his mark as an editor, rather than as a poet, for after *Great Slave Lake Suite* was published, he released only two poems in the remaining eleven years of his life. *Bachy*'s final issue appeared in 1981, and Hickman started a new magazine, *Boxcar*, in collaboration with Paul Vangelisti. *Boxcar* lasted only two issues, but its design was as important as its contents for what it portended about Hickman's final magazine, *Temblor*. Hickman had had no control over the unusual size of *Bachy* magazine, which had shifted from the standard 8 and 1/2 inches by 5 and 1/2 inches of little magazines for its first half-dozen issues and expanded to the size of a typewriter sheet. His decision to continue using this size page did not mean that he was satisfied with the typesize, and Hickman began using the down time and afterhours at his job to produce the magazine. Beginning in the late 1940s, editors aspiring to start publishing began using mimeograph equipment to produce their magazines, and by the late 1960s, a number of such publications had reinforced the image of a literary underground in which the limited circulation of texts confirmed the autonomy of the reading community. In a sense, the physical production of the text became the equivalent of a performative speech act. The gesture itself initiated the community's existence and marked the site of resistance to the normative standards of cultural distinction. Other poets, however, were less enthusiastic about the presentation of their art in a format that suggested bohemian hipness and improvisational poetics. *Temblor*'s professional appearance with a slick cover and crisp type seems to argue that if experimental maverick poets are to gain an astute audience, the editor must signal the potential readers that the work has first been taken judiciously enough by the publisher to be presented with a firm sense of the theatricality of the page (of the poem as an image/sculpture of ink), and that if the poem's argument seems initially obscure, the reader should persist in her investigation, or at least linger momentarily, out of respect for the presentation itself. Hickman at no point suggests that all publishers of independent work ought to choose this strategy, but his choice of this approach is related to his struggles to achieve a literary identity that his own upbringing would not have predicated.

Temblor required a ferocious amount of energy to sustain, even in comparison with the usual little magazine effort. His full-time job as a typesetter provided him with only a few weeks of vacation per year, and Perloff's question is worth considering again: *How did he do it?* Certainly, Hickman had a talent for editing, and while Keats's "negative capability" is usually thought of in terms of the poetic imagination, it is perhaps even more required by anyone aspiring to edit a poetry magazine. While this concept of talent provides us with an intellectual understanding of how that task is accomplished, the emotional motive for taking on the burden of cultural work is still missing. "Talent is perhaps nothing more than successfully sublimated rage," Theodor Adorno observed (*Minima Moralia* 109). "Could shed rage / Shd love come," was one of the refrains in *Great Slave Lake Suite*, and in producing *Temblor* magazine with exactitude and fidelity to the poet's requests for placing the poem on the page, Hickman sublimated much of the rage that tunneled through his poetry. Few editors have ever drawn upon such vivid masochistic energy to surrender their hopes for their own writing in hopes of succoring a community imagined within the ongoing labor of a man at his keyboard. Hickman lived in Hollywood, Silverlake, and North Hollywood the last quarter century of his life, and worked for close to a decade in Glendale, where he often stayed after work to put together the magazine. Although his influence as a poet remained palpable at the Beyond Baroque workshop for many years, his own life and editorial energies profoundly shifted the locus of Los Angeles poet-editors towards the refracting interchanges looping through the Hollywood Hills.

Hickman's tenure as an editor of *Bachy/Boxcar/Temblor* magazines occurred during the most abundant period of poetic activity in Southern California. In 1977 and 1978, the following magazines were appearing on a regular basis and were being sold at no less than a dozen bookstores in the

Los Angeles area, as well as being distributed at other independent literary bookstores throughout the United States: *Invisible City, rara avis, Little Caesar, Momentum, (Beyond Baroque) Magazine, Third Rail*. One notices what is missing immediately from this list is any magazine connected with a university. The major academic poetry magazines tend to have the word "review" attached to their title, and their impetus derives from the support that the institution gives to the publication. The University of California, Los Angeles was no different from its older sibling rival in Berkeley: both institutions had little interest in anything that smacked of contemporary poetry that was not already validated by East Coast publishers. The reading series at UCLA typically featured poets such as James Merrill, W. S. Merwin, Louise Gluck, Mark Strand, and Adrienne Rich.

The particular subversion which Hickman's editorial choices engages in is his juxtaposition of poets from incompatible communities, or at least major members of communities who have been deliberately ignored in accounts of experimental writing. The clusters of writers who belong to no particular faction or camp are the ones who need to be taken into account if the fiction of what Hank Lazer calls "opposing poetries" is to be understood as a cul-de-sac which disables a full engagement with the subversive practices of postmodern poetry. Lazer's essays implicitly affirm the same kind of dichotomy that the Beats and the academics used to define their legitimacy and centrality, ignoring the large number of poets who do not fit into either category. *Boxcar* and *Temblor*, on the other hand, insist that those who would claim center stage as the major impetuses within the avant-garde must acknowledge the work of others outside of their immediate practice and poetics, and that the failure to do so serves as a measure of their limited reciprocity as readers and members of interpretative communities.

Lazer is fond of citing Bernstein's tirade against "official verse culture," repeating the passage twice in *Opposing Poetries*; Bernstein's critique of the MFA-workshop-*American Poetry Review*-National Endowment for the Arts cycle of publication-judges-awards includes the blunt accusation that poets with these affiliations are in constant denial of the ideological work which their poetics valorizes. This accusation stops short of claiming that such poets are in direct complicity with the bourgeois goals of global capitalism, but the hint is there, and it is meant to demean with a wide brush. In *Content's Dream*, which Lazer quotes frequently, Bernstein proposes theoretical guidelines for what poets should strive to accomplish in their poems if they are to actively discharge energy which questions or investigates the real conditions of the relationship between readers and writers. If one examines the anthologies edited by Hoover and Silliman, however, all of which are listed by Lazer in his volume, one notices that several poets whose work is repeatedly published in *Boxcar/Temblor* are not included in any of these anthologies. What all of these poets share in common is an adult lifetime in Los Angeles, and while it seems strange to think that a group of poets *in a specific city* would find themselves marginalized by another group of poets who are vociferous about their own marginalization as advocates of the avant-garde, nevertheless the coincidence of residence and of the canonical invisibility of Paul Vangelisti, John Thomas, Bob Crosson, Holly Prado, and Harry Northup deserves consideration. Both Thomas and Crosson died during the winter of 2001–2002 within four months of each other, each of them over seventy years old, and the other three are close to an average of sixty years old. Subversive poetry can claim that distinction only if it works at each and every moment, and especially in the final instance, to destroy the hierarchies which the commodification of texts, no matter how avant-garde, precipitates. The reluctance of a community to accept maverick and experimental interlopers into its self-narrative is a gauge of its willingness to risk a real challenge to the possessive individualism which "language-centered" poetry claims to mount. The failure of critics and commentators on the past quarter century to examine these outsiders generates the suspicion that these critics have privileged an implicit and fallible narrative of textuality in which certain poets are held up as exemplary members of the avant-garde, and others relegated to a category of provisional curiosity, a distinction based on contingencies as basic as the alleged unavailability of marginal texts. If, however, the work of a poet such as John Thomas remains unacknowledged by critics over forty years after his first public reading, one must turn to the editors whose magazines provide the broadest possible context for the adamant dispersal of textuality, exemplified in Thomas's and Crosson's work, which marks and problematizes an entire strand of postmodern poetics. Hickman's editorial work remains a monumental destabilization of the usual categories of avant-garde communities. As a literary composition, it deserves the prolonged attention accorded to any masterwork. It is not meant to be background music to footnotes on the imagination any more than Mahler's symphonies can be adapted to elevator music.

Sun & Moon / Green Integer

The final major press committed to "experimental," "avant-garde," or "maverick post-Language" (P=O=L=A) writing to be considered in this study is not indigenous to Southern California. Doug Messerli founded Sun & Moon Press in the mid-1970s in Maryland, and moved his operation to Los Angeles in the mid-1980s only because his companion, Howard Fox, had been appointed a curator at the Los Angeles County Museum of Art. He arrived around the time that *"Poetry Loves Poetry"* and *In the American*

Tree were published and Lee Hickman began editing *Temblor*. Papa Bach Bookstore had folded, and Dennis Cooper was relishing his literary life in New York City. In San Francisco, Howard Junker ascertained that a quarterly literary magazine that published only West Coast writers could achieve national recognition and launched *ZYZZYVA*, which has by now published more than a hundred issues. Messerli first caught attention in Los Angeles with a novel by Paul Auster, *City of Glass*, which proved to be a crossover hit with readers throughout Los Angeles, including those who frequented stores such as Scene of the Crime in the San Fernando Valley, which usually favored authors such as P. D. James, Dick Francis, Paula Gosling, and (later on) Michael Dibdin. I remember Scene of the Crime's owners, who prominently displayed *City of Glass* at the front counter, told me how much they liked the novel, and within months of publication, Auster's novel caught on surprisingly well, won an Edgar, and instantly made Messerli not only a publisher with an interesting backlist, but a force to be reckoned with in Los Angeles. Within two years, he had edited an anthology of Language poetry, and during his first two decades in Los Angeles published a variety of writers that challenged the output of venerable east publishers such as New Directions for the title of best independent publisher of avant-garde writing.

With a PhD from Temple University, Messerli was unique among Los Angeles publishers in that he had academic credentials to accompany his publishing portfolio, and his editorial interest in international literature complemented and solidified Vangelisti's long-standing convocation of Italian as well as Polish poets as part of the reckoning required by any poet with a serious interest in the craft. He opened up his residence to the first public salon in Los Angeles that had ever been able to feature a mixture of fiction writers and poets from out of town. I remember in particular a very fine reading by Richard Ellman of his novel, *Tar Beach*. One could argue that Messerli would have published many of the same poets whose manuscripts he selected or solicited regardless of where he might have moved, and I would concede that if Howard Fox had ended up working at a museum in Houston, Chicago, or Boston, the odds substantially favor the retention of poets such as Charles Bernstein, Ted Greenwald, Bruce Andrews, David Antin, and Lyn Hejinian as featured writers of the Sun & Moon venture. Messerli's eventual inclusion of poets such as Will Alexander, Nathaniel Mackey, Dennis Phillips, Martha Ronk, and Paul Vangelisti as Sun & Moon stalwarts, however, is primarily due to his immersion in a scene that had been slowly but steadily gaining momentum for several decades. If not love at first sight, Messerli's marriage with Los Angeles has yielded a palpable congeries of unexpected linkages.

Messerli's impact on the Los Angeles scene continued well beyond the end of the cold war. Young (or at least younger) poets who had arrived or developed after Messerli took up residence and began their own magazines during the final decade of the twentieth century. Both Mark Salerno's *Arshile* and Standard Schaeffer's *Rhizome* reverberate with the aura of the legendary, if gruff, integrity that Hickman's *Temblor* is still celebrated for; the tables of contents of their magazines marks the resilience of the intelligent editing of poetry in Los Angeles. Salerno was born in New York in 1956, showed up briefly in the mid-1980s in Los Angeles, returned to the East Coast for a couple of years, and then returned to Los Angeles "for the duration," an expression used to remind soldiers sworn into the army during World War II of what lay ahead. His most recent book of poetry, *Odalisque*, is from Salt Publishing in England. Schaeffer has moved from his birth city, Los Angeles, to San Francisco in recent years, becoming the most recent example of how the West Coast itself seems to provide a haven that is difficult to extricate oneself from, unless sheer economic pressure demands an exit.

Douglas Messerli's *Intersections: Innovative Poetry in Southern California* is the most recent anthology to assemble affiliated poets living in this region. Messerli's twenty-seven-page introductory essay enumerates several precedents in poetry publishing in Los Angeles, taking care to cite the work of Vangelisti and Hickman in particular as being as important not just in any local sense, but for its national and even international scope and stature. Confronting the same problem that has nagged almost every editor of a nongeneric anthology since Donald Allen, Messerli points to the prevalence of editing, film/theater/performance, and narrative as concomitant linkages between poets such as Rae Armantrout, Michael Davidson, David Antin, and Jerome Rothenberg (all of whom teach or have taught at the University of California, San Diego) and now deceased poets such as Robert Crosson and John Thomas in Los Angeles. Although appearing to be "regional," Messerli's anthology serves as a singular instance of an editorial willingness to encompass the elastic flourish of the potential canon becoming actual.

The writers Messerli published after moving to Los Angeles were hardly unfamiliar to longtime residents. As mentioned earlier, Ted Greenwald had first read in Los Angeles at a bookstore I worked at in 1979, and then had read on a follow-up visit to Los Angeles at Beyond Baroque, and Barrett Watten and Bruce Andrews had also read at Beyond Baroque. Messerli almost immediately established himself as an independent ally of Hickman's editorial poetics. The departure of Black Sparrow Press in the early 1980s had left the city without a publisher in residence who was interested in producing books by the maverick avant-garde. In a manner similar to John Martin's commitment to poets such as Bukowski, Coleman, Eshleman, Wakoski, and Bromige, Messerli assiduously began integrating poets such as Dennis Phillips and Paul Vangelisti into his production schedule.

The Vinyl Canon and Stand Up Poetry

If Beyond Baroque has survived an almost endless series of challenges, its status as the eldest sibling has also been constantly diluted by the expanding kinship of other reading series. Al's Bar in downtown Los Angeles, for instance, attracted a vigorous audience for several years in the early 1980s. One small press that tended to have its publication parties at Al's Bar was Peter Schneidre's Illuminati Press, which managed to produce a set of books over a ten-year span that were often difficult to find in local bookstores, and yet managed to stay visible enough so that each new book seemed to provide a firm sense of why the editor had made the choice to engage in the ordeal of publishing. Schneidre's full-length books as well as tall, narrow items he called "tad books" included titles by William Pillin, James Krusoe, Kate Braverman, Michael C. Ford, Laurel Ann Bogen, Suzanne Lummis, Nichola Manning, and Janet Grey, who collectively provide a through-line from the beginning of this study to the present moment. Schneidre had a subtle, impish sense of humor; his annual magazine, *Nude Erections*, was intended as a jibe at James Laughlin's New Directions. Some of the poets he published have gone on to considerable fame, including Amy Gerstler, Dave Alvin, and Henry Rollins. Schneidre's willingness to juxtapose all these poets within his backlist provides a glimpse of the peculiar curiosity that seemed to impel his project. It should be noted that his reclusive presence as a poet in Los Angeles was at odds with his ability to publish his own poems in a variety of magazines outside California.

Record stores also served as a site for poets whose primary interest in writing was to connect with the kind of audience that Dennis Cooper had envisioned for his magazine, *Little Caesar*, back in the late 1970s. McCabe's Guitar Shop in Santa Monica and BeBop Records in the San Fernando Valley were two of the most prominent locations for these poets, and they had the advantage of being the outlets for Harvey Kubernik's work in the recording studios of Los Angeles. Most of the interest centered around writers and performers whose recordings on record albums produced by Harvey Kubernik exemplified the low culture divide of postmodernism. Kubernik was born and raised in Los Angeles; his father had operated a dry-cleaning store, on Adams Boulevard, that pressed the suits of Buddy Colette, one of the premier figures of the jazz scene in Central Avenue. Kubernik had first aspired to be in the record business, and had spent time in the studio with Phil Spector and Leonard Cohen. The transition from producing songs for an all-female band, The Runaways, to spoken word impresario included failed attempts to get record deals for young comedians such as Richard Lewis and Robin Williams. When Kubernik lost his job with A&M records in the bloodbath of 1979, he committed himself to "spoken word," and traded his work in studios doing janitorial work for the right to record between midnight and 6:00 AM. In the early 1970s, he produced a trilogy of albums that served as vocal anthologies of Los Angeles poets and performance poets. *Voices of the Angeles*, *English as a Second Language*, and *Neighborhood Rhythms* contained short tracks by dozens of well-known figures, such as Dennis Cooper, as well as obscure poets. It must be said that if the poets associated with Beyond Baroque, Papa Bach Bookstore, Chatterton's Bookshop, and Sisterhood Bookstore felt alienated from the mainstream, Kubernik's pangs over being dismissed were even more intense. Even events that might have provided a solid crossover audience for Kubernik kept him at arm's length; it wasn't until 1993 that Lummis's L.A. Poetry Festival opened up its doors to Kubernik.[16] The "Heard Word" reading in downtown Los Angeles on November 6, 1993, was a major success, though, and Kubernik's recordings found themselves on steady rotation on Liza Richardson's late-night show, "Man in the Moon."

Although performance poetry attracted widespread media attention through the marketing of itself as "slam poetry," the primary school of poets in Los Angeles who were interested in a blend of page and stage had little use for the unwillingness of performance poets to read assiduously from every canonical level. If anything could be said to raise the hackles of poets such as Charles Webb, Suzanne Lummis, and Laurel Ann Bogen about their kinship with proto-Stand Up poets such as Bukowski, Koertge, and Locklin, it was the slightest hint, no matter how casually uttered, that their reading of other poets did not extend much beyond those with whom they were regionally affiliated. In part, this belief that the Stand Up poets were not serious may have derived from their preference for poetry that could generate laughter that was spontaneously thoughtful. No other group of poets seemed to seek a renewed version of what the *Coastlines* editors had called for in asking for a third path.

Through anthologies such as *Grand Passion* and *Stand Up Poetry*, Webb and Lummis seemed to be compiling a potential canon that was far different from anything that would be found in an anthology to which Vangelisti and Messerli would ever contribute their work. Yet Vangelisti had not just featured individual poems of Koertge and Locklin in *Invisible City*, but had also published their book-length collections of their writing. Exemplified by pieces such as "The Bear Is Ill," Koertge's *12 Photographs of Yellowstone*, in particular, was a proto-Stand Up collection of poems.

The Bear Is Ill

said the sign on the box-office
and people were turning away left
and right

I guess they wanted to see Timmy
the Bear wrestle The Masked Marvel
as much

as I did, and when they couldn't
see the bear they just wouldn't
see anything

at all. I started to turn away too
when the ticket man stopped me.
Hey, he said,

don't go. We've got a great card.
Who needs bears with what I got
lined up?

I want to see the bear, I told him.
How about this, he said. The
1000 Pound

convict vs. Super Hog. Nope, I said.
Well, then, would you go for a
round-robin

Tag-team match featuring Snow White
and the 7 Dwarfs Vs. The Wicked
Queen and

Her Elfin Retinue? Nope, I said
again. Then how about Sphincter Man
vs. The Stinking

Mess? No deal, I said. When are you
planning to have the bear again?
Never, he said.

The fucking bear's dead. Son of a bitch
died in his sleep last night.
Jesus, I said.

Does that mean the bear's gone forever?
That's right, kid, forever. Now
shove off

somebody behind you wants to buy a ticket.

The headquarters for the Stand Up congeries of poets is Long Beach, where Gerald Locklin has unabashedly held firm to a poetics that steadfastly gazes askance through its dime-store sunglasses at the overwrought intellectual infrastructure of avant-garde programming. Publishing exclusively with small presses both in England and the United States, Locklin has firmly established himself as an archetypal Stand Up artist, the one most capable of bantering the foibles of Los Angeles when its resident artists take themselves too seriously, and taking them seriously when all others are expeditiously primed to chortle in disbelief. In one of his poems, he laments his daughter's ineluctable loss of primal joy at seeing him return home. In the poem's narration, she has not yet lost it, but he knows she will. The poem itself will never lose that joy, nor will any reader who gives herself or himself over to the emotional risk that Stand Up poetry subtly encourages its readers to accept.

Ultimately, the poets in Los Angeles whose strategies seem almost irreconcilable are the ones who most likely will enable readers of the poets in other regions to understand how poets learn to talk with each other by accepting the presence of the astonishing opposite. If Locklin, Vangelisti, and Hickman have all managed to find themselves sharing the pages of the same anthologies and magazines, surely other recombinations only await our assent to complicate the enormity of multitudinous voices refusing to blend, even as in bending to listen more closely to each other, the chorus sustains a precarious density.

Conclusion

The Subjunctive Legacy
of the West Coast Poetry Renaissance

"sweetzer & sunset let me out sold poor torn patience"
—Harry E. Northup, "The Lord Is My Preposition"

James Harding and Cindy Rosenthal, the editors of *Restaging the Sixties: Radical Theaters and Their Legacies*, argue that cultural work has a proleptic character, built into its assemblage, which may not be visible to those who are encased within immediate spheres of self-sacrificing labor. At the end of their introductory essay, Harding and Rosenthal ask "When do we begin to speak of legacy? For there must be a threshold and a crossing, beyond which a legacy no longer looms on the horizon but stands before us" (23). In the case of the small press movement, especially on the West Coast, the need to address its legacy requires that its efforts be examined within a discursive context far larger than the length of this study permits. I have hardly touched, for instance, on the matter of compulsory military service during the Vietnam War and yet the choices confronting young men born between 1945 and 1954 could be said in some instances to be a conscious part of their commitment to publishing projects in the 1970s.

The legacy of the small press movement will require that the errors and oversights of those who contributed to its development be used as an impetus for theoretical evolution as well as beneficial praxis by those who wish to make literature a site of cultural engagement and communal affirmation rather than passive consumption. First, though, before a legacy can be utilized, the full contents of what might constitute a legacy need to become more widely known. One can hardly be influenced by knowledge that is padlocked within an obscure warehouse. In May 2010 I gave a talk at the American Literature Association conference in San Francisco that focused on book production at the West Coast Print Center. David Kippen, who was on the panel with me and who had headed up the Literature Program at the

National Endowment for the Arts for several years, said that he had never heard of this site. Yet the importance of the West Coast Print Center to the resurgence of literary activity in the Bay Area during the 1970s can be read in the colophons at the back of dozens of books typeset by John McBride, Johanna Drucker, and Barrett Watten. Beyond Baroque's NewComp Graphics was perhaps even more crucial to the poets in Los Angeles. As a scholar digs into libraries, both public and personal, to find these books and generate a bibliography, the colophons are crucial clues. They are a residual, unfading beam that backlights the fulminating resistance of poets as well as maverick editors and publishers.

If the NEA has forgotten its own contribution to this period, perhaps the lapse could be attributed to a desire to suppress the possibility that writers would demand such facilities again in order to expedite the distribution of a new generation of writers. The Web and the Internet create an illusion that all that is needed is a hard drive for works of imaginative literature to gain an audience. It is arguably true that if the small press movement had had these technological tools in 1980, then many of the small presses that were publishing in 1980 might well have continued their production for another decade or two. Depending on cyberspace to achieve literary value, however, would be like fantasizing that political change can be inculcated without leaving the creature comforts installed alongside pixilated screens.

As I worked on the final drafts of this study, I became all too aware that one of the central assumptions I had mentioned to friends as I began my initial research was in danger of fading away. The emphasis on Los Angeles poets must not be used as a way to fragment important questions that can develop out of considering the legacy of the West Coast Poetry Renaissance as a whole. Legacy is not local; the Los Angeles poetry renaissance of the 1970s and 1980s, backlit by those who struggled against even greater odds in previous decades to find a "third path," does not have an autonomous patrimony. What happened in the plenitude of community formation in Venice and Ocean Park, and at KPFK-FM radio station, and at the editorial desks of Leland Hickman, Paul Vangelisti, Dennis Cooper, and Aleida Rodríguez is only a legacy if all of its implicit manifestations are in conscious dialogue with the small presses in Berkeley, Oakland, San Francisco, and Bolinas, never forgetting that a significant number of poets moved between these areas during this period.

On a smaller scale, though not necessarily any less intense, one could find parallel efforts emerging out of the coalescences of fluctuating migrations in the Northwest and the Midwest as well as the South. Minneapolis-St. Paul has had a vibrant poetry "scene" for many years, but is that scene singular, and what features do the layers of those scenes share with the poets working in Duluth? While the upper Midwest hardly has a full-scale enter-tainment industry to contend with in the same manner as the poets in Los Angeles, Detroit's music scenes—from the greatness of Motown onward—and the more recent vigor in Minneapolis should hint that a complex set of poetic projects await our examination as indicators of alternatives to the development of sustainable poetics as our mutual legacy as well as new mod-els of social configuration. In looking back at the political forces that beset the aspirations of poets working out of specific environments, it would behoove us to revisit Paul Goodman's influence on the baby boom generation. "In Goodman's view," Terrence Diggory argues, "the intimate acquaintances are themselves alienated, 'estranged from themselves, from one another, and from their artist.' 'Intimate community' does not exist in modern society, but the poet 'takes the initiative' toward forming such community as *if* it did exist. Reciprocally, the reader is invited to read as *if* he were a member of the community the writer has imagined" (18–19). One major contention of this book is that the manifold interactions involved in the production and distri-bution of books as a primary gift within communities of poets constitute a significant portion of those alternative, subjunctive activities.

Legacy *bequeaths*: a familiar, almost archaic chord of association. The noun-verb combination is almost Bakhtinian in its immediate conjunction. Perhaps community is archaic, even as an existential yearning. Nevertheless, I have written this book *as if* it still could provide the knowledge to hope for more than can be justifiably claimed as aspirations for the social value of poetry. In the work of those I have mentioned, however, lingers the notion of a paradoxical gift, a blessing bestowed with all the unresolved aspects of the initial conflicts that generated these particular, improvised but hopeful responses. A legacy is an adamant rebuke: why have you not given your-self the same permission that those who assembled the possibility of legacy awarded themselves? Legacies suffuse the thresholds of the next generation, which must find new motives as well as means to delineate its portion of omniscience.

Notes

Introduction

1. Michael Davidson's *Ghostlier Demarcations: Modern Poetry and the Material Word* and *Guys Like Us: Citing Masculinity in Cold War Poetics* both contain essays which pertain to the construction of marginality. Chapter 2 of the latter book, "From Margin to Mainstream: Postwar Poetry and the Politics of Containment," builds on careful distinctions between various increments of marginality. "The Beats . . . neither sold out to the mainstream nor rejected it; rather, they worked strategically *within* it to develop an immanent critique." (Chicago: University of Chicago Press, 2004) Davidson argues that it was the cold war ideology that marginalized the Beats more than any other literary establishment.

2. In *Poetic License: Essays on Modernist and Postmodernist Lyric*, Marjorie Perloff regards class, gender, and race as categories that all lead towards an essentialist impasse in the hands of critics who regard it as their "role . . . to characterize the dominant discourse and then to read against it that writing it has excluded or marginalized, thus redefining the canon so as to give pride of place to the hitherto repressed" (2). She suggests that the critics of poetry consider "redefining the term *dominant class* as what Charles Bernstein has called 'official verse culture.' For increasingly, in the twentieth century, the opposition arises not from, say, a working-class 'us' against a middle-class or upper-class 'them' (or even female against male, gay against straight, black against white) but from those who, whatever their actual status in the social order, refuse the norms of mainstream publishing, book reviewing, university curricula, creative writing programs, and so on" (3). A genuine opposition, however, does more than "refuse" norms. During the 1970s, especially, the small press movement attempted to generate and establish a set of alternative norms that specifically addressed issues of class, race, and gender. Unfortunately, a phrase such as "increasingly, in the twentieth century" is far too vague to be reliable as a cultural gauge. Even if Perloff provided a better focused claim that proved to be accurate for the 1990s, it would not cancel the need to

address the dialogue between gender, race, and class and the material conditions of access in the small press movement of the 1970s.

3. Leland Hickman was the first poet-editor I know of to layer Everson's book into the groundswell of poetry magazine production on the West Coast in the 1970s and 1980s. Four years after Everson's book was published, Hickman quoted a long passage from *Archetype West* at the end of his interview with John Rechy, which ran in issue number 17 of *Bachy: A Journal of the Arts in Los Angeles* (Spring 1980). *Bachy*'s subtitle was an addition by Hickman to the original title, *Bachy*; the staff box listed as contributing editors Paul Vangelisti, Joseph Hansen, Robert Peters, Barry Brennan, Kate Braverman, and Rod Bradley. The first half of the quoted passage reads: "For popular success stands opposite the individual critical spirit as alternate or rival, just as the Dionysian and Apollonian archetypes stand opposed. There is no more solution to the anguish of blocked archetypal tension. It is an anguish which genius must sustain to achieve full stretch, and which creative form, like an angel of deliverance, arrives to resolve. But lacking such an angel the recourse to virtuosity, which talent implements and success, like a devil of ensnarement, arises to confer, is insidiousness itself" (11). Almost one hundred pages later, Hickman's interview with Martha (Lifson) Ronk ends with a similar skepticism of the seductive power of virtuosity, which Ronk associates with East Coast poetry.

4. Los Angeles as a singular postmodern urban space has received considerable attention the past twenty-five years from critics such as Roger Keil (*Los Angeles: Globalization, Urbanization, and Social Struggles*), Mike Davis (*City of Quartz* and *Ecology of Fear*), Edward Soja, Rosalyn Deutsche, Dolores Hayden (*The Power of Place*), and Jean Baudrillard. None of their writing, Eric Avila notes, can be read outside of the massive preliminary work produced by Carey McWilliams; despite all these efforts, Avila observes that "after several decades of inquiry, scholars agree that Los Angeles defies the conventions of urban theory" (McNamara, *The Cambridge Companion to the Literature of Los Angeles*, 177). In part, this antithetical elusiveness derives from the fact that the urban figuration of Los Angeles is always already complicated by its proximity to a regional landscape resembling Shelley's "Ozymandias." On the other hand, the city's legal boundaries simultaneously dissolve into government-owned parks that are far more riparian than might be expected. Of recent books that address this intermingling of the civil and chthonic, Bradley John Monsma's *The Sespe Wild: Southern California's Last Free River* is a fine meditation on the congruency of nature abutting urban nurture. Books of memoirs or personal essays are increasingly making use of Los Angeles as an instantiating trope. *Making Time: Essays on the Nature of Los Angeles* by William L. Fox, who began his literary career as the editor of *West Coast Poetry Review*, provides a general reader with an exceptionally intelligent, closeup perusal of iconic sites of Southern California such as the La Brea Tar Pits, Mt. Wilson, Forest Lawn Memorial, and the Jet Propulsion Laboratory. With a casual tone that belies its deftness, D. J. Waldie's *Holy Land*, a memoir of growing up in Lakewood, demonstrates on a ground-level basis how suburban cartography remains anchored in the aftermath of global warfare. Waldie's book serves as a counterbalance to other

incisive memoirs set in California, such as Joan Didion's *Where I Was From.* The unique urban scale of Los Angeles is the canvas for a projected trilogy of books by Jeremiah Axelrod, the first of which, *Inventing Autopia: Dreams and Visions of the Modern Metropolis in Jazz Age Los Angeles,* was published in 2009 by the University of California Press. The second volume, "Constructing Autopia: Freeways, Suburbs, and Sprawl in Postwar Southern California," is scheduled to be published in the near future. A special issue of *American Quarterly: Los Angeles and the Future of Urban Cultures,* edited by Raúl Homero Villa and George J. Sanchez (Baltimore: Johns Hopkins University Press, 2005), is a superb collection of diverse essays on the culture and politics of Los Angeles. Dolores Hayden's *The Power of Place* poignantly argues that any sincere analysis of the problems confronting the singularity of Los Angeles must deliberately foreground "ethnic and women's history as the missing mainstream experience." David James's *The Sons and Daughters of Los: Culture and Community in L.A.,* which I will draw upon later on in this book, is an exemplary volume of essays that present "diverse social history as part of the public landscape" (*The Power of Place,* 244). James's essay, "Los Angeles, Writing and Space" in *Seeing Los Angeles: A Different Look at a Different City,* is simultaneously replete and compact in its interrogation of the relationship of ethnic writers to culture industry.

1. The Cartography of Dissidence

1. The tone of Murphet's argument suggests that mutually repellant social forces are at work which disallow any meaningful contact between these groups. While Coleman's early editorial supporters, such as Lee Hickman and myself, were not part of any academic culture in the 1970s, her maturation as a poet was not completely separate from any contact with the academy. For instance, Coleman's early encounter, as an 18-year-old poet, with CSU Los Angeles professor (and winner of the Lamont Prize) Henri Coulette demonstrates the importance, for those whose beginnings are confined to limited expectations, of finding astute mentors. Ryan Van Cleave, *Contemporary American Poetry: Behind the Scenes.* While the impetus toward "becoming-minor" in Los Angeles is vigorous unto the present moment, I would agree with Meiling Cheng that "becoming minor is never free from the possibility of becoming major. . . . The boundary between different becomings is porous and elastic." *In Other Los Angeleses: Multicentric Performance Art* (Berkeley: University of California Press, 2002), 232.

2. Jay Clayton in *The Pleasures of Babel: Contemporary American Literature and Theory* focuses on fiction and takes a different tack in coming to a similar conclusion. "We live in a great period of writing, certainly the equal of any in the comparatively short history of this nation," Clayton asserts. However, he adds that "today's society is constructing a literature without masterpieces." (New York: Oxford University Press, 1993), 148.

3. Kevin McNamara has assembled an invaluable set of essays in *The Cambridge Companion to the Literature of Los Angeles.* This volume astutely surveys Los

Angeles-inflected fiction writers produced by the usual suspects (Nathaniel West, F. Scott Fitzgerald, John Fante, Thomas Pynchon, John Rechy, Carolyn See, Alison Lurie, T. C. Boyle) as well as by figures who might not be as familiar to general readers (Steve Erickson, Hisaye Yamamoto, Acosta).

4. In a book of essays, *Married to the Icepick Killer*, Carol Muske-Dukes appoints herself as someone worthy of taking on the questions raised by Starr toward the end of his book: "Could California nurture excellence? And who was in charge of authenticating excellence?" (480) Muske-Dukes has little use for non-academic poets in Los Angeles, whom she claims without any evidence whatsoever have very limited knowledge of poetry outside of their self-enclosed communities. Ironically, Muske-Dukes recently served as the poet-laureate of California, appointed to that position by Arnold Schwarzenegger.

5. In "The Beat Writers: Phenomenon or Generation," Thomas Parkinson observed that "From about 1944 on, the area has been distinguished by . . . a group of people—mainly poets—who were interested in creating and establishing a community of literary interest. They were like coral insects building a reef that might ultimately create the calm and pleasure of a lagoon" (*Poets, Poems, Movements* 173). Parkinson's use of an ecological image for community formation is worth further commentary; any critic's examination of Parkinson's role as a poet-critic within this community should take note of Robert Duncan's letter to Denise Levertov dated January 25, 1961. Robert J. Bertholf and Albert Gelpi, eds., *The Letters of Robert Duncan and Denise Levertov* (Stanford: Stanford University Press, 2004), 276–277.

6. *Restaging the Sixties: Radical Theaters and Their Legacies*, edited by James M. Harding and Cindy Rosenthal, looks at theaters from across the United States, including the Free Southern Theater and the feminist group, At the Foot of the Mountain. The last chapter of *Playing Underground: A Critical History of the 1960s Off-Off-Broadway Movement* by Stephen J. Bottoms cites Murray Mednick's observation about the Padua Hills Theater Festival that "In many ways, Padua was a furthering and even a fulfillment of what began at (Theater) Genesis." (Ann Arbor: University of Michigan Press, 2004), 355. Neither book, however, mentions the Provisional Theater Company in Los Angeles, which deserves a critical study in its own right as a left-wing, agit-prop theater company that toured the United States with such group productions as "Inching Through the Everglades."

7. A literal street-level view of life as a small press editor and publisher at work at this time can be found in *American Odyssey: A Book Selling Travelogue* by Len Fulton with Ellen Ferber (Paradise, CA: Dustbooks, 1975). Popular enough to require a second printing, *American Odyssey* recounts Fulton's and Ferber's seven-week trip in 1974 across the United States to hustle his novel, *The Grassman*, as well as the tenth edition of the *International Directory of Little Magazines & Small Presses* and the *Whole COSMEP Catalog*. They sold five hundred copies of *The Grassman* and two hundred copies of the *Directory*. They also attended the COSMEP conference in New York City. COSMEP co-sponsored a book fair with the American Library Association that year in New York, which lured fifteen thousand people to its tables over a three-day period (*American Odyssey* 14). I doubt that more than

2 percent, if that, of the independent book stores listed in "Appendix B: An Anno-tated List of Bookstores" are still in operation. For mid-1970s idealism at its best, see "On the Road with Two Small Press Missionaries in a White Whale," *Coda: Poets & Writers Newsletter*, May 1975, pages 1–3 (New York: Poets & Writers).

8. One of the most comprehensive books documenting the proliferation of underground newspapers during the 1960s is *Voices from the Underground: Insider Histories of the Vietnam Era Underground Press* (volume 1), edited by Ken Wachs-berger (1993). Not all of this writing stayed underground. By 1971, for instance, a Laurel Edition paperback from Dell Publishing Company entitled *Liberation Now! Writings from the Women's Liberation Movement* gathered articles from under-ground publications such as *Up From Under*. Although this study will not be able to consider the relationship between underground newspapers and poetry magazines and literary small presses, I would urge critics who are interested, for instance, in the work of Alta, the editor and publisher of Shameless Hussy Press, to acknowl-edge the contributions made by feminist newspapers during that period. *Are We There Yet?: A Continuing History of Lavender Woman, A Chicago Lesbian News-paper 1971–1976*, edited by Michal Brody (1985) is a valuable account of one such newspaper.

9. A. D. Winans, an editor and publisher based in San Francisco, wrote a memoir, *The Holy Grail: Charles Bukowksi and the Second Coming Revolution,* that focuses on "Hank" more than Winans's magazine and press, which among many titles published an anthology of California poets coinciding with the bicentennial celebrations in the United States. Chapter 12 provides some anecdotal sense of how COSMEP disintegrated as it became large enough to lobby with some effectiveness for grant projects.

10. In an interview which remains only partially transcribed, Barrett Watten talked with me on October 25, 2000, about the years he worked at the West Coast Print Center, a facility located on the outskirts of Oakland which provided techno-logical assistance to literary small presses. For once, at least, I knew that I was not the only one who understood that giving birth to books is not some magical process akin to storks bringing babies. I have read autobiographies, memoirs, and biogra-phies of individuals, such as Alfred Kreymberg, who worked on little magazines back in the modernist period, but none of them provide even a hint of the physical process of putting out the magazine. A thorough materialist-culture account of the small press movement would integrate the technological changes that facilitated the insurgency of the small press movement.

11. Jahan Ramazani, "Introduction," *The Norton Anthology of Modern and Con-temporary Poetry*, lx. Embedded in tautological assumptions of who qualifies to be described as a poet, Ramazani's account of the development of contemporary American poetry raises disturbing questions of how well he has read the poetry produced in the 1970s. The majority of poets who were young in the 1970s, and who are still writing and publishing, did not receive their training in MFA programs.

12. Daniel Halpern, *Young American Poets*. The publisher and manager of *Will-more City* was Alex N. Scandalios, and it was published out of Carlsbad, California,

which is slightly north of San Diego. Scandalios was using Gemini Graphics in Marina del Rey to print his magazine by issue no. 6–7. Stephen Paul Miller's *Surveillance in the Seventies* provides another survey of social reorganization and artistic response in that decade.

13. Report of Judy of July 11, 1974, COSMEP meeting in New York. *Cosmep Newsletter*, August 1974. 6–7. Hogan, who was primarily a poet then, became a well-recognized novelist. She was very active in organizing the southern regional branch of COSMEP. Her reference to the CCLM portion of the meeting could easily be developed into a chapter in and of itself. In my recollection of this period, the level of hostility between the members of COSMEP and the board of directors of CCLM exceeds my capacity for description. Caustic activists in COSMEP might have considered lions and hyenas as an appropriate analogy. An attempt to negotiate a truce occurred on April 30, 1974, when COSMEP chair Len Fulton met with William Phillips and Ron Sukenick of CCLM and arrived at a seven-point settlement that was published in a special issue of *COSMEP Newsletter* (April 1974). *Coda: Poets & Writers Newsletter* is a quick source for a list of magazines that received grants; in 1976, for instance, see issues April/May and September/October. The issue of the lack of democracy in government-sponsored or government-affiliated operations at that point unfortunately remains all too relevant; when was the last time, for instance, poets were asked to vote on who would serve on the "peer panels" that hand out grants from the National Endowment for the Arts?

14. The choice of a multitude of poets in the United States to break the constraints of the author-function and to challenge the limited social identity of writing was in part a response to the immense social upheaval which rippled through American society in this period, but the headwaters of this development can be traced back to crises, tribulations, and minor triumphs for writers in many societies during the evolution of print culture. Disputing Foucault's periodization of literary and scientific texts, Roger Chartier emphasizes that "the trajectory of the author (of vernacular texts) can be thought of as a gradual change" (*The Order of Books* 58), and proposes that the transitions involved in the emergence of the social role of the author are not simply proleptic instances of juridical force and penal impositions in the early modern period. Chartier points to the physicality of texts, both in their production as commodities and in their consumption, as central elements for any analysis of the social meaning of literacy, and proposes a "fundamental question" which must permeate any assessment that includes a multivalent perspective of "textual criticism, bibliography, and cultural history: in the societies of the *ancien regime*, how did increased circulation of printed matter transform forms of sociability, permit new modes of thought, and changes people's relationship with power?" Although Chartier's analysis does mention the oral reading of texts as part of the distribution of a writer's works, I would emphasize that the increased circulation of texts through performances and public readings is crucial to the notions of a shift away from a national literature or an ineffable canon.

15. Poets in the United States who are identified as part of the countercultures that emerged between 1948 and 1968 seem to have the misfortune of being analyzed

by critics who are very vague on details, and yet vehement in their condemnation. Andrew Ross's sweeping condemnation of the poets in Donald Allen's *The New American Poetry* (*Marxism*, Nelson, Grossberg) misses crucial aspects of the social challenges, such as gay sexuality and drug use, that their work poses. This lapse occurs because Ross imagines that the only kind of cultural impact Allen's anthology had was on the world of poetry itself. One of the interesting ways that Allen's anthology works is as a gay text. If any book could be said to initiate the process of queering the canon, *The New American Poetry* not only put its queer shoulder to the wheel, it did so without even including the poem by Allen Ginsberg that concluded with that ironic jibe! This is the first anthology to come out of the closet, even if its editor never did. Take note, for instance, of Robert Duncan's "bio note" in which he matter-of-factly announces the fact that he lives with the man he loves, Jess. There is also the deeply divisive issue of drug use. One senses that lurking behind Ross's all-out attack is a fear of being tainted in any way, shape, or form with any writer or cultural worker who advocated even the mildest of drugs. Aspiring radicals are usually as Calvinist as the oppressors they want to subdue. I have yet to find, in fact, any article that addresses the valorization of drugs in Allen's anthology. It's not a subject that can be easily avoided, but academics have managed to do so ever since the book appeared. It's possible they do not want to see it as an issue that needs to be addressed.

16. "A few years after I came to Los Angeles there was a fine little group around a magazine called *Coastlines*. There were Thomas McGrath and Bert Meyers, exceptionally gifted poets. There were Gene Frumkin, Stanley Kiesel and Alvaro Cardona-Hine, true poets, complex and sincere men. I contributed many poems to *Coastlines*. In some manner that I can't analyze, they must have influenced my writing. Probably because they were the first group of poets with whom I was more or less associated. Not that I was ever a part of this group—I was always on the periphery, never integral to any group. Still, when I wrote my little book *Passage after Midnight* (Inferno Press, San Francisco), there was a new feeling in the poems, more energetic, more urban, more modern. Is it because of my association with *Coastlines*, and all those fine poets?" William Pillin's interview by Leland Hickman appeared in issue 16 of *Bachy* magazine. Pillin's claim that he was "never integral to any group" may be an accurate approximation of his subjective experience, but Perkoff's letter is firmly categorical in its assignment of Pillin to the *Inferno* group. It should be emphasized that Perkoff seems to have thoroughly enjoyed Pillin's company as a poet and to have respected his work. Four years after writing that letter, they met at KPFK-FM studios and read back to back as part of a poetry program. William Margolis published a detailed account of Perkoff's portion of the reading in issue number 4 of *Bachy*.

17. William Margolis could properly be said to be a typical example of the overarching and encompassing quality of the West Coast Poetry Renaissance. It is quite simply impossible to limit Margolis to one group. My assignment of Margolis to the *Inferno* group occurred before I met with Marsha Getzler, one of the few surviving members of Robert Alexander's Temple of Man in Venice, California.

Margolis's archive, housed at Getzler's residence, has a substantial body of photographs, including many in which Margolis and Bob Kaufman are standing together at various street corners in San Francisco. The cache includes the only known photograph of Bruce Boyd, who at the time of the picture was living in Venice.

18. Jeff Weddle's *Bohemian New Orleans: The Story of the Outsider and Loujon Press* is a literary biography of Jon and Louise Webb, who published books as well the *Outsider* magazine. The book contains an appendix listing, issue by issue, each author and the title of every poem or story. As an editor, Webb's attitude toward conventional poetry would have been obvious to all but the most obtuse reader. "Fondly dedicated to the Academic Quarterlies" by Jon and Louise Webb, Russell Edson's editorial, "One night a horse quit its barn," opens the first issue with a meditation, in the guise of a "fable," on a horse who uses the open window of a house as a place to back up to, lift its tail and shit.

The *Outsider*'s editorial and production format significantly influenced Los Angeles poet and actor Jack Grapes, who moved from New Orleans to Los Angeles to launch his own publishing ventures in the late 1960s.

2. Thinking Alone in Company

1. As literary communities developed and matured after World War II, both in northern and Southern California, an antinomian critique of pastoral self-reliance enabled them to reassess the dominant canon. De Beauvoir used Henry Miller for an example: "He's not important at all in New York, but on the West Coast where he lives, he is regarded as a genius" (199). The willingness to acknowledge the superior gift and talent of another writer is not a casual or superfluous detail. If community is missing in modernist thinking, the problem can partially be traced to an ideology of individual careers and a notion of autonomous authorship. The first step in creating community involves a generous reading of the manuscripts and books of others and being willing, as one shares one's knowledge of their imaginative wisdom, to concede within a selfless critique their potential value as possibly greater than your own.

2. Frona Lane worked as a teacher of poetry for many years in the Los Angeles area and had a book of poems published by Alan Swallow.

3. Hendrick's quote is from a clipped newspaper article in the author's possession. Grover Jacoby, Jr., was the oldest child, and only son, in a prosperous Los Angeles family of six children. His poems appeared several times in *Voices* magazine, which was published in Maine. Its tables of contents in the 1950s included contributors such as Wallace Stevens, Thomas McGrath, Harold Norse, Marcia Masters, Jesse Stuart, Jean Burden, Galway Kinnell, Frank O'Hara, Eve Merriam, Allen Ginsberg, and William Pillin. In 1953, for instance, in issue number 151 of *Voices*, Jacoby appeared alongside May Sarton, Langston Hughes, and Louis Simpson, and two issues later, in 1954, was featured in a "California Issue," which included Robinson Jeffers, Josephine Miles, Joan La Bombard, Brother Antonius, Kenneth Rexroth, and Edwin Fussell.

4. Although never achieving the prominence of *Variegation*, *Line* magazine was distributed and read outside of Southern California. Letters to the editors included notes of appreciation from the Midwest. Although it primarily published poetry, the two most important pieces it published were prose. The first is a virtually unknown short story called "The Silk Kimono and the Vase" by Hiroshi Kashiwagi, which is an account of a young boy watching his mother having to choose what possessions to pack as the family prepares to enter the concentration camps for Japanese Americans. It may well be the first short story by a Japanese American to appear in a literary magazine after World War II. For those interested in internment camp literature, it should be noted that this short story is not reprinted in Kashiwagi's *Swimming to America*. Kashiwagi appeared in the documentary film, *Rabbit in the Moon*, in 1999. The other prose piece was Charles Newman's piece of experimental prose. *Line* magazine did mount what was termed a "Modern Poetry Exhibit" during the first three weeks of March 1948 at the studio of Jacquelyn Segall (7391 and 1/.2 S. Hope Street, Los Angeles). The editorial staff of *Line* included Sam Bluefarb, Helen and Richard Curry, Art Casey, and Gordon Kinzer.

5. Poems from *Variegation* were reprinted alongside poems from the *Kenyon Review*, *Saturday Review*, and *Sewanee Review*. One of the poems which the *New York Herald-Tribune* reprinted from *Variegation*, "Big Sur" by Eric Barker, went on to be reprinted again in the *New York Times* on May 3, 1953.

6. Jacoby's *Variegation* was also one of the few poetry magazines at that time to address in any specific detail the dangers faced by workers inside the factories mentioned in Miles's poem. A long poem, "Assignments," by Aveline Perkins was serialized in *Variegation* by Jacoby, and although its rhetoric is often florid, it is at times quite vivid in its depictions of the toll exacted on industrial laborers: work is not just tedium, but constant exposure to the risk of being killed or crippled. Depictions of danger at work in American literature are not new—*The Jungle* broke that literary ground several decades before Perkins wrote "Assignments"—but one reads this poem and wonders how it was possible that it took until 1970 for Congress to pass a law that specified "that workplaces must be free from recognized hazards" (Cohen 444). A quarter century after the passage of that law, a survey showed that ten thousand amputations occur every year on jobs in the United States. Even if each incident were only a single finger or a toe, that's an average of a finger or toe of a worker on the hour, twenty-four hours a day, seven days a week, no holidays. The point made by "Assignments" has hardly become irrelevant. It is possible, by the way, that "Aveline Perkins" was a pen name for Jacoby.

7. Biographical details are scarce. According to the issue of *Poetry (Chicago)* that Hanson Kellogg appeared in, he was a professional puppeteer who lived in Glendale. Alan Swallow published his full-length collection of poems, *Attics Own Houses*.

8. His selection of incoming correspondence included more than letters from poetry magazine editors. In issue number 15 in early 1956, May ran a letter from Ann Carll Reid, editor of *One* magazine in Los Angeles, in which she insisted that her magazine was "not limited in scope as some would suppose—even though

devoted primarily to the homosexual. Its purpose presents a challenge . . . to anyone interested in the problem of civil rights and equality for all people." His willingness to provide a gay magazine space to publicize its existence alongside magazines that were predominantly devoted to contemporary poetry indicates that May perceived his project as involving more than a challenge to institutional literature.

9. In contrast to May's reaction to major magazines and the implicit adversarial position taken by West Coast writers and poets, Schrag's book on the emergence of a major arts scene in Los Angeles during the 1950s cites *Time* magazine articles on that scene in a manner that suggest Los Angeles artists welcomed, if not courted, the approval of high culture forces on the East Coast. Her footnotes contain several citations of articles in *Time* magazine, many of which contribute to a general valorization of what was regarded by the East Coast as a provincial or culturally dormant region.

May's magazine is useful in many respects, especially in regard to the historical record. One of the most frequent misconceptions about the development of alternative literature on the West Coast is that the only book that ran into censorship troubles during the summer of 1957 in San Francisco was Allen Ginsberg's *Howl and Other Poems*. Gil Orlovitz's *Statement of Erika Keith*, which was published as a special issue of *Miscellaneous Man*, a magazine edited by William Margolis, but to which James Boyer May was a contributing editor, was also subject to obscenity charges. Charges were brought against Orlovitz's book, but eventually dropped. May published a considerable amount of poetry and criticism by Orlovitz. Neither of them was considered a member of the Beat movement. The erasure of Orlovitz from the standard narrative allows the contrast between straight and Beat to seem a dichotomy without any nuance, whereas an editor such as May perceived the tumult on the West Coast as a far more complicated affair.

10. A representative figure in this regard would be poet and spoken word artist Michael C. Ford, who was born in Illinois around 1940, but spent almost all his childhood and youth in Southern California. As a teenager, he attended the jazz and poetry event that is discussed in the Venice West chapter. Ford published a special issue of his magazine, *Mt. Alverno Review*, as a fundraiser for Patchen in 1971. He went on to found and edit the *Sunset Palms Hotel*, which published poetry by a wide range of poets, including Tom Waits. Ford's record album, *Language Commando*, was nominated for a Grammy, and for many years he performed his poetry in venues such as McCable's Guitar Shop in Santa Monica, with keyboardist Ray Manzarek of The Doors. After being billed at McCabe's with Ford and Manzarek, Michael McClure began to collaborate in public performances with Manzarek.

11. In issue number 35 of *Trace*, May published an impassioned note from Clarence Major, the editor of the *Coercion Review*, urging every young poet to launch a poetry magazine and to keep it "going for as long as possible." Although Major ended up teaching at UC Davis, he spent the most significant portion of the period this book primarily addresses outside of California.

12. May's praise for the authors in *Evergreen Review* seems to be reserved for writers associated with the West Coast, in general, and Venice West in particular.

May was especially fond of Henry Miller. However, in praising Alexander Trocchi and Charles Foster, whose "The Troubled Makers" went on to be reprinted in a major anthology, May was hardly bestowing his blessing on Venice West. He had little use for Lawrence Lipton or Lipton's idea of a literary community. In giving a report of the Los Angeles scene to the national audience enjoyed by *Trace*, May included his own attendance at public events such as Langston Hughes reading his poetry backed up by the Ralph Pena quartet.

13. In February 1956, *Coastlines* merged with CFLA, which included dancers, filmmakers, and theater people. Dahl described CFLA as "A non-profit, non-political public affairs organization to encourage individual growth in those activities not now served adequately by mass communications media. Without being narrowly partisan, we look for new forms in the art, in political education, and in science. We are conservative in the sense that we try to retain the best traditions, and we are radical in our demand for development and restatement of the universal problems of existence" (*Coastlines*, Spring 1956, 38).

14. William Pillin shared the ambivalence, if not antipathy, that many poets in May's "Sensible School" felt toward both the "raw" and the "cooked" schools. Years later, in an interview conducted by Leland Hickman, Pillin made his disdain for both abundantly clear: "All Black Mountain poets bore me." "Robert Lowell is a bore."

On the other hand, he did not see himself as part of the Sensible School, either, although he acknowledged their impact.

15. Information about the lives of Lawrence Ferlinghetti and James Laughlin is not difficult to come by, but considering the impact that his editorial projects had on American poetry, comparatively little is known about the trajectory of Donald Allen's life and career. Unfortunately, he does not seem to have written a memoir. In well-known biographies of Charles Olson and Frank O'Hara, he puts in appearances so brief as to utterly belie his stature and accomplishment. If ever a biographical project was needed before too many more witnesses to his life pass from the current scene, then Donald Allen's biography should be undertaken immediately, if only to gather as much material as possible. After spending a fair amount of time with his archives at UCSD's Geisel Library, I put together a series of questions that he eventually answered in a detailed letter dated April 19, 1998, which I will be happy to share with anyone interested in such a project.

16. While New Directions has added very accomplished poets such as Jerome Rothenberg, Michael Palmer, Susan Howe, Nate Mackey, and Will Alexander to its publication list, the majority of poets whose books remain in print with New Directions consists of the same names as made up the bulk of New Directions' backlist in 1960. In addition to several of Allen Ginsberg's close friends, such as William Burroughs, Carl Solomon, and Peter Orlovsky, City Lights went on to add poets such as Robert Bly, Charles Bukowski, and Jack Hirschman to its roster.

17. Swallow's poetics as an editor as well as a poet can be found in the letters he wrote to the authors he published as well as in his own poems. A letter he wrote to Ann Stanford on May 1, 1956, reveals not only his ability to criticize in a useful manner the work of his authors, but his own attempts to resolve the conflict

between traditional poetics and artistic revolt. He concedes in the letter that "there is a point at which one must step out on one's own," but this seems to refer not only to an autodidactic poetics, but to a challenge to articulate the enjambments of social experimentation. "Surely this idea at the opposition of the younger generation to an older ought to be automatic. . . . I am pretty confident that the way is not one of direct revolt—and certainly not to method in the deepest sense—but to find one's own attitudes about the world, which become the subject matter of the poems and emotions of the poems. That is a bigger problem, probably, than the literary one of attitudes toward poetry, method, etc." (Claire 23–24).

18. *Trace* magazine ran a negative review of *Displaced Persons* written by Gil Orlovitz, a poet and fiction writer who frequently appeared in May's magazine. Gordon's longtime association with McGrath was noted in a letter dated November 7, 1972, Gordon wrote to William L. (Bill) Fox at *West Coast Poetry Review* in which he thanked Fox for requesting poems for his magazine. "It is not often that this happens. It must be due to something Tom McGrath said, something probably not true. Good old Tom—he's one of my oldest and dearest friends. One of his characteristics, as you probably know, is that he is forever doing something for someone else. My unbiased opinion is that Tom is the finest poet in the country today."

19. The biographical details I mention draw upon the information provided by Fred Whitehead's long essay on Don Gordon in the *Collected Poems* published by the University of Illinois Press. Cary Nelson's introductory essay to Edwin Rolfe's *Collected Poems* (University of Illinois Press, 1993) provides far more details about his life than the ones I have cited.

20. Don Gordon lived an exceptionally quiet life as a poet in Los Angeles. His public appearances were very intermittent. He showed up, for instance, at an event at California State University, Los Angeles in 1982 that featured an exhibition of books and magazines by Los Angeles poets. Laurel Ann Bogen has a program signed by over a dozen of the poets in attendance, including Don Gordon. His poems did not appear in many of the area's more prominent magazines, although an issue of *Electrum* magazine contains his writing alongside other Los Angeles poets such as Laurel Ann Bogen. In the late 1970s, he sent signed copies of two books, including *On the Ward*, to Beyond Baroque, one of which was inscribed to James Krusoe.

21. The death of Alan Swallow in 1965 from a heart attack was a major loss to American letters in general and to poets such as Don Gordon in particular. Over a decade and a half would go by after *Displaced Persons* was published before Gordon would find an editor willing to give a serious reading to his next manuscript. Bill Fox carefully read Gordon's manuscript in September 1974, but informed him that West Coast Poetry Review Press would not be able to publish Gordon's book for at least a year. Gordon's alignment of his social critique with the small press movement can be detected in a response he sent Fox on October 14, 1974: "You suggest that I try the trades. By trades I suppose you mean major commercial publishers. I have not tried any of them and do not intend to. It would use up a lot of time, in my opinion, and to no purpose. What I had in mind was small presses. It is very good of you to say, 'I think you deserve more attention than you would get by publishing with us.' But

nothing is farther from my thoughts than this idea. I would be happy to stick with you on all counts. The only reason for sending it elsewhere is not to find something *bigger* or *better*—only something *quicker*. I am thrown a bit at what I understand about your time schedule. It sounds like a year or more from now and that resembles forever." Gordon's *On the Ward* did not, in fact, get published until 1977.

22. Six pages later, Filreis mentions Pillin again, this time as a contributor to *Golden Goose,* which he describes as "a mix of radical and avant-garde verse." In this instance, Pillin's company includes Robert Creeley, Lorine Niedecker, Theodore Enslin, Norman Macleod, and Robert McAlmond.

23. In an interview on September 2, 1979, conducted by Leland Hickman and published in issue number 16 of *Bachy,* Bill Pillin said, "Any poem that requires a professional explainer is not worth a goddamn. Young poets! Study data-processing, become a checker in a supermarket, or a mechanic. Stay away from universities, unless you want to study a real subject, like medicine. Don't get tamed by the Mandarinate." Pillin's life as a poet was much more social than Don Gordon's, though encounters with other poets did not always end well. For one such instance, see "Poetry in Los Angeles 1945–1975" (*Bachy* 12: 138–140; 13: 146–149), in which Alvaro Cardona-Hine recounts an evening at Pillin's residence that included himself, Gene Frumkin, James Dickey, and Ann Stanford. On the whole, though, Pillin was friendly and known for generously encouraging young poets in Los Angeles, such as Doren Robbins and Suzanne Lummis. Lummis dedicated the first of her Los Angeles poetry festivals to Pillin.

24. *Pacifica* was a twelve-inch record of several poet-editors and their favorite contributors released in 1952. Emerson (*Golden Goose*), Hedley (*Inferno*), and May (*Trace*) were joined, in reading their own poems, by Pillin, Lawrence Lipton, and James Schevill. With three poets each from Los Angeles and San Francisco, *Pacifica* represented an indication very early in the 1950s that the West Coast Poetry Renaissance would ripple throughout the major urban areas of California.

25. Pillin's "credits" for *Everything Falling* include *Ante, Café Solo, Coastlines, Illuminations, kayak, The Nation, New Mexico Quarterly, Poet and Critics, Sur* (Argentina), and *Triquarterly.* Robert Bly wrote a seven-page introduction, "Words Emerging from Objects Again." Bly mentions the titles of seven poems he considers first-rate, among them "You, John Wayne," a poem that future anthologists should not neglect. Pillin's work, in some ways, reveals the influence of European models, but Pillin was adamant about his particular path to those affiliations: "I had read George Trakl and Gottfried Benn and other Europeans long before *The Fifties* came out" (*Bachy* 16: 10).

3. I Cannot Even Begin to Imagine the Extent of Their Aloneness

1. I owe the citation of Nathaniel Hawthorne's phrase "paved solitude" to Burton Pike's *The Image of the City in Modern Literature* (Princeton: Princeton University Press, 1981), xi–xii.

2. Sarah Schrank's *Art and the City: Civic Imagination and Cultural Authority in Los Angeles* traces the history of visual art in Los Angeles from the struggles

of modernism to get a foothold in Southern California to the exuberant days of proliferating galleries on La Cienega Boulevard in the 1950s. She also addresses the reactionary forces that hounded some of the area's best-known artists in an attempt to reify a sanitized version of California. "One of the many ironies of the struggle over art and civic identity in the postwar period," Schrank points out, "is that the efforts to push avant-garde, experimental and modern art out of the public realm resulted in alternative art communities that, though initially marginalized, would eventually in the 1960s put the city on the international art map. Los Angeles' Beat and bohemian artists self-consciously undermined the postwar culture of domestic suburban life at the same time that they celebrated the opportunities offered by prosperity: cheap cars, low rent, voluminous urban detritus and ample space" (95). Although her book devotes several pages to Venice West, it focuses on visual artists such as Ed Kienholz, Ed Ruscha, Billy Al Bingston and gallery owners such as Walter Hopps, "who linked the San Francisco and Los Angeles (art) scenes together in creative ways no one had previously tried" (115).

3. Zeitlin's talk harks back to the kind of cultural map established in Emory Stephen Bogardus's *Southern California: a Center of Culture* (Los Angeles: University of Southern California Press, 1938). Those interested in how Zeitlin's bookstore functioned as "one of the central flash points of Los Angeles cultural and intellectual life" in the first half of the twentieth century should consult chapter 2 of Daniel Hurewitz's *Bohemian Los Angeles and the Making of Modern Politics* (Berkeley: University of California Press, 2007).

4. Ann Charters's *The Portable Beat Anthology* and Anne Waldman's *The Beat Book: Writings from the Beat Generation* are representative of an inexplicable erasure of the poets of Venice West from the Beat movement. In late summer of 1996, I visited a substantial exhibit of Beat generation materials at the University of California, Berkeley library; not a single book or placard made mention of anything other than Beats who were active in New York or the San Francisco area.

5. The front cover of this issue of *Life*, which featured a photograph of the wives of seven astronauts, announced only two stories: the wives' "inner thoughts, worries" and "Kansas Squares vs. Coast Beats." John Arthur Maynard sizes up the article in chapter 6 of *Venice West: The Beat Generation in Southern California*: "In spite of (the article's) deceptively trivializing tone, 'Squaresville vs. Beatsville' was not a piece of fluff. It was a major feature in the most important weekly picture magazine in America—expensively produced, prominently positioned, and surrounded by advertisements costing between fifteen and twenty thousand dollars per page, not counting what the advertisers may have paid to have their ads placed within or near it (It would be interesting to know how many had insisted on *not* having their ads placed near it.)" (129). The article, according to Maynard, generated a sufficient volume of mail from readers that *Life* devoted twenty column inches in a subsequent issue to reflect the generally positive responses to the article. For a total contrast between concurrent cultural scenes in Los Angeles, see Suzanne Muchnic's *Odd Man In: Norton Simon and the Pursuit of Culture*, in which she surveys the life of a man who was featured in June 1960 in *Time* magazine as a distinguished

art collector on the West Coast, and yet nevertheless perceived himself as a "belea-guered outsider." (Berkeley: University of California Press, 1998), 4–5.

6. According to Maynard, Lipton turned in his final manuscript on February 9, 1959 (100), and the book went on sale in June (108). Schrank's *Art and the City* includes a full-page reproduction of the front cover of the dust jacket.

7. As in the previous instance, the cover of the November 30, 1959, issue of *Life* highlighted only two articles, and once again, the Beats were prominent. The subtitle for "The Only Rebellion Around," which ran from pages 114–130, was "But the shabby beats bungle the job in arguing, sulking, and bad poetry."

8. Lipton's title was reinforced in the book by Perkoff's poem, "The Barbar-ians from the North," which he wrote in response to a reading by Allen Ginsberg and Gregory Corso at the household headquarters of *Coastlines* magazine in Los Angeles. O'Neil mentions this reading in his article without attributing any source, and O'Neil most likely cribbed the report of Ginsberg's disrobing from *The Holy Barbarians*, in which Lipton appended Perkoff's poem as corollary substantiation to his highly subjective account of the event.

9. Allen, in fact, had visited Venice West in the summer of 1957. In response to one of my questions about his trip to the West Coast to gather material for *Ever-green Review*, Allen stated, "From San Francisco I went to Los Angeles to visit a relative and to meet Lawrence Lipton, who introduced me to Stuart Perkoff, Alex Trocchi and others. There was a vague idea that the LA/Venice scene might work for an issue of *ER*, but that soon faded." The portrait of Lipton in Perkoff's letter suggests that Allen was probably wise in steering clear of any project involving Lip-ton. In a book of interviews with San Francisco Beat poets, David Meltzer recalls his youth in Los Angeles and how he got a ride with Jonathan Williams to Lipton's house in Venice. "Lipton . . . was an older guy who looked like anyone of my Jewish uncles—balding, thick horn rims, cigar-chomping, and a spoken word evangelist before his time. Lipton's stuff was kind of corny to me . . . Perkoff was, hands down, the major poet there, and his work bears it out" (*San Francisco Beat: Talking with the Poets*, ed. David Meltzer, San Francisco: City Lights Books, 2001), 201–202.

10. In addition to Maynard's book, researchers can find an immense amount of detail about minor figures and their lovers in the artistic underground on the West Coast during the 1950s and 1960s in *Beach and Temple: Outsider Poets and Artists of Western America 1953–1995* by David B. Griffiths. *Beach and Temple* was published by International Scholars Publications in 1998, and appears to be a barely modified version of a PhD dissertation. Neither Maynard nor Griffiths seem to have been aware of the archives of Donald Allen at the University of California, San Diego, and both labored under the disadvantage of not having easy access to Perkoff's poetry. Griffiths refers to the forthcoming edition of Perkoff's poetry, so *Voices of the Lady* had not yet appeared as he worked on the chapter he devotes to Perkoff. Almost none of the journal entries I cite are mentioned by Griffiths, though many of his notes refer to Perkoff's journals. Maynard's book is a lively account of the social impact of Venice West on Venice as a neighborhood in Los Angeles. By giving as much, if not more, time to Lawrence Lipton as Perkoff, Maynard is able to

suggest the impact of the friendly rivalry between Lipton and Kenneth Rexroth on Venice West. Linda Hamalian's *A Life of Kenneth Rexroth* includes several passages about Rexroth and Lipton, but Perkoff is misidentified as a musician who backs up Rexroth at the Los Angeles Jazz and Poetry Festival in 1957. Lipton's archive of tape recordings of interviews and readings by Venice West poets at USC includes material by some of the poets that has never been published.

11. Eileen Aaronson Ireland, a poet who is cited in Perkoff's journals at several points, is still alive and writing poems in Las Vegas, New Mexico. In September 2010, she loaned me her personal copy of Maurice Lacy's second collection of poems, *Twinkling Split from Hell*, which I had not been aware of until she sent it along. Its copyright page and what passes at the end of the book for a combination of colophon and editorial statement contain some surprising information. In the late 1950s, the Unicorn Bookshop (8907 Sunset Blvd., Hollywood, 46, California) seems to have housed "a battered mimeograph machine" which was used to produce several chapbooks of poetry, including at least two by San Francisco poet, Lenore Kandel, whose *Love Book* was prosecuted for obscenity. Lacy's book contains a short biographical note: he was born in 1937 in Fort Worth, Texas, and some of the poems in *Twinkling Split from Hell* had appeared in an earlier collection, *Mystic Perch*, also published by Three Penny. Lacy's name is alternately listed in the book as W. M. Lacy. The editorial address of Three Penny is a house address on Laurel Canyon Blvd., in Studio City. Grover Haynes is listed as the editor and Rosie Haynes, who would eventually marry John Thomas, contributed production assistance. This publishing project seems to have been the only one located in Los Angeles in the 1950s that published any individual titles by poets associated with the Beat movement.

12. The final poem in *Voices of the Lady* gives Stuart Perkoff's birth date as July 29, 1930, and his death date as June 25, 1974. Griffiths's book also provides these dates. Although his father spent almost his entire childhood in the United States, he had been born in Russia in 1904. Perkoff's mother was a year younger (Griffiths 5). *Resistance*, edited by Jackson MacLow (his last name was not yet two separate syllables), was the successor to an antiwar publication, *Why?*, published in the United States during World War II. Perkoff's poem, "At the End of the Uprising," appeared in vol. 9, no. 2 (Oct.–Nov., 1950), page 8, of *Resistance*. In Perkoff's first book, *The Suicide Room*, "Uprising" was dedicated to MacLow. *The Diaries of Judith Malina 1947–1957* (New York: Grove Press, 1984) provides glimpses of Stuart and Suzanne Perkoff's participation in the anarchist community in New York between late May and mid-December 1950. It should be noted that, in Olson's archives at the University of Connecticut, at least one letter that Perkoff sent Olson from the West Coast contains several unpublished poems.

13. Perkoff read with Bruce Boyd and Saul White at the San Francisco Poetry Center on Sunday, March 30, 1958, though tape recordings in the archive at the SFPC contain two complete "sets" of readings and it appears that they read both in the afternoon and the evening. Recordings of Perkoff and Boyd reading their poems can also be found in Lawrence Lipton's archives at the University of Southern California. In addition to Creeley, Jack Spicer attended at least one of these readings.

According to a letter Robert Duncan sent Denise Levertov on Thursday, April 3, Creeley gave a reading on Wednesday night, April 2, "in the midst of a savage rain storm," and then drove to Los Angeles the next morning "a little grimly." Both Creeley and Bobbie Louise Hawkins seemed to be "reticent" and to have "visible misgivings" about giving Perkoff a ride, though Duncan gives no specifics (Robert J. Bertholf and Albert Gelpi, eds., *The Letters of Robert Duncan and Denise Levertov*, Stanford: Stanford University Press, 2004).

14. The back cover of Donald Allen's *The New American Poetry* repeats an assertion that appears on the first page of Allen's "Preface": "most of the work presented here has appeared only in a few magazines, as broadsheets, pamphlets, and limited editions, or circulated in manuscript; a larger amount of it has reached its growing audience through poetry readings" (xi). Four pages later, in the final paragraph, Allen makes the point again. "As I have said, only a fraction of the work has been published, and that for the most part in fugitive pamphlets and little magazines." Between the back cover and the preface, one could not blame too many readers for feeling that they were lucky to get hold of this book. After all, what intelligent, imaginative person wouldn't want to be thought of as hip back in the 1950s? The only problem is that, like most sales pitches, Allen leaves something out of the story. An avid reader in the 1950s in a rural town in Pennsylvania would have been familiar with a substantial number of the names in Allen's anthology by 1960. Here is a list of contributors to a single magazine in a five year period just before the appearance of Allen's anthology: Frank O'Hara, 12 poems; Kenneth Koch, 7 poems; Robert Creeley, 7 poems; Robert Duncan, 9 poems; Denise Levertov, 8 poems.

While our theoretical reader of *Poetry* magazine would not have known of the work of Michael McClure or Stuart Perkoff, it is fair to say that *The New American Poetry* had the benefit of several of its contributors appearing repeatedly in the nation's best-known poetry magazine. While *Poetry* is listed in a bibliography at the back of *NAP*, one would never guess from the preface that *Poetry*'s affirmation of this new writing was very generous. In fairness, Allen's contextual statement is true. "Most of the work presented" in the anthology first appeared in obscure magazines. The book, however, has gained the aura of being a version of an iceberg on a very foggy night about to hit the *Titanic* of conventional verse. In actuality, several distinguished contributors to Allen's anthology were conspicuously visible. Allen could have corrected this image in an afterword he wrote for the reprint of *The New American Poetry* by the University of California Press (1999), but he chose instead to reiterate just one side of the story: "More than a fourth of the poems finally selected for the anthology were culled from current issues of *Black Mountain Review, Measure, Yugen, Chicago Review, Big Table,* and *Evergreen Review*" (448–449). He goes on to cite hostile reviews of his anthology in *Hudson Review* and *Audit*, which was published at SUNY Buffalo. Allen obviously wished to maintain his investment in a strict bifurcation of the underground and those who had the academic seal of approval with no intermediaries in sight.

15. On March 22, 1957, Donald Allen wrote Allen Ginsberg that he had "received a remarkable long poem from Perkoff, which we'd like to run in the next issue, but

may have to hold over." The poem is not named, but given that Perkoff's journals show he wrote this poem in the late winter/early spring of 1957, and that he refers to this poem in his long letter to Allen as "FDFL" (the casual manner implying that Allen would know which poem he meant since he had sent it to him), in addition to its inclusion in *The New American Poetry*, it's a very reasonable guess that Allen's praise is for this particular poem. Allen's correspondence reflects a man who was not given to effusion; he rarely singles out poems for praise. During one of the readings with Bruce Boyd and Saul White at the Poetry Center in San Francisco, Perkoff mentions that "FDFL" had been published in the "current issue" of John Wieners's *Measure* magazine. Issue number 2 of *Measure* contained ten contributors to Allen's anthology, including Blaser, Creeley, Olson, Duncan, Dorn, McClure, and Kerouac. "FDFL" is the major poem in the issue; it takes up seven full pages (34–40). The first two pages, facing each other, end up sharing the title, which is split in two, with "Feasts of Death" on the left-hand page and "Feasts of Love" on the right. "FDFL" is not the only poem that included prose in *Measure*'s second issue. Duncan's "The Dance," the poem (on pages 32 and 33) that immediately precedes Perkoff's, concludes with a prose paragraph "But that was my job that summer." And the piece before Duncan's is all prose (Ed Dorn's "The Magick of Place Skaget Valley"; pages 29–31).

16. As far as I have been able to determine, Lipton's use of the term "Disneyfication" is its first recorded instance.

17. "Part 2: The Venice Years" of Tony Scibella's *The Kid in America* is a prose memoir that provides a fair amount of correlating detail to Perkoff's journals; pages 80–82, in particular, reinforce Perkoff's account about his valiant attempt to create a communal coffeehouse. Perkoff's brief but intense period as a painter as well as a poet is described on pages 90–91. Other figures cited include Bruce Boyd ("our zen poet"), Arnold Wagman, Bill Stanton, and Arte Richer.

18. During almost the entire time I worked on this project, I could find little evidence of this workshop outside of references in Perkoff's journals. Once again, however, Eileen Ireland recently proved to be an invaluable resource. Lawrence Lipton tape-recorded an interview with her in the early 1960s in which she talks about the workshop. Surprisingly, perhaps, the workshop emphasized formal poetry much more than anyone might guess. One of the first assignments Ireland received from Perkoff, for instance, was to write a sonnet.

19. John Maynard's *Venice West*, however, points out that the bohemian lifestyle was still very much present in Venice throughout the early 1960s. John Haag, for instance, a political activist "who had been coming to poetry readings in Venice since 1959" (163), had purchased the Venice West Expresso Café from John Kenevan when its popularity had waned, and established the Venice Music and Arts Center in its place. They encountered the same kind of police hostility to poetry readings during this period that is recounted in *Welcome All Poets*. Bob Alexander's Temple of Man continued to operate, too. Other social experiments were also taking place in nearby Ocean Park. One fairly radical one for drug addicts was called Synanon. Other poets were also present in Venice at this time. Jack Hirschman was visibly present in Venice in the early 1960s as was Harold Norse, who would later move to

San Francisco and start a magazine called *Bastard Angel.* One could argue, in fact, that the "scene" in Venice did not become extinguished with the dispersal of the core membership of Venice West and the eventual incarceration of Stuart Perkoff. Certainly, from the point of view of the police department, the pursuit of artists in Venice remained an active case. In the fall of 1966, for instance, Steve Richmond was arrested on the charge of obscenity for an issue of his newspaper, *Earth Rose,* an event noted by Charles Bukowski in a letter to Carl Weissner on November 2, 1966 (*Screams from the Balcony: Selected Letters 1966-1970,* 273-274).

20. *Beach and Temple* states that a warrant for Perkoff's arrest was served on August 5, 1966 (82), and that he was confined at Terminal Island, San Pedro, and at the minimum security prison at Chino, California. He was released in late September 1970 (90). Although for understandable reasons Perkoff is almost automatically relegated to the Venice West scene, he did spend over two years living in northern California after his release from prison. The composition dates for his book-length poem, *Alphabet,* which was published by Red Hill Press in December 1973, follow his standard pattern of an annual cycle (April 8, 1972 to April 8, 1973). Underneath these dates, Perkoff assigns the place of composition to Larkspur, California; the publisher's address is listed as 6 San Gabriel Drive, Fairfax, CA 94930. Perkoff's work, therefore, is not just representative of the Southern half of the West Coast Poetry Renaissance but is textually part of the work written and published in northern California, too. Boyd and Thomas were perhaps more visibly active up and down the coast, but Perkoff cannot be confined to Los Angeles, even if it was his central and primary point of poetic identification.

On a familial level, Perkoff reunited with Suzan while living in northern California. His daughter, Rachel DiPaola, wrote me in an e-mail dated November 8, 2010, that she remembered it "as a warm and fun time in my life. Lots of life and laughter in the house," though she adds that it was "far from (a normal family), of course when your parents and their friends drop acid on Thanksgiving while cooking the turkey with all the trimmings."

21. Perkoff included the poem for Gary Cooper among a group of nineteen he recorded at KPFK studios on September 9, 1961. Perkoff was paired with William Pillin for the program. William Margolis attended the session and recollected the evening in an article published in the fourth issue (Autumn 1974) of *Bachy* magazine as a tribute to Perkoff. Perkoff and Pillin had known each other for several years. Perkoff's journals refer to Pillin more than once, but the following extended entry from 1957 is the one that indicates a degree of reciprocal interest on the part of three different groups in Southern California: Venice West, the Dynamo group, and the *Coastlines* contingent. "Tonite on the way home from Pillin's house Charley sounded me: every day, at the word. & he is right, especially now, as I am at a turning point of some sort—and my hand does not move across the paper . . . . where am I without / the ones who love me? / lost lost / Pillin is one of the Dynamo / group, grown older & he is also / like lost / how he dug having us come / onto the scene to talk to him." Pillin also claims that McGrath expresses appreciation for both Newman's and his poems at a reading and Perkoff admiringly cites McGrath's

poems in *Mainstream*. At a certain point in the entry, Perkoff seems to be writing a kind of diarist free verse, which I have indicated with virgules.

22. E-mail to Bill Mohr from Gary Snyder, Friday, November 21, 2008. Donald Allen, in his written responses to my questions, said that he had met Boyd briefly in San Francisco in 1957.

23. "Venice Recalled" is dated 1959 in *The New American Poetry*; Boyd had moved back to Berkeley in 1958 from Venice West and attended Duncan's poetry workshop. By June 4, 1959, he wrote Snyder that he was living at 1990 Filbert St., San Francisco and attending Zazen at the Zenshu Soto Mission on Bush Street "every morning from 5:45 to 7." He seems to have worked at Brentano's for most of the next twelve months; in a letter to Snyder after he moved back to Venice in May 1960, he said he "grew to hate the job" at the bookstore and had returned to Los Angeles to find better paying work. In the spring of 1961, work was sufficiently scarce that he became eligible for unemployment, which he described as "not altogether unpleasing leisure. I've done two parts of a long (15 pp., so far) peyote poem wh, if it turns out, will be more political than anything else one could call it. (Having been turned back on to politics by the Cuba Revolution, wh I think of as the only hopeful thing that's happened for a long while. Matter of fact, had I known Spanish I'd have gone to Cuba last summer. Am studying it now.)" By November 1961 he had found steady work at a narcotics warehouse and in February 1962 he took up residence in the same apartment he had lived in (450 C Carroll Canal, Venice) before he had returned to San Francisco in 1958. (Boyd added the parenthetical remark "'s truth") after telling Snyder about his job. Snyder and Boyd apparently discussed the distinction between the scenes in San Francisco and Venice in their letters; Boyd's comment to Snyder was that "San Francisco was *mythologized*" whereas Venice "got *publicized*; because while San Francisco had Kerouac, Venice had Lipton, & that man is a publicist." Boyd added that Lipton's financial success with the book irritated those who had served as his "characters" in the book, although Boyd seems to have been more adept at converting any envy he felt into actual remuneration in one form or another: "It was much harder for the people here to exploit him than it had been for him to exploit them; but some of us succeeded, to a certain small extent, & I'm glad to say I'm amongst them." By April 1962 Boyd wrote Donald Allen that he found work in a factory making medical respiration equipment for $1.75/hr., but was laid off that around the time of the Cuban missile crisis. Boyd mentions that he had visited Margolis in Long Beach and that Margolis believed that "Perkoff will die very soon." Boyd seems to have worked for the Congress of Racial Equality in the mid-1960s. The last known address I have been able to locate for Boyd is 1536 6th Street, Apt. 4, on Santa Monica in November 1969. Larry Fagin reprinted some of Boyd's poetry in *Adventures in Poetry* in the early 1970s, but wrote me that he did not have any personal contact with Boyd in doing so. Diane DiPrima published some of Boyd's work in *Floating Bear*, and she too comments on his disappearance: "Bruce Boyd is a poet from Venice, California, who is very highly thought of. Hard to know what he's doing now. He doesn't answer letters when you write him. These

poems came from a whole book-length manuscript called *Toward Morning: From Apotropeia Instead of an Alba*, probably finished in the late fifties." (*Floating Bear* 16, notes adapted from taped interview with Diane DiPrima, July 29–August 1, 1970.)

24. Both Joseph Hansen and I wrote reviews in the early 1970s that made special mention of Thomas's work. My appreciation of Thomas's poetry began with Leland Hickman's enthusiastic recommendation of his first spiral-bound collection, *John Thomas*. I was visiting Hickman in late 1972, and he had a copy of it in his writing room. Within a week I went to Papa Bach and bought a copy and was equally impressed. My review was published in the second issue of *Bachy*. Joseph Hansen wrote a review of Paul Vangelisti's *Specimen 73*; Thomas was the only poet to receive Hansen's unqualified praise. It should be noted that John Thomas wrote most of the poems that went into his first book not in Venice, but in San Francisco. Thomas had told me a story about being at a party where Donald Allen was a guest, and in a letter to Donald Allen, I asked him if he remembered Thomas. "No," Allen wrote back, inquiring quite naturally about whether it was a pen name.

25. Thomas primarily shared the final portion of his life with Beat poet Philomene Long, who as Stuart Perkoff's companion at the very end of his life, escorted him to Papa Bach Bookstore for a brief reading. Thomas's love poems to Philomene Long in *"Poetry Loves Poetry"* are among his best poems, a collection of which Philomene's twin sister, Pegarty, is working on as his literary executor.

4. Left-Handed Blows

1. In the encyclopedic history of post–World War II little magazines entitled *A Secret Location on the Lower East Side*, the notion of community as a primary mode of literary identity is invoked by many of the featured editors and poets, including Ron Silliman, Lyn Hejinian, Charles Bernstein, and Bruce Andrews. In their brief recollections of their experiences in the small press world, "community" remains undefined, a gesture used to conjure a nostalgic glimpse of the glory days of baby-boom idealism. But however unfocused their citation of the concept might be, community formation was willy-nilly one of the central concerns of non-university poets in this country between the end of World War II and the beginning of the Gulf War.

2. A brief list would include Robert Crosson, Harry Northup, Michael Lally, Jack Grapes, Jed Rasula, Exene Cervenka, Dave Alvin, John Doe, Henry Rollins, Michael C. Ford, Viggo Mortenson, and even Charles Bukowski, who wrote the script for *Barfly*. Some individuals, such as Kenneth Atchity, have even been active as poets and editors and then become full-scale entrepreneurs in the entertainment field.

3. The details of George Drury Smith's life are taken from an unpublished chronology that he shared with me. Smith is finishing up a memoir that should provide much additional background. An interview with George Drury Smith and Alexandra Garrett about the first years of Beyond Baroque's operations appears in Noel Peattie's *A Passage for Dissent*, pages 142–150.

182 / NOTES TO PAGES 92-94

4. One of Leland Hickman's first decisions after he became one of the editors of *Bachy* was to run a three-part article by Joseph Hansen (1923–2004) about the history of the Beyond Baroque poetry workshop. *Bachy* 9—"Forgetting the Bridge" (122–125); *Bachy* 10—"The Thursday of the Small Rains" (136–139); *Bachy* 11—"Odd Sabbaths" (136–139). Joseph Hansen's archives are located at the Huntington Library, but are not yet available for research.

5. The films Northup has acted in include *Mean Streets, Alice Doesn't Live Here Anymore, Taxi Driver, The Silence of the Lambs,* and *Philadelphia.* He was one of the stars in *Fighting Mad.* One film he is particularly fond of is *Over the Edge,* which is finally receiving recognition as a minor classic of teenage rebellion. *Over the Edge* is now available on DVD, but it was perceived as so provocative when it was first released that it was almost immediately withdrawn from theaters. Northup has also been a member of the Academy of Motion Picture Arts and Sciences for over thirty years. As an activist poet, Northup ran the Gasoline Alley reading series in the mid-1980s and is one of the founder-members of Cahuenga Press, a poets' cooperative in Los Angeles that has published over a dozen books, including a posthumous collection by Ann Stanford.

6. My biographical essay on Leland Hickman, "When You Put Your Ear Down to It," is the afterword to Hickman's posthumous *Tiresias: The Collected Poems of Leland Hickman,* published by Nightboat Books in 2009. Hickman's life and accomplishments as a poet and editor deserve a chapter in some future study of American poetry at least as substantial as that which I have accorded Stuart Perkoff. In brief, Leland Hickman was born in 1934 in California, went to high school with Joanne Kyger, studied at University of California, Berkeley, but did not graduate, and moved to New York City to study acting. He moved back to the West Coast in the late 1960s, and spent almost all of the rest of his life in Los Angeles, where he died in 1991. He edited *Bachy* magazine from 1977–1981 and *Temblor* magazine from 1985–1989.

7. Other reading series were also taking place in Los Angeles. A poet named Ted Simmons, who was deputy director of the Pacific Coast Writers Conference at Los Angeles State College in the mid-1960s, established a project called the Venice Poetry Company which put on readings in Venice, Santa Monica, Hermosa Beach, and San Pedro. The readers included Charles Bukowksi, Jack Hirschman, Ron Koertge, John Thomas, K. Curtis Lyle, Gerald Locklin, William and Barbara Margolis, Deena Metzger, John Montgomery, and the English poet Michael Horowitz, who had edited *Children of Albion.* Other readings were held at Chatterton's Bookshop on Vermont Avenue, next door to the Los Feliz Movie Theater. William Iwamoto had left his job as a clerk at Papa Bach's shortly after I met him in 1971 in order to launch his own store. He appeared in a cameo role in a film, *The Competition.* After he died of AIDS, Chatterton's closed, though the space was eventually leased again, and turned into another independent bookstore called Skylight. Papa Bach Bookstore closed in 1984, and the building became a computer outlet. The building was demolished in the 1990s, and is now a car lot.

8. *Out of This World: An Anthology of the St. Mark's Poetry Project 1966–1991,* ed. Anne Waldman (New York: Crown, 1991), 3–4.

9. The attrition rate for independent arts organizations is, not unexpectedly, very high. One important arts organization elsewhere in Los Angeles in the early to mid-1970s was Theater Vanguard, which lasted for five years, but succumbed to a lack of funding. It was located more centrally in Los Angeles and included live performances as well films in its programming. Typical screenings would be *The Anxiety of the Goalie Keeper at the Penalty Kick* and David Larcher's *Mare's Tail*.

10. Other alternative institutions, such as the Inner City Cultural Center, began giving coverage to the workshop. *Neworld*, a magazine that was primarily devoted to dance and theater, ran two articles on poetry workshops in Los Angeles. The second article, which appeared in the summer of 1975, evaluates the workshop with an implicit warning to anyone who was not serious about the craft: "The workshop is characterized by extreme intellectualism, and pointed, hard-hitting criticism." (*Neworld*, Summer 1975, 62).

11. Interview with Jim Krusoe, October 28, 1996.

12. Although Lyle has not lived in Los Angeles for many years, his poetry continues to be supported by Beyond Baroque, which published *Electric Church*, a selection of over 150 pages of his work in the spring of 2004.

13. Laurel Ann Bogen covered the official opening-night reading for the *Los Angeles Herald Examiner*. Bogen had written a favorable review of *The Streets Inside* for the *Herald Examiner* (February 18, 1979, sec. E). Braverman was interviewed in *L.A. Weekly* by Laurel Delp for an article called "The Angry Shaman, Triumphantly": "I think there's some extraordinary poetry being written in Los Angeles, in part because we exist in such isolation here" (May 25–31, 1979).

14. The Burbage Theater as the site for a multi-arts project was covered in a series of articles in the *Los Angeles Times*: Barbara Riker, "A Showcase for Unknown Artists," West Side, *Los Angeles Times*, August 30, 1973; Kenneth J. Fanucchi, "Stage Troupe: A Moving Experience," West Side, *Los Angeles Times*, November 22, 1973; West Side, *Los Angeles Times*, July 28, 1974.

15. Prado's work first appeared in the *Lamp in the Spine* in issue no. 2. By early 1974, Prado's work in that magazine was beginning to attract serious attention. "Issue 6, Spring 1973, is 112 pages long, and begins with 2 of the most remarkable prose poems I have ever seen; those by Holly Prado." Angela Peckingpaugh, "Rich Yellow Flame: A Look at *The Lamp in the Spine*," *Margins*, February 1974.

16. According to a note by Alexandra Garrett in her archives at UCLA, the typesetting machine was first put to work on November 30, 1975, when Leonard Randolph typeset one of his own poems on the machine, which was located in a pagoda-like building behind Beyond Baroque's storefront headquarters. The poem, "An Open Letter to the Poets of America," cites Tom McGrath, Denise Levertov, Maxine Kumin, William Meredith, Michael Moos, Ramona Weeks, Jenne Andrews, and Ken McCullough.

17. Ironically, although the Momentum workshop had begun to fade as I assembled the anthology, clues that it functioned as a kind of coterie remain visible in the poems that Hickman selected for his portion of *The Streets Inside*. The first poem, "The Hidden," was dedicated to Harry Northup, and his four successive

poems made a bow in the direction of Jim Krusoe, Kate Braverman, and myself, as well as Deena Metzger. Robert Kirsch, in his review in the *Los Angeles Times*, noted how many of the poets "seemed to know each other," though he claimed that this was not a problem in itself. There were, in fact, frequent dedications in the poems in *The Streets Inside*: Holly Prado, Harry Northup, Deena Metzger, and Eloise Klein Healy in particular assigned their poems a social role in reinforcing a sense of community in the renaissance of poetry in Los Angeles in the 1970s. In addition to dedications, poets in Los Angeles are named as "characters" within poems by both Hickman and Jim Krusoe, whose prose poem, "Saxophone," begins: "I am reading a poem called 'Saxophone.' With me is Barry Simons, a friend of mine who I am beginning to recognize as the symbol of my unconscious whenever he appears. He has brought his saxophone, and I am standing on stage leaning into a mike." Simons (1943–2009) was a visual artist who also gained a reputation in the early 1970s for giving readings off of books with blank pages. In *Frank O'Hara: The Poetics of Coterie*, Lytle Shaw has characterized coterie as community's "problematic twin" because its self-referentiality amounts to a heresy that disturbs canonical models of literary "kinship" by challenging "an interpretative community's tacit standards" (16). In extending the antinomian principle to create a haven of kinship between poets, a coterie ultimately raises issues of how claims for value attain sufficient legitimacy to be taken seriously. If a coterie, however, is conceived as a group of writers "whose primary, or at least initial, audience was those involved," (58) were the poets in *The Streets Inside* actually a coterie? All of the poets in *The Streets Inside* were giving many well-attended public readings, so it could hardly be said that these poets were each other's cultivated audience. On the other hand, John Bernard Myers's definition of coterie, cited by Shaw, certainly would at least partially align itself with many poets in my first anthology: "a group of writers rejected by the literary establishment who found strength to continue with their work by what the anarchists used to call 'mutual aid'" (7–8). Kirsch's review perhaps marks the point at which the Momentum workshop and the poets associated with the Woman's Building began to lose their aura of coterie. In *Frantic Transmissions*, Kate Braverman writes about Los Angeles as a cultural wasteland, but oddly enough makes no mention of this workshop whatsoever and how her early work was shaped by the ambition of the oldest poets in it to devote themselves to the composition of long poems.

At that point, I was working at the Department of Social Services for the Medi-Cal program in an office near Pico and Sepulveda, and was living in an apartment in Ocean Park, about three blocks west of a Methodist church whose pastor, Jim Conn, was opening up the space to alternative artists, theater groups, and consciousness-raising workshops. The address, 512 Hill St., Apt. 4, eventually served as the editorial address for Momentum Press. The Church in Ocean Park became known as the launching point for the rent-control campaign in Santa Monica and also held many poetry events over the years. Doren Robbins, Denise Levertov, and Clayton Eshleman, for instance, read together in an evening of protest against U.S. intervention in Central America. I ran a series of the brief essays Jim Conn sent out with the church's monthly mailing in the final issue of *Momentum* as a way of enfolding his activist ministry into the poetry community that his church supported.

18. Laura Meyer, "The Los Angeles Woman's Building and the Feminist Art Community 1973–1991," *The Sons and Daughters of Los* (Philadelphia: Temple University Press, 2003), 39–62.

19. Interview with Holly Prado by Leland Hickman. *Bachy* 12: 6.

20. Ibid. Lee Hickman: "I feel that *Feasts*, coming as it does into the Los Angeles community—it comes into a wider community than Los Angeles, of course—but as it does appear, amongst us all as writers and poets, it stands as kind of a keystone—cornerstone—for a depth of feeling we all share. I don't think it's any accident that it was written in Los Angeles." Eloise Klein Healy used the phrase "communities of intention" at a conference of Los Angeles women poets at the Huntington Library.

21. "What makes these poems special are their concrete images: words that floor the reader with their power, their drive. They contain the kind of energy one finds in Rimbaud and Van Gogh's pictures and in the writings of Charles Bukowski." Ben Pleasants, untitled reviews, *Los Angeles Times Book Review,* May 12, 1978.

22. Stephen Kessler, "Inside the Streets: A Curb's Eye Lowdown on L.A. Poetry: An Essay/Review," *Bachy* 14, 141–144.

23. *Los Angeles Times.* Kirsch's review was not the first notice taken of the book. On Sunday, February 18, 1979, both the *Los Angeles Times* and the *Los Angeles Herald Examiner* ran reviews of *The Streets Inside*. "Los Angeles is a reservoir of poetic genius," Warren Wood declared in the first notice the *Times* took of the book, and then pointed to both the headwaters that fed that reservoir, and the social management of that cultural resource that created our distinctive predicament. "Unfortunately, it bleeds into small presses suffering from bad circulation. As a result, this excellent anthology may stay buried in the small circle of L.A.'s literary influence. For the sake of this city, *The Streets Inside* should be discovered and enjoyed beyond its boundaries, an example of Los Angeles' power and sensitivity that few people believe exist." (*Los Angeles Times*, February 18, 1979, *Los Angeles Times Book Review,* 14) Besides the previously cited review by Stephen Kessler of *The Streets Inside* in *Bachy* 14, Robert Peters wrote a largely favorable review in the same issue, "Scribbling in Journals, and Other Poetry Matters: An Essay/Review," pp. 138–141. The same issue also contained a review of James Krusoe's *Small Pianos* by Eloise Klein Healy, pp. 148–149, and my review of Bob Flanagan's *The Kid Is the Man*, pp. 149–150. Peters's review was reprinted in *The Great American Poetry Bake-Off,* second series, pp. 244–255. The death of Robert Kirsch (1922–1980) was a genuine loss to the Los Angeles poetry community. He was willing to champion us at a pivotal moment in the late 1970s, and if he had lived another ten years, our books would probably have received much more thorough attention in the book review section of the *Los Angeles Times.*

24. When Philomene Long, the widow of John Thomas, died of a heart attack in the summer of 2007, I asked John Harris at an informal memorial service about Hickman's pay as editor of *Bachy*. "It wasn't enough to live on," said Harris, and added, "Lee earned every penny of it." The interviews Hickman conducted with

poets in Los Angeles end up being fairly revealing of himself and his own percep-
tions of his relationship with a poetic community that was largely heterosexual.

The sequence of interviews, their dates, and the issues in which the interviews
were published is as follows: Deena Metzger (August 24, 1977) *Bachy* 10; Harry Nor-
thup (December 11, 1977) *Bachy* 11; Holly Prado (May 20, 1978) *Bachy* 12; James Kru-
soe (September 10, 1978) *Bachy* 13; Eloise Klein Healy (December 3, 1978) *Bachy* 13;
William Mohr (January 7, 1979) *Bachy* 13; Dennis Ellman; Marine Robert Warden
(April 29, 1979) *Bachy* 15; Wanda Coleman (August 26, 1979) *Bachy* 16; William Pil-
lin (September 2, 1979) *Bachy* 16; Dennis Phillips (December 14–15, 1979) *Bachy* 17;
Martha (Lifson) Ronk (January 20, 1980) *Bachy* 17; John Rechy (February 7, 1980)
Bachy 17. All of the interviews by Lee Hickman in the final issue of *Bachy* were
undated: Joseph Hansen, Jon-Stephen Fink, Kate Braverman, and Peter Levitt. An
undated interview with Dennis Cooper by David Trinidad and with George Hitch-
cock by George Fuller also appeared in the final issue.

25. *Alternate: The International Magazine of Sexual Politics*, Vol. 2, No. 13 (May/
June 1980). John Preston, "Detective David Brandstetter: California's Avenging
Angel," 24–26. George Whitmore, "Hansen's Briefs" (a 500-word review of *The Dog
and other stories*), 63. According to an editor's note on the letters to the editor page,
Alternate had begun focusing on gay literature in issue number 11, which was fol-
lowed by an issue focusing on gay art (March/April 1980). A national survey of gay
publishing houses was planned for issue number 15. Issue number 13 included both
a prize-winning short story and a one-act play in addition to articles about gay life
in New York, Los Angeles, and San Francisco.

26. Rudy Kikel, *Contact II*.

27. Robert Peters had singled out Lee Hickman's poems for special praise in his
review of *The Streets Inside*, in *Bachy* 14 (1979): "Here are five long sections from his
almost epic-length poem in progress, 'Tiresias.' The modest price of this anthology
is worth it for these poems alone. They are real discoveries. . . . Finding (his work)
so well-represented here is a rare treat. Hickman is writing an incredible symphony
of the tortured self." His review, "Scribbling in Journals and other Poetry Matters,"
was reprinted in Peters's *The Great American Poetry Bake-Off*, second series. In the
same issue of *Bachy* Stephen Kessler reviewed *The Streets Inside*, too, and although
he gave the volume a mixed review, praised Hickman's work unstintingly, predict-
ing that the completed poem could be "a very astonishing work."

28. Peace Press was located at 3828 Willat Avenue, Culver City, California
90230.

29. Kevin Killian was the first to write an enthusiastic review of Hickman's
Tiresias (http://www.amazon.com/Tiresias-Collected-Poems-Leland-Hickman/dp/
0982264518). Ron Silliman's assessment was that Hickman unfinished project
seemed "*Tiresias* is . . . one of the most interesting / problematic of all the longpoems
to come out of the New American (& behind it, the Pound-Williams-Zukofsky) tra-
dition. . . . *Tiresias* at times feels like the launching pad for a tremendous poem that
has yet to be written" (ronsilliman.blogspot.com; Thursday, March 11, 2010). Cal

Bedient, a poet who teaches at the University of California, Los Angeles, reviewed it in the summer issue of *Boston Review.*

30. In an interview I conducted with Alicia Ostriker on October 15, 2002, she told me that the Beyond Baroque workshop in particular had enabled me to write about her body with less self-consciousness. Mary Kinzie's review of *The Mother/ Child Papers* appeared in *The American Poetry* Review, July–August 1981. *The Mother/Child Papers* was subsequently reprinted by Beacon Press and the University of Pittsburgh Press.

31. Paul Vangelisti wrote a report of this tentative effort that was published in *Contact II.*

32. Giovanni's Corner in Philadelphia not only ordered and paid for books, but was also fairly prompt about *reordering* books. Books were also distributed through Truck Distribution, which became Jim Sitter's Bookslinger in the late 1970s when David Wilk became the head of the Literature Program at the National Endowment for the Arts. Wilk went on to launch another project, Inland Book Company, which also carried my books. Several distribution projects ended on less than a happy note and generated considerable acrimony within the small press world. Wings Distribution, for instance, was a particularly egregious failure. For an account of the relationship between an editor of a small press projects, A. D. Winans of Second Coming Press in San Francisco, COSMEP, and one of the proprietors of Wings, see *The Holy Grail: Charles Bukowski and the Second Coming Revolution.*

33. Even at this early stage, Cooper began making claims for the national importance of some of the poets in the city. "(T)wo of the area's most stalwart luminaries, James Krusoe and Jack Grapes, have been writing poetry which is as exquisitely clear and literate as any in the country." His article went on to cite Bob Flanagan and Martha Lifson (now Martha Ronk) as other poets in Los Angeles who are "reading vociferously and honing their craft." Cooper himself would soon be profiled alongside the poets and editors whose projects he admired ("The License to Write: L.A.'s Poets Start a New Tradition of Their Own," Laurel Delp, "California Living," *Los Angeles Herald Examiner,* January 31, 1982). In addition to reflecting is cultural interests, ranging from punk music to classical ballet, his diary at Fales Library, New York University, provides a glimpse at his early efforts to get published in Los Angeles.

34. James Cushing, "Beyond Baroque's Poetic License Expired." "Metaphors be with you" was a bumper sticker produced by Peter Schneidre, the editor of Illuminati Press. Cushing, who has lived and taught in San Luis Obispo since the mid-1980s, contributed several important articles and reviews to the scene during the early 1980s, including a long piece on Harry Northup's *Enough the Great Running Chapel,* which I published in 1982, as well as a full page of commentary about a one-day conference on L.A. poetry at UCLA ("L.A. Poets Drive Alone on Metaphysical Freeways"). The plight of Beyond Baroque was also examined in detail by journalist Elaine Woo, whose article included excerpts from an interview with NEA honcho Frank Conroy, who admitted that the panel's decision was "subjective, to be sure ... you're talking about the judgment of things like literary quality" Conroy also

said that the eight-member panel of writers and editors whom he had chosen for the panel were "struck by the low literary quality" of books that were published at NewComp. "You can't get around the question of who's using the services and are they good enough" to warrant support, Conroy asserted. As rebuttal, Woo's article cited Momentum Press as an example of a publisher making use of NewComp; in point of fact, even as Conroy slammed down his gavel in judgment, I was typesetting on NewComp equipment the poems that would go into *"Poetry Loves Poetry."* The Endowment gave grants to five literary centers in that round of application, and not one of them was on the West Coast.

35. Interview with Dennis Phillips, June 18, 2009.

36. Letter to Leland Hickman from Dennis Phillips. Letter in the Leland Hickman archive at the Archive for New Poetry, University of California, San Diego.

37. Sylvia Drake's theater column in the *Los Angeles Times* recorded how one of the primary spokesmen for LATW was a lawyer who at one point had been on the board of directors at the Center Theater Group for the Mark Taper Forum. In New York, this would be the equivalent of a lawyer associated with Lincoln Center going to work for the Ontological Theater, which is also located at St. Mark's in the Bowery, in order to minimize the Project's access to church space.

Part of the skirmishing between Beyond Baroque and LATW involved the maintenance of the building, which by the mid-1980s had not been painted for many years. In my interview with Dennis Phillips, he cited the nonliterary work he was called up to do in order to sustain Beyond Baroque as a site for the public presentation of poetry. "One of the ways that Susan tried to get the building was that she went on a campaign that it needed to be painted, and she cast it as a big public affairs thing. . . . (Beyond Baroque) had no money, so I wrote a letter to the guy who was the head of Builders Emporium and he donated several thousand dollars worth of paint." The details of this battle are available in Alexandra Garrett's archive, including exchanges between major law firms working for both sides. I should add a disclaimer to this particular portion of the history. I was employed in the early 1980s by LATW in its artists-in-the-prisons program.

38. Eshleman's comments appeared in an article in the *Los Angeles Times,* "Poetry: Is There a Los Angeles Sound" by Nancy Shiffrin, January 25, 1987. His attitude did not surprise any poets in Los Angeles. He cannot claim that no one ever paid any attention to him while he was here. His reading at Chatterton's Bookshop with Robert Kelly, for instance, was attended by 150 people, according to a letter (June 16, 1981) to Peter Schneidre from Laurel Ann Bogen, who noted that those in attendance included Wanda Coleman, Lee Hickman, Dennis Phillips, Kate Braverman, Martha (Lifson) Ronk, Charles Webb, Dennis Cooper, and Barbara Einzig. "And they charged $3.00," she added. Illuminati Archives, University of Southern California.

39. The most insightful and comprehensive reviews of *"Poetry Loves Poetry"* were by Joe Safdie and Sharon Doubiago. Safdie was born and grew up in Los Angeles, but was living in Bolinas when he reviewed my anthology for *Poetry Flash.* Doubiago's review appeared in an issue of *Electrum* magazine that featured Manazar Gamboa. Doubiago, a widely published poet born and raised in Los Angeles,

received a master's degree at Cal State Los Angeles in the late 1960s and then lived on the beach for a half-dozen years raising her children. Although she has spent the bulk of her poetic career in the Northwest, she is a requisite poet in any comprehensive critical examination of West Coast writing in the future. Michael Ventura, "With Her Own Eyes in her Own Body: The Life and Art of Sharon Doubiago," *LA Weekly*, May 1993, 16–17, 28–31. Christopher Beach seems to have been the first significant academic critic to have acknowledged the accumulative contribution of Stand Up poetry to the visibility of Los Angeles within the West Coast Poetry Renaissance. "Los Angeles has quietly emerged as an important center of West Coast poetry, where a form of populist performance poetry variously called 'Standup Poetry,' 'Easy Poetry,' or 'Long Beach Poetry' has combined stand-up comedy and post-Beat poetry exemplified by Charles Bukowski" (*Poetic Culture* 36).

40. One major element was missing by the time St. John settled in Los Angeles: the bookstore scene. By the mid-1980s, most of the important stores of the previous decade and a half had folded, cut back on their operations, or had to shift locations due to economic pressures. Lawrence Weschler's article in the *Reader* in 1979 on the closing of Intellectuals & Liars was reprinted in a book of his essays. Lionel Rolfe's article on the closing of Papa Bach appeared in the *Reader* on June 22, 1984. Page 12 of Rolfe's article contains especially pertinent passages about the pressures of the real estate market on culture in Los Angeles in 1980s, a period that saw a massive immigration of people from New York City, proportionately few of whom bought books other than nonfiction or novels they hoped to option for screenplays.

41. Interview with Phillips, June 18, 2009.

42. Interview with St. John, summer 2009.

43. *Invocation L.A.* was published by John Crawford, whose West End Press (named for a bar in NYC) had published poet, playwright, and cultural critic Cher'rie Moraga, lived in Los Angeles for several years. One of the poets he published was William Oandassan (1947–1992), a Native American poet whom I remember meeting at NewComp during the 1980s. Beyond Baroque's chapbook library has over a half-dozen of his chapbooks.

44. Interview with Fred Dewey, August 21, 2009.

45. Dewey, ibid.

46. Dewey, ibid. Another disclaimer must be interjected: it needs to be acknowledged that I served on the board of directors of Beyond Baroque for at least two years in the late 1990s, and my activism on the board was directly responsible for an outcome in a vote of confidence that allowed Dewey to continue in his joint position of administrative director and artistic director.

47. Dewey, ibid.

5. Fault-Line Communities

1. In 1989, Harry Northup organized a day-long celebration of Los Angeles small presses at Chatterton's Bookshop and recorded the talks by the editors and publishers, who included Rodríguez and DeAngelis as well as representatives from

Chrysalis magazine. Copies of these tapes are available at the Archive for New Poetry at the University of California, San Diego. A history of the Woman's Building, with a considerable number of photographs, is available as an e-book on the Internet.

2. The best account of the Watts Writers Workshop is Daniel Widener's "Writing Watts: Budd Schulberg, the Watts Writers Workshop, and the War on Poverty," which first appeared in *Journal of Urban History* 34, no. 4 (May 2008). This article is now part of his book, *Black Arts West: Culture and Struggle in Postwar Los Angeles, 1942–1992.* I would note that, although one of the plays developed in the Watts Writers Workshop, *Big Time Buck White*, ended up getting a Broadway production, the poetic legacy of the Watts Writers Workshop remains its most significant accomplishment, as many of the poets who emerged from it are still writing today, including Eric Priestley, K. Curtis Lyle, and Quincy Troupe. An anthology of writing from the workshop was published by a major New York house in 1969, but unlike the poets just named, none of the writers who appeared in *From the Ashes: Voices of Watts* were able to develop a literary career. I wish to thank Kevin McNamara for calling my attention to Widener's superb article. Another account and analysis of the Watts Writers Workshop can be found in a portion of chapter 5 of James Edward Smethurst's *The Black Arts Movement: Literary Nationalism in the 1960s and 1970s* (University of North Carolina Press, 2005), pages 290–318.

3. "Our literature won't be like the South's literature of remembered guilt or the East's literature of transgression and assimilation or the West's literature of isolation by nature's indifference. The best of our literature will be tragic. The standard for the excellence of our stories won't have been set in the Iowa Writers' Workshop, but by women talking at a hearth baking *chipati* and men whispering in Spanish before slipping between strands of barbed wire across any border south of here. It will be a literature that cures our willful amnesia about Los Angeles." (D. J. Waldie, *Where We Are Now: Notes from Los Angeles* (Santa Monica: Angel City Books, 2004), 123–124. Both emerging after the period that forms the arc of this study, the Taco Shop Poets, who are primarily based in San Diego, and Los Angeles poet Marisela Norte deserve much more attention within contemporary critical discussion.

4. *Urban Exile: Collected Writings of Harry Gamboa Jr.*, edited by Chon A. Norigea, is a massive and intriguing volume of scripts and prose pieces, some of which contain poems, but the section entitled "poetry" comes at the very end of the book (pages 508–543). While the twenty-one poems set aside from the other writing are worthy contenders for any anthology of L.A. poets, the placement of this section suggests that Gamboa sees himself in broader literary terms than being just a poet. Ruben Martinez is another example of a writer primarily known for his journalism, but whose performances as a poet—including one memorable afternoon at the Gasoline Alley Poetry Series I ran in the late 1980s—contributed to the poet performance scenes in Los Angeles.

5. On the other hand, Bukowski never asked to read at Beyond Baroque. He did read at other places at which poets associated with Beyond Baroque also read. I remember, in particular, a reading he gave at Papa Bach Bookstore in the early 1970s. He is said to have called the next day and asked if anyone found his

eyeglasses, which he had lost at some point in the evening. Bukowski's poems appeared in both the first and last issues of *Bachy* magazine, as well as making frequent appearances in Helen Friedland's *Poetry/LA* and *ONTHEBUS*, edited by Jack Grapes and Michael Andrews. If the day-to-day poets in Los Angeles did not fawn over him, neither did they pretend that he did not deserve their admiration. On Saturday, October 3, 1987, for instance, over a dozen poets gathered at Barnsdall Art Gallery Theater in Los Angeles to pay public tribute to Bukowski. In the publicity for the event, Loss Pequeño and I worked very hard to emphasize that the celebration was about Bukowski and would not include an appearance by the poet himself. The poets who agreed to be part of the evening included Ron Koertge, David James, Gerald Locklin, Susan Hayden, Mike Meloan, Tulsa Kinney, Loss Pequeño Glazier, Doren Robbins, Brooks Roddan, and John Thomas. Much to our surprise, and the delight of the two hundred people who attended, Bukowski did show up and took the stage for a little over ten minutes. The top of the front page of a four-page photocopied-on-green-paper program had a disclaimer by the guest of honor:

> To pay tribute
> to a man
> is to make him
> less dangerous.
> —Charles Bukowksi
> On HOMAGE TO BUKOWSKI:
> An Evening of Writing By, For, and About Charles Bukowski.

6. Martin's publishing career deserves a book-length account, and his absence from this study is not meant to discount his contribution to Los Angeles literature. This study focuses on writer-editors, however, and Martin dedicated himself first to book collecting and then to publishing. Martin only lived in San Francisco for the first decade of his life. His father was killed in an auto accident in the late 1930s, and by 1942 Martin's family was living in San Francisco. At the age of eighteen, Martin began working, and eventually proved to be a successful salesman with Office Supplies Unlimited in West Los Angeles. In 1965, Martin pocketed thirty thousand dollars from selling his rare book collection to the University of California, Santa Barbara. Within a few years, he started Black Sparrow Press while still working full-time. In order to keep it afloat, Martin recounted in his interview, he kept dipping, with increasing dismay and a touch of incredulity, into his nest egg at the rate of five and ten thousand dollar increments. In the late 1960s, Black Sparrow finally began to turn a small profit, and he soon became a full-time publisher. No one should underestimate his acumen as an editor or the enormous contribution he made to the West Coast Poetry Renaissance. Robert Dana, *Against the Grain*, 113–150.

7. "Gab Poetry." Review of Charles Bukowski in *Margins* and reprinted in *The Great American Poetry Bake-Off*, second series, 169–184.

8. In terms of being visible to poets across the country who might be interested in Language poetry, Silliman first sent out a call for work to *Trace* magazine

in the late 1960s, and by 1973 he was emphasizing the distinction between Language poetry as an avant-garde movement and other "experimental" work. As a term attributed to a specific poet which in turn became applicable to a large number of other poets, "Stand Up" was first used in an article by Gerald Locklin and Charles Stetler to describe the qualities that Field's poetry exuded. The term was ready-made for their use, of course, in that it was directly inspired by the title of Edward Field's second book, *Stand Up, Friend, with Me*. It should be noted that Field was the *only* poet in Donald Allen's anthology to go on to edit his own volume of alternative poets. Richard Howard led off his commentary on Field's first two volumes of poetry in *Alone with America* by noting that Field's poems demonstrate an "extreme resistance to the habitual conventions of literature," a quality that also underlies the writing of Field's progeny. *Alone with America: Essays on the Art of Poetry in the United States Since 1950*, enlarged ed. (New York: Atheneum, 1980), 143. The two poetry magazines that have provided the most significant outlets for these poems are *Wormwood Review*, edited by Marvin Malone, and *Pearl*, edited by Joan Jobe Smith, Barbara Hauk, and Marilyn Johnson.

9. Jim Stingley, "The Rise of L.A.'s Underground Poets," *Los Angeles Times*, April 21, 1974.

10. In an interview in *South Bay* magazine (1981), Jack Grapes asked Bukowski about a Los Angeles school of poets. He dismissed the notion, but pointed to Locklin as a poet deserving of further consideration. However, when I wrote to Bukowski three years after this interview and asked for poems for my second anthology of Los Angeles poets, *"Poetry Loves Poetry,"* he called me at home on the telephone to discuss which poems might best fit into such a project. His willingness to allow me to include his poems and to waive any royalties was an incredibly generous act, for which I remain grateful.

11. One of the first times I heard Paul Vangelisti read his poetry was at the Beyond Baroque workshop, and I was immediately attracted to the forthright political stance of his poetry. As soon as the workshop ended, I introduced myself and offered to publish his poem in the first issue of *Bachy* magazine.

12. See Bill Mohr, "Likelihood: The Avant-Garde Poetry of Paul Vangelisti."

13. The title for the magazine was decided upon well before the publication of Calvino's *Invisible Cities*.

14. Harry Northup Archive, University of California, San Diego, Archive for New Poetry. The Chatterton Bookstore Tapes.

15. Robert Peters, *The Great American Poetry Bake-Off*, 231.

16. This summary of Kubernik's background and career owes a substantial debt to "Would you buy poetry from this man? Better say yes, or Harvey Kubernik will talk your head off" by Erik Himmelsbach (Front cover lead). Internal headline: "At long last, we introduce the supersalesman of words: lighten up, Harvey Kubernik, we *really* do love you." *Los Angeles Reader*, September 17, 1993, 8–10.

Permissions

Temple" and "Aphroditos Absconditus" were originally published in *The Streets Inside: Ten Los Angeles Poets*. "Tiresias I: 1" was first published in *Bachy* magazine. All poems were eventually published in *Tiresias: The Collected Poems of Leland Hickman*, Seismicity Editions, 2010. Reprinted by permission of Cliff Hickman.

Judy Hogan: From a report on 1974 COSMEP conference. Copyright © 1974. Originally published in the *COSMEP Newsletter* (1974). Reprinted by permission of the author.

Ron Koertge: "The Bear Is Ill." Copyright © 1976 by the author. Originally appeared in *12 Photographs of Yellowstone*, published by Red Hill Press. Reprinted by permission of the author.

Gerald Locklin: "Do you remember the scene in *The Godfather* where James Caan says, 'Now make sure that the gun gets stashed in the rest room—I don't want my kid brother walking out of there with nothing but his dick in his hand'?" Copyright by the author. Originally published by *Wormwood Review*. Reprinted by permission of the author.

Suzanne Lummis: "Letter to My Assailant." Copyright © 1985 Momentum Press. Originally published in *Poetry Loves Poetry: An Anthology of Los Angeles Poets*, published by Momentum Press (1985). Reprinted in a revised version in *In Danger*, published by Roundhouse Press (1999) and in *Stand-Up Poetry*, published by the University of Iowa Press, 2002. Reprinted by permission of the author.

Bob Perelman: "The development of presses. . . . " Copyright © 1996 Bob Perelman. Originally appeared in *The Marginalization of Poetry*. Reprinted by permission of the author.

Stuart Perkoff: "Feasts of Death, Feasts of Love" first appeared in *Measure* magazine. "On Unloading a Boxcar" was originally published in *The Holy Barbarians*. "In Pound's Last Years in Venice, Italy" was originally published in *Invisible City*. Two untitled poems were published in *Voices of the Lady*. All reprinted by permission of Rachel DiPaola. Journal excerpts and the letter by Stuart Perkoff to Donald Allen are published here for the first time and are copyright © 2011 Rachel DiPaola. Printed by permission of Rachel DiPaola.

William Pillin: "Notes on Making Pottery," copyright © 1946. Originally published in *Theory of Silence*. "That Which Is Good Is Simply Done" and "Dance without Shoes" copyright © 1956. Originally published in *Dance without Shoes*. Reprinted by permission of Boris Pillin, literary executor of William Pillin.

Ron Silliman: "The libraries are filled with the wrong books. . . ." Copyright © 1968 Ron Silliman. Originally published in the *COSMEP Anthology*. Reprinted by permission of the author.

Bibliography

Adorno, Theodor. *Minima Moralia: Reflections from Damaged Life*. Translated from the German by E. F. N. Jephcott. London: Verso, 1974.

Allen, Donald. Archive. Mandeville Special Collections Library. University of California, San Diego.

———, ed. *The New American Poetry*. New York: Grove Press, 1960.

Bartlett, Lee. *The Sun Is But a Morning Star: Studies in West Coast Poetry and Poetics*. Albuquerque: University of New Mexico Press, 1989.

Beach, Christopher. *Poetic Culture: Contemporary American Poetry between Community and Institution*. Evanston: Northwestern University Press, 1999.

Bennett, Guy, and Beatrice Mousli, eds. *Seeing Los Angeles: A Different Look at a Different City, Proceedings of a Conference at the Bibliogtheque National de France, June 15–17, 2006*. Los Angeles: Otis Books/Seismicity Editions, 2007.

Bernstein, Charles. *A Poetics*. Cambridge: Cambridge University Press, 1992.

Bertholf, Robert J., and Albert Gelpi, eds. *The Letters of Robert Duncan and Denise Levertov*. Stanford: Stanford University Press, 2004.

Bérubé, Michael. *Marginal Forces/Cultural Centers Tolson: Pynchon, and the Politics of the Canon*. Ithaca and London: Cornell University Press, 1992.

Boyd, Bruce. Archives of Gary Snyder. Library, Special Collections. University of California, Davis.

Braverman, Kate. *Frantic Transmissions to and from Los Angeles: An Accidental Memoir*. Minneapolis: Graywolf, 2006.

———. *Milk Run*. Santa Monica, California: Momentum Press, 1977.

Breslin, James E. B. *From Modern to Contemporary, American Poetry, 1945–1960*. Chicago: University of Chicago Press, 1984.

Brodhead, Richard H. *Cultures of Letters: Scenes of Reading and Writing in Nineteenth-Century America*. Chicago: University of Chicago Press, 1993.

Brunner, Edward. *Cold War Poetry*. Urbana: University of Illinois, 2001.

Bukowski, Charles, Paul Vangelisti, and Neeli Cherry. *Anthology of L.A. Poets.* Los Angeles/San Francisco: Laugh Literary/Red Hill Press, 1972.

——, ed., and Neeli Cherry. *Laugh Literary, or Man the Humping Guns.* Los Angeles, 1968–1970.

——. *Living on Luck: Selected Letters, 1960s–1970s.* Vol. 2. Ed. Seamus Cooney. Santa Rosa, California: Black Sparrow Press, 1995.

Chambers, Ross. *Room for Maneuver: Reading (the) Oppositional (in) Narrative.* Chicago: University of Chicago Press, 1991.

Chartier, Roger. *The Order of Books: Readers, Authors, and Libraries in Europe between the Fourteenth and Eighteenth Centuries.* Trans. Lydia G. Cochrane. Stanford: Stanford University Press, 1994.

Claire, William F., ed. *Publishing in the West: Alan Swallow.* Santa Fe, New Mexico: Lightning Tree, 1974.

Clay, Steven, and Rodney Phillips. *A Secret Location on the Lower East Side: Adventures in Writing, 1960–1980.* New York: New York Public Library and Granary Books, 1998.

Clinton, Michelle T., Sesshu Foster, and Naomi Quinonez. *Invocation L.A.: Urban Multicultural Poetry.* Albuquerque: West End Press, 1989.

Cohen, Rob. *Scream When You Burn: An Anthology from the Editor of Caffeine Magazine.* San Diego: Incommunicado Press, 1998.

Coleman, Wanda. *African Sleeping Sickness: Stories and Poems.* Santa Rosa: Black Sparrow Press, 1990.

——. *Mercurochrome: New Poems.* Santa Rosa: Black Sparrow Press, 2001.

——. *Native in a Strange Land: Trials and Tremors.* Santa Rosa: Black Sparrow Press, 1996.

Cooper, Dennis. *Coming Attractions.* Los Angeles: Little Caesar Press, 1980.

——. *Little Caesar.* Los Angeles: Little Caesar Press, 1977–1982.

——. "The New Factionalism," *Poetry News.* No. 5 (February 1981).

——. "The Poetry Reading." In *GOSH!,* edited and published by Terry Cannon. Pasadena, California. February 1979.

——. "Seeing the Forest for the Trees: Recent Trends in American Poetics," in *GOSH!,* issue 11.

Cushing, James. "Beyond Baroque's Poetic License Expired." *Los Angeles Reader,* March 8, 1985.

——. "L.A. Poets Drive Alone on Metaphysical Freeways." *Los Angeles Reader,* June 10, 1983.

Damon, Maria. *The Dark End of the Street: Margins in American Vanguard Poetry.* Minneapolis: University of Minnesota Press, 1993.

Dana, Robert, ed. *Against the Grain: Interviews with Maverick American Publishers.* Iowa City: University of Iowa Press, 1986.

Davidson, Michael. *The San Francisco Renaissance.* Cambridge: Cambridge University Press, 1989.

——. *Ghostlier Demarcations: Modern Poetry and the Material Word.* Berkeley: University of California Press, 1997.

de Beauvoir, Simone. *L'Amerique au jour le jour.* Paris: Editions Gallimard, 1954.

Dewey, Fred. Interview by Bill Mohr. Venice, California. Fall 2009.

Diggory, Terrence, and Stephen Paul Miller. *The Scene of My Selves: New Work on New York School Poets.* Orono, Maine: National Poetry Foundation, 2001.

Ellingham, Lewis, and Kevin Killian. *Poet Be Like God: Jack Spicer and the San Francisco Renaissance.* Hanover, New Hampshire: Wesleyan University Press and University Press of New England, 1998.

Eshleman, Clayton. *Companion Spider: Essays.* Middletown, Connecticut: Wesleyan University Press, 2001.

Everson, William. *Archetype West: The Pacific Coast as Literary Region.* Berkeley: Oyez, 1976.

Field, Edward. *A Geography of Poets.* New York: Bantam Books, 1979.

Filreis, Alan. *Counter-Revolution of the Word: The Conservative Attack on Modern Poetry, 1945–1960.* Chapel Hill: University of North Carolina Press, 2008.

Fine, David, ed. *Los Angeles in Fiction: A Collection of Essays.* Albuquerque: University of New Mexico Press, 1995.

Flanzbaum, Hilene, ed. *The Americanization of the Holocaust.* Baltimore: Johns Hopkins University Press, 1999.

Fredman, Stephen. *Poet's Prose: The Crisis in American Verse.* 2nd ed. Cambridge: Cambridge University Press, 1990.

French, Warren. *The San Francisco Poetry Renaissance, 1955–1960.* Twayne's United States Authors Series 575. Boston: G. K. Hall, 1991.

Fulton, Len. *International Directory of Little Magazines & Small Presses.* 9th ed. 1973–74. Paradise, California: Dustbooks, 1974.

Gamboa, Manazar, ed. *Obras.* Venice, California.

———. *Memories Around a Bulldozed Barrio: Book One.* Los Angeles: Copies Unlimited (self-published), 1996.

Garrett, Alexandra. Archives. University Research Library, Special Collections, University of California, Los Angeles.

Ginsberg, Allen. *Collected Poems: 1947–1980.* New York: Harper & Row, 1984.

Gioia, Dana. *Can Poetry Matter? Essays on Poetry and American Culture.* Saint Paul: Graywolf Press, 1992.

Golding, Alan. *From Outlaw to Classic: Canons in American Poetry.* Madison: University of Wisconsin Press, 1995.

Gordon, Don. *Collected Poems.* Edited with an essay by Fred Whitehead. Urbana: University of Illinois Press, 2004.

———. *On the Ward.* Reno, Nevada: West Coast Poetry Review, 1977.

Griffiths, David B. *Beach and Temple: Outsider Poets and Artists of Western America 1953–1995.* San Francisco and London: International Scholars Publications, 1998.

Grossberg, Lawrence. *Bringing It All Back Home: Essays on Cultural Studies.* Durham, North Carolina: Duke University Press, 1997.

Gubar, Susan. *Poetry After Auschwitz: Remembering What One Never Knew.* Bloomington: Indiana University Press, 2003.

Guillory, John. *Cultural Capital: The Problem of Literary Canon Formation*. Chicago: University of Chicago Press, 1993.

Hamalian, Linda. *A Life of Kenneth Rexroth*. New York: W. W. Norton, 1991.

Hansen, Joseph. "Forgetting the Bridge." *Bachy* 9 (Summer 1977): 122–125.

———. "Odd Sabbaths." *Bachy* 11 (Spring 1978): 136–139.

———. "The Thursday of Small Rains." *Bachy* 10 (Winter 1977–1978): 136–139.

Harding, James. M., and Cindy Rosenthal. *Restaging the Sixties: Radical Theaters and Their Legacies*. Ann Arbor: University of Michigan Press, 2006.

Harrington, Joseph. *Poetry and the Public: The Social Forms of Modern U.S. Poetics*. Middletown, Connecticut: Wesleyan University Press, 2002.

Hayden, Dolores. *The Power of Place: Urban Landscapes as Public History*. Cambridge: MIT Press, 1995.

Hedley, Leslie W. *Inferno*. San Francisco, California.

———. *The Edge of Insanity*. Los Angeles: Modern Writers Club, 1949.

Hejinian, Lyn. *The Language of Inquiry*. Berkeley: University of California Press, 2000.

Hendrick, Kimmis. "A Serving of Free Verse: Magazine and Muse Enter Third Year." Author's photocopy of article from newspaper, title of paper and date unknown, although "Spring, 1948" is typed at the bottom.

Hickman, Leland. Archive. Archive for New Poetry. Geisel Library. University of California, San Diego.

———, ed. *Boxcar: A Magazine of the Arts*.

———, ed. *Temblor*. North Hollywood, California.

———. *Tiresias I:9:B: Great Slave Lake Suite*. Santa Monica: Momentum Press, 1980.

———. *Lee Sr Falls to the Floor*. Los Angeles: Jahbone Press, 1991.

———. *Tiresias: The Collected Poems of Leland Hickman*. Edited by Stephen Motika. Introduction by Dennis Phillips. Afterword by Bill Mohr. New York/Los Angeles: Nightboat Books/Seismicity Editions, 2009.

Higgins, Dick. *Whole COSMEP Catalog*. Paradise, California: Dustbooks. 1973.

Himmelsbach, Erik. "Would you buy poetry from this man?" *Los Angeles Reader*. September 17, 1993.

Hoover, Paul. *Postmodern American Poetry*. New York: Norton, 1994.

Horkheimer, Max, and Theodor W. Adorno. *Dialectic of Enlightenment*. Translated by John Cumming. New York: Continuum, 1999.

Ireland, Eileen Aaronson. Interview by Larry Lipton. Lawrence Lipton Archives, Special Collections. University of Southern California.

Jacoby, Jr., Grover. Archives. University Research Library, Special Collections. University of California, Los Angeles.

James, David, ed. *Power Misses: Essay across (Un)popular Culture*. London: Verso, 1996.

———. *The Sons and Daughters of Los: Culture and Community in L.A.* Philadelphia: Temple University Press, 2003.

Kane, Daniel. *All Poets Welcome: The Lower East Side Poetry Scene in the 1960s*. Berkeley: University of California Press, 2003.

Kaufman, Alan. *The Outlaw Bible of American Poetry*. New York: Thunder's Mouth Press, 1999.

Kessler, Stephen. "Inside the Streets: A Curb's Eye Lowdown on L.A. Poetry: An Essay/Review." *Bachy* 14 (1979): 141–144.

Kirsch, Robert. Untitled review of *The Streets Inside*. *Los Angeles Times*. April 27, 1979.

Klein, Norman M. *The History of Forgetting: Los Angeles and the Erasure of Memory*. London: Verso, 1997.

Koertge, Ronald. *12 Photographs of Yellowstone*. Los Angeles: Red Hill Press, 1976.

Kolin, Philip C., and Colby H. Kullman. *Speaking on State: Interviews with Contemporary American Playwrights*. Tuscaloosa: University of Alabama Press, 1996.

Kowalewski, Michael, ed. *Reading the West: New Essays on the Literature of the American West*. Cambridge: Cambridge University Press, 1996.

Krech, Richard, and John Oliver Simon, eds. *The anthology of poems read at COS-MEP, the conference of small-magazine editors & pressmen, in Berkeley, California, May 23–26, 1968*. Berkeley: Undermine Press, 1968.

Krusoe, James. Interview by Bill Mohr. Santa Monica, California. Fall 1996.

Lacy, Maurice. *Split from Twinkling Hell*. Los Angeles: Three Penny Press, 1959.

Lazer, Hank. *Opposing Poetries. Vol. One: Issues & Institutions*. Evanston, Illinois: Northwestern University Press, 1996.

Lefebvre, Henri. *Writings on Cities*. Translated and edited by Eleonore Kofman and Elizabeth Lebas. Malden, Massachusetts: Blackwell, 1996.

Lehman, David. *The Last Avant-Garde: The Making of the New York School of Poets*. New York: Random House, 1999.

Lentricchia, Frank. *Modernist Quartet*. New York: Cambridge University Press, 1994.

Lipton, Lawrence. *The Holy Barbarians*. New York: Julian Messner, 1959.

Lorence, James J. *The Suppression of Salt of the Earth: How Hollywood, Big Labor, and Politicians Blacklisted a Movie in Cold War America*. Albuquerque: University of New Mexico Press, 1999.

Lowney, John. *The American Avant-Garde Tradition: William Carlos Williams, Postmodern Poetry, and the Politics of Cultural Memory*. Lewisburg: Bucknell University Press, 1997.

Lummis, Suzanne, ed. *Grand Passion: The Poetry of Los Angeles and Beyond*. Los Angeles: Los Angeles Poetry Festival anthology, 1995.

———. *In Danger*. Berkeley, California: The Round Press, 1999.

Maclay, Sarah, Holaday Mason, and Jessica Pompei, eds. *Echo 681*. Venice: Beyond Baroque Books, 1998.

Margolis, William. "In Memoriam: Stuart Perkoff." *Bachy* 4 (Autumn 1974): 1–3.

May, James Boyer. Archive (1932–1972). Editorial papers, *Trace* magazine. Special Collections. California State University, Fullerton.

———. Archive (1932–1972). Editorial papers, *Trace* magazine. Special Collections. California State University, Fullerton.

May, James Boyer, Thomas McGrath, and Peter Yates. *Poetry Los Angeles:I*. London: Villiers Publications, Ltd., 1958.

Maynard, John Arthur. *Venice West: The Beat Generation in Southern California*. New Brunswick, New Jersey: Rutgers University Press, 1991.

McNamara, Kevin. *The Cambridge Companion to the Literature of Los Angeles*. New York: Cambridge University Press, 2010.

Meltzer, David. *The San Francisco Poets*. New York: Ballantine, 1971.

Messerli, Douglas. *Intersections: Innovative Poetry in Southern California*. The PIP Anthology of World Poetry of the 20th Century, Vol. 5. Los Angeles: Green Integer, 2005.

Mohr, Bill. Archive for Momentum Press. Mandeville Special Collections Library. University of California, San Diego.

———. ed. *Momentum*. Santa Monica, California.

———. "Likelihood: The Avant-Garde Poetry of Paul Vangelisti." *Chicago Review* (Fall 2004).

———. ed. *"Poetry Loves Poetry": An Anthology of Los Angeles Poets*. Santa Monica: Momentum Press, 1985.

Mohr, William. ed. *The Streets Inside: Ten Los Angeles Poets*. Santa Monica: Momentum Press, 1978.

Murphet, Julian. *Literature and Race in Los Angeles*. Cambridge: Cambridge University Press, 2001.

Muske-Dukes, Carol. *Married to the Icepick Killer: A Poet in Hollywood*. New York: Random House, 2002.

Nelson, Cary. *Repression and Recovery: Modern American Poetry and the Politics of Cultural Memory 1910–1945*. Madison: University of Wisconsin Press, 1989.

Northup, Harry. Archive. Mandeville Special Collections Library, University of California, San Diego.

———. *Enough the Great Running Chapel*. Santa Monica, California: Momentum Press, 1982.

Novak, Estelle Gershgoren. *Poets of the Non-Existent City: Los Angeles in the McCarthy Era*. Albuquerque: University of New Mexico Press, 2002.

Ostriker, Alicia. *The Mother/Child Papers*. Santa Monica, California: Momentum Press, 1980.

Parkinson, Thomas. *Poets, Poems, Movements*. Ann Arbor, Michigan: UMI Research Press, 1987.

Peattie, Noel. *A Passage for Dissent: The Best of Sipapu, 1970–1983*. Jefferson, North Carolina: McFarland and Company, 1989.

Perelman, Bob. *The Marginalization of Poetry: Language Writing and Literary History*. Princeton, New Jersey: Princeton University Press, 1996.

Perkins, David. *Is Literary History Possible?* Baltimore: John Hopkins University Press, 1992.

Perkoff, Stuart. *Voices of the Lady: Collected Poems*. Edited by Gerald Perkoff, M.D. Orono, Maine: National Poetry Foundation, 1998.

———. Archives. University Research Library, Special Collections. University of California, Los Angeles.

Perloff, Marjorie. *Poetic License: Essays on Modernist and Postmodernist Lyric.* Evanston, Illinois: Northwestern University Press, 1990.

Peters, Robert. "Chairing the Visible-Invisible: Ten Years of Vangelisti and McBride." *Invisible City.* Reprinted by permission from *Bachy* 17 (June 1980): 149–153. *The Great American Poetry Bake-Off*, 2nd series. Metuchen, New Jersey: Scarecrow Press, 1982.

Phillips, Dennis. Interview by Bill Mohr. Pasadena, California. June 18, 2009.

Pike, Burton. *The Image of the City in Modern Literature.* Princeton, New Jersey: Princeton University Press, 1981.

Pillin, William. *Dance Without Shoes.* Francestown, New Hampshire: The Golden Quill Press, 1956.

———. *Everything Falling.* Santa Cruz, California: Kayak Books, 1971.

———. *Pavanne for a Fading Memory.* Denver: A. Swallow, 1963.

———. *Theory of Silence.* Los Angeles: G. Yamada, 1949.

———. *To the End of Time: Poems New and Selected (1939–1979).* Los Angeles: Papa Bach Editions, 1980.

Plimpton, George, and Peter Ardery, eds. *The American Literary Anthology* 2. New York: Random House, 1969.

Poulin, Jr., A., and Michael Waters. *Contemporary American Poetry.* Boston: Houghton Mifflin, 2001.

Prado, Holly. *Feasts.* Los Angeles, California: Momentum Press, 1976.

Preston, John. "Detective David Brandstetter: California's Avenging Angel." *Alternate: The International Magazine of Sexual Politics* 2, no. 13 (May/June 1980): 24–26.

Ramazani, Jahan, ed., and Richard Ellmann and Robert O'Clair. *The Norton Anthology of Modern and Contemporary Poetry, Volume 2 Contemporary Poetry.*

Rasula, Jed. *The American Poetry Wax Museum: Reality Effects, 1940–1990.* Urbana: National Council of Teachers of English, 1996.

Rexroth, Kenneth. *American Poetry in the Twentieth Century.* New York: Herder and Herder, 1971.

Roberts, Andrew Michael, and Jonathan Allison, eds. *Poetry and Contemporary Culture: The Question of Value.* Edinburgh, Scotland: Edinburgh University Press, 2002.

Rolfe, Lionel. *In Search of Literary L.A.* Los Angeles: Classics Books, 1991.

Ross, Andrew. *The Failure of Modernism: Symptoms of American Poetry.* New York: Columbia University Press, 1986.

Russell, Charles. *Poets, Prophets, and Revolutionaries: The Literary Avant-Garde from Rimbaud through Postmodernism.* New York, Oxford: Oxford University Press, 1985.

Said, Edward W. *The World, the Text, and the Critic.* Cambridge, Massachusetts: Harvard University Press, 1983.

Salas, Charles G., and Michael S. Roth, eds. *Looking for Los Angeles: Architecture, Film, Photography, and the Urban Landscape.* Los Angeles: Getty Research Institute, 2001.

Schaeffer, Standard. "Impossible City: A History of Literary Publishing in L.A.," in *The World In Time and Space: Towards a History of Innovative American Poetry in Our Time*. A Special Issue of *Talisman: A Journal of Contemporary Poetry and Poetics* 23–26.

Schneidre, Peter. Archives of Illuminati Press. Research Library. University of Southern California.

Schrank, Sarah. *Art and the City: Civic Imagination and Cultural Authority in Los Angeles*. Philadelphia: University of Pennsylvania Press, 2009.

Scibella, Tony. *The Kid in America*. Los Angeles: Black Ace Books/Passion Press, 2000.

Shaw, Lytle. *Frank O'Hara: The Poetics of Coterie*. Iowa City: University of Iowa Press, 2006.

Shoemaker, Lynn. *Venice 13*. Venice, CA: no publisher listed; printed by Bayrock Graphics, located at the premises of Beyond Baroque, 1971.

Silliman, Ron, ed. *In the American Tree*. Orono: University of Maine, 1986.

Sinfield, Alan. *Faultlines: Cultural Materialism and the Politics of Dissident Reading*. Berkeley: University of California Press, 1992.

Smith, George Drury, ed., and James Krusoe, assoc. ed. *Beyond Baroque*. Venice, California.

———. *NewLetters*. Venice, California: Beyond Baroque, 1972–1973.

———. *The Newsletter*, no. 2 (March–April 1969).

———. Unpublished personal chronology.

Smith, Richard Candida. *Utopia and Dissent: Art, Poetry, and Politics in California*. Berkeley: University of California Press, 1995.

Stanford, Ann. Correspondence File of the Archive of Ann Stanford. San Marino: Huntington Library.

———. *The White Bird*. Denver: Alan Swallow, 1949.

Starr, Kevin. *Coast of Dreams: California on the Edge, 1990–2003*. New York: Vintage Books, 2004, 2006.

St. John, David. Interview by Bill Mohr. Idyllwild, California. Summer 2009.

Stingley, Jim. "The Rise of L.A.'s Underground Poets," *Los Angeles Times*. April 21, 1974.

Thomas, John. *John Thomas*. San Francisco: Red Hill Press, 1972.

Thompson, E. P., "Homage to Thomas McGrath," in *The Revolutionary Poet in the United States: The Poetry of Thomas McGrath*, edited by Frederic C. Stern. Columbia: University of Missouri Press, 1988.

Thurston, Michael. *Making Something Happen: American Political Poetry between the World Wars*. Chapel Hill: University of North Carolina Press, 1991.

Van Cleave, Ryan G. *Contemporary American Poetry: Behind the Scenes*. New York: Longman, 2002.

Vangelisti, Paul. Archive. Archive for New Poetry, Geisel Library. University of California, San Diego.

———, and John McBride, eds. *Invisible City*. San Francisco: Red Hill Press, 1971–1981.

——, ed. *L.A. Exile: A Guide to Los Angeles Writing 1932–1998*. New York: Marsilio, 1998.

——, ed. *Specimen 73: A Catalog of Poetry*. Pasadena: Museum of Modern Art, 1973.

Villa, Raúl Homero. *Barrio-logos: Space and Place in Urban Chicano Literature and Culture*. Austin: University of Texas Press, 2000.

von Hallberg, Robert, ed. *Canons*. Chicago: University of Chicago Press, 1984.

Webb, Charles Harper. *Stand Up Poetry: An Expanded Anthology*. Iowa City: University of Iowa Press, 2002.

Weddle, Jeff. *Bohemian New Orleans: The Story of the Outsider and Loujon Press*. Jackson: University Press of Mississippi, 2007.

Weinberger, Eliot. *Works on Paper, 1980–1986*. New York: New Directions, 1986.

Weschler, Lawrence. "L.A. Glows." *New York Times*, February 23, 1998.

Widener, Daniel. *Black Arts West: Culture and Struggle in Postwar Los Angeles*. Durham, North Carolina: Duke University Press, 2010.

Wieners, John, ed. *Measure* 2 (1958).

Winans, A. D. *The Holy Grail: Charles Bukowski and the Second Coming Revolution*. Paradise, California: Dustbooks, 2002.

Wolverton, Terry. *Insurgent Muse: Life and Art at the Woman's Building*. San Francisco: City Lights, 2002.

Woo, Elaine. "Federal Agency Writes Off Literary Center." *Los Angeles Times*. December 30, 1984.

Zeitlin, Jake. *Small Renaissance, Southern California Style*. Los Angeles: Richard Hoffman/California State University, 1972.

Zukofsky, Louis. *A Test of Poetry*. Hanover, New Hampshire: Wesleyan University Press, 2000.

Index

Industrial Poetics: Demo Tracks for a Mobile Culture
By Joe Amato

Postliterary America: From Bagel Shop Jazz to Micropoetries
By Maria Damon

On Mount Vision: Forms of the Sacred in Contemporary American Poetry
By Norman Finkelstein

Jorie Graham: Essays on the Poetry
Edited by Thomas Gardner
University of Wisconsin Press, 2005

Gary Snyder and the Pacific Rim: Creating Countercultural Community
By Timothy Gray

Urban Pastoral: Natural Currents in the New York School
By Timothy Gray

We Saw the Light: Conversations between the New American Cinema and Poetry
By Daniel Kane

History, Memory, and the Literary Left: Modern American Poetry, 1935–1968
By John Lowney

Paracritical Hinge: Essays, Talks, Notes, Interviews
By Nathaniel Mackey
University of Wisconsin Press, 2004

Behind the Lines: War Resistance Poetry on the American Homefront
By Philip Metres

Hold-Outs: The Los Angeles Poetry Renaissance, 1948–1992
By Bill Mohr

Frank O'Hara: The Poetics of Coterie
By Lytle Shaw

*Renegade Poetics: Black Aesthetics and Formal Innovation
in African American Poetry*
By Evie Shockley

Radical Vernacular: Lorine Niedecker and the Poetics of Place
Edited by Elizabeth Willis